THE SLAVE TRADE AND THE
ECONOMIC DEVELOPMENT OF EIGHTEENTH-CENTURY LANCASTER

Dedication

For my parents,
James and Betty Kay

The Slave Trade
and the Economic Development
of Eighteenth-Century Lancaster

Melinda Elder

Ryburn Publishing

First published in 1992
Ryburn Publishing Ltd
Krumlin, Halifax

© Melinda Elder

ISBN 1 85331 030 1

Composed by Ryburn Publishing Services
Originated by Ryburn Reprographics

Printed by Ryburn Book Production, Halifax, England

Contents

List of Illustrations

Lists of Tables, Graphs and Family Trees

List of Abbreviations

P.R.O.	Public Record Office, Kew
Lancs. C.R.O.	Lancashire County Record Office
L.P.L.	Lancaster Public Library
Liv.R.O.	Liverpool Record Office
Adm.	Admiralty
B.T.	Board of Trade
C.O.	Colonial Office
T.	Treasury
P/C.	Lancaster Port Commission Records (manuscript).
Free/App.Rolls	Lancaster Freemen, Apprentice and Waste Rolls, vols. 1–3 (manuscript).
F.R.	The Rolls of the Freemen of the Borough of Lancaster, 1688–1840, vols. 87 and 90 (The Record Society of Lancashire and Cheshire, 1935 and 1938).
ARR/11	Lancaster Marriage Bonds (manuscript).
M.B.	Lancaster Marriage Bonds, vols. 74, 80, 83, 100, 115 (The Record Society of Lancashire and Cheshire).
L/c.P.R.	The Registers of the Parish Church of Lancaster, vols. 57 and 88 (Lancashire Parish Register Society, 1920 and 1948).
Ulv.P.R.	The Registers of Ulverston Parish Church, ed. C. W. Bardsley (Ulverston, 1886).
H/h.P.R.	The Registers of the Parish of Hawkshead, ed. K. Leonard (London,1969–71).
WRW/A,F,K.	Richmond Wills/Amounderness, Furness, Kendal.
WCW	Chester Wills.
G.L.A.	Gore's Liverpool Advertiser.
W.L.A.	Williamson's Liverpool Advertiser.
L.L.	Lloyds' Lists.
Ec.H.R.	Economic History Review.
T.H.S.L.C.	Transactions of the Historic Society of Lancashire and Cheshire.

Preface

During the eighteenth century Lancaster witnessed a commercial revolution which transformed it from a local agricultural centre to an important west-coast port employed in overseas shipping. It was Lancaster's transatlantic trade which was largely responsible for this development. This is a study of a significant part of that commerce, the African slave trade, and of its relative importance to Lancaster's economic development. Lancaster's participation in the slave trade began in 1736. Between this date and the abolition of the British trade in 1807, Lancastrians sent vessels on more than 180 ventures to the West African coast in search of slaves. Their commitment to the trade established Lancaster as Britain's fourth slaving port after Liverpool, Bristol and London, and distinguished it from other small ports in the North West.

This book examines the reasons for Lancaster's interest in this notorious trade, looks at the structure and organization of its typically small-scale enterprises, analyses its participants and evaluates its impact on Lancaster's commercial and economic development. At the same time, it endeavours to set the trade at Lancaster in a regional and national context.

Slave trading at Lancaster offered local opportunists, eager to benefit from the expanding wealth of the plantations, a means to overcome the limitations that Lancaster faced as a developing colonial port. By pursuing a determined and individual brand of slaving, these operators of marginal status prospered, amidst the competition of eighteenth-century African commerce, to become influential members of their merchant community. The cumulative effect of their enterprise played a significant role in Lancaster's development as a colonial port and regional centre, which was in turn to stimulate, and on occasions fund, industrial development.

A variety of source materials have been used, including national and regional shipping records, contemporary newspapers, insurance records and merchants' correspondence, as well as local freeman and apprentice rolls, probate records and parish registers.

This book, based largely on my research as a graduate student at Lancaster University, has profited from the help and advice of a good many people. The History Department at Lancaster has been most supportive and encouraging both during my time as a graduate student and subsequently. I should especially like to thank my two supervisors, Bob Bliss and John Walton, for their generous and scholarly guidance throughout and also Mike Mullett for his many valuable comments. I am most grateful to former student, Janet Nelson, not only for our informal discussions on eighteenth-century Lancaster, but also for letting me see some of her notes, in particular those on the Insurance Records kept at the Guildhall Library, London.

I am, at the same time, indebted to the staff at the various record offices, libraries and museums I have visited in London, Liverpool and elsewhere. In particular, I should like to thank the staff at the Lancashire County Record Office, Lancaster Public Library and Lancaster Maritime Museum.

A number of people have assisted me in the collection of material to illustrate this book. Here I am especially grateful to Nigel Dalziel at Lancaster Maritime Museum for all his patience, time and trouble on my behalf. I would also like to thank the staff at Hull City Museums and Art Galleries, Whitehaven Museum, Liverpool Central Library, the British Library and Keele University Library.

For the publication of this book, I owe a debt of gratitude initially to Steve Constantine of Lancaster University for his encouragement and introduction to Ryburn Publishing, and then to Richard, Lucia and everyone at Ryburn for taking it on board with such enthusiasm and friendly cooperation.

Finally, untold thanks are due to my husband, John, who not only produced the original typescript, but also gave me the support and time at home needed to complete this work.

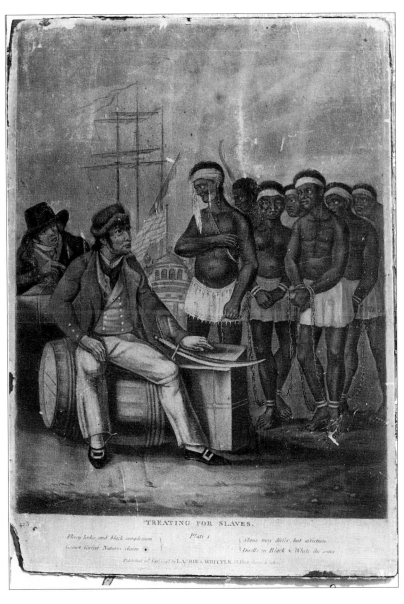

'Treating for Slaves' published in 1798. A captain negotiates for his human cargo. *Courtesy of Hull City Museums & Art Galleries*

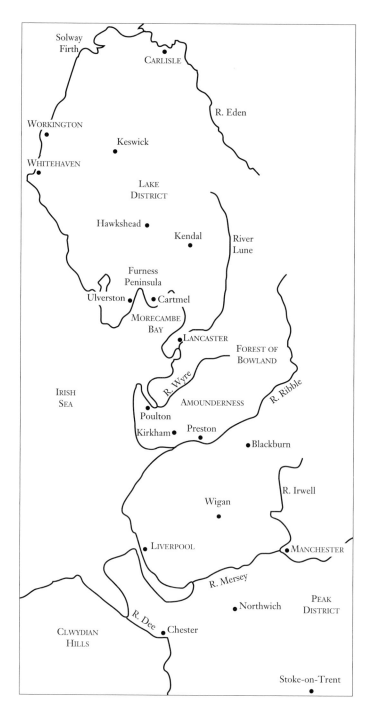

Sketch map of North-West England

Introduction

Lancaster experienced a remarkable period of economic development and expansion during the eighteenth century. The number of fine Georgian buildings, still standing in today's city, bears witness to this former period of prosperity. St. George's Quay, with its tall warehouses and noble customs house fronting on to the River Lune, is a powerful reminder that eighteenth-century Lancaster owed its prosperity primarily to maritime commerce and the associated industries that this supported and encouraged. As a consequence, Lancaster's situation towards the end of the eighteenth century was very different from what it had been at the outset. It changed from being an agricultural centre to a predominantly commercial one. In 1698 Celia Fiennes wrote this description of the port. "Lancaster town is old and much decay'd ... the town seems not to be much in trade as some others."[1] Although this description concealed commercial developments initiated in the late seventeenth century that were of some local significance, Lancaster's experience in trade at this time, relative to many other ports, was limited. In contrast, by the 1780s, Lancaster ranked behind, admittedly some way behind, only London, Liverpool and Bristol as an English colonial port.

Lancaster's commercial success was inextricably bound up with slavery. The port was renowned for its West India trade and, to a lesser extent, for its trade with the North American mainland colonies. Lancaster merchantmen carried English manufactures and local produce to the plantations and returned laden with colonial produce. The trade, which had begun in the 1680s, developed apace in the second half of the eighteenth century, especially during the later decades. It depended on slave-based economies, on the plantations which relied on regular shipments of slaves from Africa. This relationship is highlighted in the attitudes of West India merchants. When the island economies were threatened by those pressing for the abolition of the British slave trade in the later decades of the eighteenth century, many West India merchants expressed anxiety over the consequences of their actions. One of Lancaster's most

Lancaster's 18th-century warehousing along St. George's Quay is still very much in evidence today.

eminent West India merchants made the following cynical entry in his letter book in 1792, concerning abolitionists:

> ... the people in England want to lower the prices of sugar and yet continue presenting petitions from all quarters to Parliament to procure the abolition of the slave trade, many have left off the use of sugar, for the purpose of putting a stop to the slave trade, if the custom become prevalent of eating and using nothing that has been touched by slaves, we may soon expect to see people in the state of their first nature, naked in the field, feeding like Nebuchadnezzar upon grass, what wonders their philanthropy or Enthusiasm will produce is unknown.

In a subsequent letter he was more openly pessimistic, expressing fears that the numerous petitions from the abolitionists "may produce dreadful consequences in the islands".[2]

Lancaster's bilateral trade with the colonies was not its only commercial connexion with slavery. The town had, at the same time, more obvious and direct links with the enslavement of black Africans. It was engaged in the enforced shipment of men, women and children across the Atlantic to the New World colonies. Lancaster's association with the African slave trade began in 1736 and was to last until the trade was finally outlawed by an Act of 1807. The port's greatest participation in the trade took place in the third quarter of the century,

14

when Lancaster established itself as Britain's fourth slave-trading port, again some way after Liverpool, Bristol and London.

The Atlantic slave trade has received a lot of attention from historians over the years, and various aspects of the trade, explored in some detail in recent research, have provoked and continue to provoke much controversial discussion. The slave trade's relationship with Britain's economic development remains a central historiographical issue. It has promoted discussions on the trade's profitability and has called for a greater understanding of its mode of operation. Various viewpoints will be referred to in subsequent chapters of this book, when they are discussed in relation to aspects of the Lancaster slave trade.

In contrast to the prolific historiography of the slave trade, relatively little has been written about Lancaster's commercial development and even less about its slave trade. Although the trade generally gets a brief mention in histories of Lancaster, it has received little serious consideration, with the exception of one, more recent article. In 1946 Maurice Schofield published a brief economic history of Lancaster in which he wrote, "Lancaster took only a small part in the triangular trade as far as can be judged from literary evidence and the entries in the Port Commission".[3] He then went on to list just a few fragmentary pieces of evidence about the trade. Thirty years later, Schofield published an article on the slave trade of the small ports of Lancashire and Cheshire.[4] In this article he looked at the slave trade at Lancaster, Chester, Preston and Poulton, examining the reasons why these small ports entered the slave trade and viewing each of their slave trades in turn. This study provides some valuable information about the slave-trading enterprises of the North West but it is, by its nature, rather generalised. Schofield does not, for example, make any distinctions between the different ports when he discusses their reasons for entry into the slave trade, even though the timing of their entry, and the extent to which they involved themselves in the trade, varied considerably. The wide scope of this article does not lend itself to a detailed discussion of the slave trade's mode of operation at any one port. Although some important characteristics of Lancaster slaving ventures are detailed, other aspects are only briefly mentioned or not discussed at all. Indeed, Schofield writes that the business connexions of Lancaster merchants and the possibility of return cargoes for slavers, important aspects in terms of the trade's profitability, all need further research.[5]

This work sets out to discuss, in detail, the Lancaster slave trade and to relate it to the important historiographical issues which surround the trade in general. It will be viewed in the wider context of the port's overall trading opportunities so as to enable an assessment of its relative importance to Lancaster's commercial and economic development.

A central aim of this study will be to discover the reasons why Lancaster participated in this particular commerce, and at a level which set it apart from other small ports in the region. It is hoped that an analysis of Lancaster's experience in this commerce will also contribute to our knowledge of the slave trade as a whole, particularly in terms of its operation and management, and will provide further comment as to its profitability and its importance in shaping the English economy.

The first chapter will examine the circumstances under which Lancaster entered the slave trade and will compare its situation with that of other ports in the region. Lancastrians' ability to operate alongside much larger competitors makes their mode of operation particularly interesting. Details of the various aspects of slaving ventures will be discussed, again in comparison with other ports, in a second chapter, in an attempt to ascertain what features enabled Lancastrians to persist in the trade. The third chapter will concentrate on the slave traders themselves and seek to provide information on their management of the trade and to suggest further reasons why the slave trade may have been important to them, and therefore to Lancaster. The final chapter will consider the impact of the slave trade on the local economy by setting it in a national context and comparing it to Lancaster's West India trade. It will also consider the circumstances that led to the decline of the slave trade at Lancaster, again relating it to opportunities in other trades.

Extant documents paint a far from comprehensive picture of Lancaster's slave trade. The greatest difficulty is the lack of business records of Lancaster slave merchants. Only one set of papers specifically concerned with African ventures has survived and it neither covers the period when Lancaster's slave trade was in full swing nor elucidates more than a small part of the operations of the merchant concerned.[6] However, despite this limitation, it is possible to construct a reasonable picture of the trade at Lancaster from more general shipping records, both national and local, and from newspapers which exist for this period, together with fragmentary evidence from the correspondence of contemporary eighteenth-century merchants both in Lancaster and elsewhere.

The term 'slave trader' or 'slave merchant' will be used to refer to those who played an active or prominent role in the slave trade. Collectively they formed what will be described as a 'slave-trading' group or community. This is not to imply that their activities were confined to this one area alone. Indeed, this was seldom, if ever, the case. Nevertheless, these were the individuals who were instrumental in the management and execution of slaving ventures to Africa and the

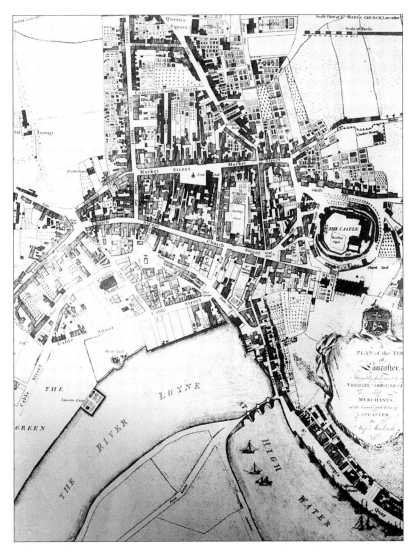

A plan of Lancaster in 1778 by S. Mackreth. *Courtesy of Lancaster City Museums*

colonies, as opposed to those who merely invested in the trade from time to time and whose interests were purely passive, fleeting and financial. Slave traders have also been variously described as 'African' or 'Guinea' merchants and their ships and captains as 'Guineamen' and 'African' or 'Guinea' captains, respectively. Finally, as it was quite common for ship owners to use the same name for successive vessels or for there simply to be more than one ship of a particular name during the period covered, Roman numerals have been added in order to distinguish them and avoid confusion.

Notes to Introduction

1. R. Craig and M. M. Schofield, 'The Trade of Lancaster in William Stout's Time', in J. D. Marshall, ed., *The Autobiography of William Stout of Lancaster 1665–1752* (Manchester, 1967), p. 31.
2. L.P.L., MS 3719, Letter Book of A. and J. Rawlinson, letters to Thomas Gudgeon and Thompson and Jackson, 2 April 1792.
3. M. M. Schofield, *Outlines of an Economic History of Lancaster* (Transactions of the Lancaster Branch of the Historical Association, No. 1, 1946), Part 1, p. 26.
4. M. M. Schofield, 'The Slave Trade from Lancashire and Cheshire Ports outside Liverpool c.1750–1790', *T.H.S.L.C.*, 126, 1977.
5. *Ibid.*, p. 54.
6. L.P.L., MS 3738, *Hope*'s Package Book and MS 5165, *Tom's* Papers.

CHAPTER I

The Emergence and Establishment
of the Lancaster Slave Trade

By 1736 Lancaster already had experience in transatlantic trade. This took place in two main directions. Firstly there was the tobacco trade with Virginia and then there was the trade with the West Indian colonies, for commodities such as sugar and cotton. This commerce began in the seventeenth century. The first recorded voyage by a Lancaster ship in the tobacco trade occurred in the 1670s,[1] and in 1689 John Hodgson made £1,500 profit on a £200 venture to Virginia.[2] Such profits doubtless encouraged other Lancastrians to send ships. Lancaster's tobacco trade, although small in national terms, soon reached a level which prompted Ralph Davis to comment on it in his "Rise of the English Shipping Industry",[3] but he does point out that this unusual scale of activity by a minor port took place during the French wars after 1689.[4] At such times there was a scarcity of colonial imports at home which meant that a successful voyage would be more profitable. William Stout, a Lancaster grocer and merchant, described the advantages of war-time trading in 1691–2,

> … the merchants have bought provisions and our manufactures low, and not above half the value of a cargo as in times of peace, and had their returns at a low price, but sold them here at a double price …[5]

Lancaster, alongside other north-western ports, was well placed for the colonial connexion, whilst eastern, southern and south-western ports were particularly vulnerable to privateering attacks. It was much safer to take a route north of Ireland. Lancaster's increased level of activity at such times tells us something about its position and development as a port. This is the first of a number of instances when trade figures go up during years of conflict. It implies that Lancaster had a need to take risks and thereby increase the value of its imports, thus hinting at its position as a small west-coast port with typically small profit margins, perhaps due to high export costs, anxious to get a foothold in the colonial trade. Lancaster's tobacco trade, which had been initiated by two grocers, John Hodgson and Augustine

Lancaster and the River Lune, c. 1730, by Ralph. The area to the right of the bridge has yet to see the building of St. George's Quay. Artistic licence has brought the open sea much closer to the town than in reality. *Courtesy of Lancaster City Museums*

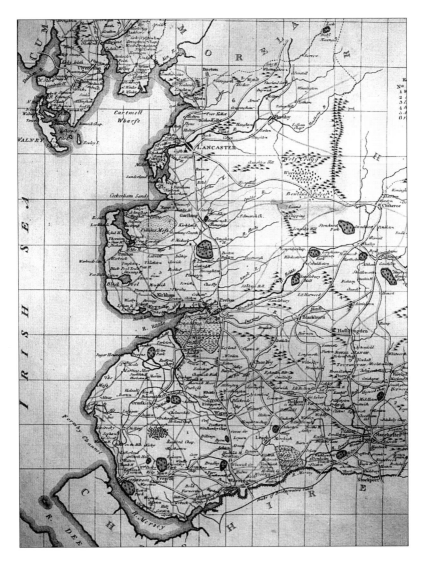

The County of Lancashire, engraved for J. Harrison in 1789. *Courtesy of Lancaster Library*

Greenwood, did continue after peace returned in 1714, with usually one or two vessels being sent each year. However, after about 1724 the trade declined markedly. This can probably be largely explained by Scotland's successful competitive entry into the trade after the Act of Union in 1707,[6] and Glasgow's eventual dominance of it.

It is interesting to note that Whitehaven, which had always had a more established trade to Virginia than Lancaster, managed to maintain some footing in the tobacco trade where Lancaster failed. In the 1720s its ships were afforded some assistance by the Scottish merchants who, finding themselves short of vessels, called upon their Cumberland neighbours to supply ships and masters for Virginia. This is reflected in the figures for 1721 when twenty-four vessels sailed from Whitehaven to Virginia. The year 1723 saw an end to this when Whitehaven and Glaswegian merchants fell out over alleged custom frauds and Whitehaven masters had to look to Ireland for freight to America which they normally avoided because of bad profit margins. However, before long, Whitehaven merchants managed to make a comeback and the 1730s and 1740s saw their tobacco trade expand apace as they succeeded in exploiting major European markets first in Holland and then in France, where buyers were especially attracted to Whitehaven's and Glasgow's cheaper tobacco after the outbreak of war in 1739. By the 1740s Whitehaven had earned itself second place after London in the level of its tobacco imports.[7] This tobacco trade, alongside Whitehaven's even more substantial coal trade, gave the port a period of substantial prosperity.

Meanwhile Lancaster, having been unable to capitalize on the tobacco trade, focused its attention on its other colonial interest, that of the sugar islands. Ships had been fitted out for the West Indies for many years. The year 1687 saw the first recorded voyage which was made from Lancaster to Jamaica by the *Lambe*, which traded for sugar, cotton and logwood.[8] Barbados was the other island visited by Lancaster ships, and it was to this island that the *Employment* made the first of several voyages in 1699.[9]

Table 1   *Comparison of Lancaster's West Indian and American Trade*[10]

	1715	1716	1717	1721	1722	1723	1724	1725	1726	1727	1728	1729	1730
W. Indies													
Vessels	2	–	1	3	3	2	5	9	3	2	6	6	7
Tonnage	100	–	60	190	172	120	240	480	185	115	360	323	405
America													
Vessels	1	1	1	2	2	2	2	1	1	1	–	1	1
Tonnage	100	80	80	140	125	220	105	70	70	80	–	60	60

In time the West Indian trade, supplying the home market with sugar, cotton and rum, replaced the tobacco trade, although one or two ships continued to trade with Virginia each year. Table 1 shows this change taking place.

Quay and warehouses of Second Terrace at Sunderland Point, scene of Robert Lawson's enterprise close to the mouth of the River Lune (photograph c. 1900). *Courtesy of Lancaster City Museums*

Clearly the number of vessels employed in the West India trade was reaching new levels. This encouraged further steps to be taken in developing Lancaster as a port. The most notable of these was taken in 1720 by Robert Lawson, a prominent Quaker merchant, who built quays and warehouses near the river mouth at Sunderland Point to avoid the difficult navigation of the Lune, from whence he conducted his transatlantic voyages. Then, in 1721, a petition by local merchants was presented to the Mayor of Lancaster, requesting that a buoy should be placed at the Shoulder of Lune, a perilous sandbank north of the entrance to the estuary, and that it should be maintained by voluntary subscriptions.

However, it was not all a matter of progress. The susceptibility to misfortune was always present. Small profits or losses persuaded William Stout to quit his transatlantic investments after 1715. These are carefully recorded in his autobiography,[11] whilst Robert Lawson of Sunderland Point was declared bankrupt in 1728 for £14,000 for living beyond his profits,[12] and no one came forward to take over his quays and warehouses close to the river mouth. Such examples again hint at the uncertain profit margins experienced by many of these early Lancaster merchants, especially in the light of a declining tobacco trade at Lancaster and given that colonial trade was often too limited to allow for the fluctuations of fortune. Its merchants also, as yet, lacked adequate contacts in the colonies.

Nevertheless, the overall trend of colonial trade remained upwards throughout the 1730s, and conditions were gradually changing. Certain Lancaster merchants were now beginning to reap the benefits of experience gained from some years of small but steady trading across the Atlantic. This enabled them to organize their business enterprises better. For instance, they began to send out regular factors to the West Indies to deal with the ships' cargoes in place of the captains or supercargoes. Their permanency there ensured a more effective distribution of the home produce and the buying of better quality and better priced return cargoes. They also had the important effect of reducing the time a vessel needed to spend in the colonial port. All these factors would undoubtedly increase the returns on a West Indian voyage. Gwalter Borranskill was one such employee, sent out to Barbados to act for several Lancaster merchants in 1735.[13] The following year saw Abraham Rawlinson, a junior member of an important Lancaster merchant family, likewise sent to the West Indies to serve his family and their partners and at the same time to afford him with valuable first-hand experience of the West Indian trade. Schofield notes, "One of the advantages of the close relationship of the Townson-Dilworth-Rawlinson group was that there was a supply of young men to go to Barbados or elsewhere in the West Indies to serve as a representative of the partners in buying and selling."[14] Meanwhile, the colonies themselves were developing fast, as more and more land was turned over to plantation, and their needs for goods from the mother country were expanding accordingly. Lancaster merchants seized the opportunity to supply the plantations with items such as Lancashire textiles, Furness iron, various local manufactures and food provisions. The diversity of their exports is well illustrated by the cargo of the snow *Sarah*, owned by Robert Lawson and Company, which traded with Barbados in 1737. It consisted of beef, butter, sundry oats, felt hats, feathers, men's shoes, tallow candles, pewter, snuff, northern cottons, cordage, potatoes, cheese, nuts and grutts (probably new ale or poor small beer or, less likely, the refuse of fish livers).[15]

However, the nature of this and other export cargoes during the same period highlights a problem that Lancaster merchants faced, namely that their region had no one staple export of value to offer the colonies. The town was not, at this time, a centre for lucrative English manufactures, rather it supported a number of small-scale industries, such as tallow chandling, cheese making and leather dressing. Likewise Lancaster had no obvious raw material to export overseas to the colonies. Consequently, its merchants were forced to export a variety of local, fairly cheap exports such as candles and cheese, take on foodstuffs such as butter and beef in Ireland and, if they could arrange and afford it, send more valuable but costly manufactures from elsewhere, such as textiles from East Lancashire, for which they were not as well placed as merchants at Liverpool. These factors would have restricted the profit margins on Lancaster's colonial ventures. More importantly, they would have favoured those who had both sufficient capital to make multiple ventures and who had good contacts in Lancaster and elsewhere, but would have made it hard for newcomers to get established. This situation is reflected in the partnerships of this time.

A study of the Colonial Naval Officers' Lists for Barbados[16] makes it possible to reconstruct, at least in part, a picture of Lancaster's early trading partnerships. It would seem that the merchants who took part in transatlantic trade of the 1730s fell into two main categories. Firstly, there were those whose names appeared frequently. These men obviously formed the more permanent partnerships. They undertook repeated voyages and owned several vessels. These men were undoubtedly in a position to develop good contacts in terms of suppliers at home as evident in some of their partnerships. Their links were especially important given the lack of a staple export at Lancaster. These merchants would also have been able to set up good contacts in the West Indies in the form of resident factors, which would enable them to speed up their operations there and maximise their returns. In the second category were the lesser, more casual traders whose names appear maybe once or twice as they made the occasional investment. They could not have organized the same network of contacts. These men would probably have been more on a par with William Stout. The financial returns experienced by these two groups no doubt varied considerably.

One family in many ways typical of the more persistent and serious traders was the Lawsons. John Lawson had pioneered commercial developments in the post-Restoration period, whereupon the family established itself in colonial trade at Lancaster in the earlier decades of the eighteenth century. For some time it produced a succession of fairly successful merchants, despite Robert of Sunderland's bankruptcy in 1728. One of these was probably Robert's uncle, also Robert (the Elder of Lancaster). He himself had experienced substantial financial losses in 1721 when the South Sea Bubble burst. It was a disaster he withstood, however, owing to his considerable investments in land.[17] His resilience demonstrates the established nature of this branch of the family through trade. He and his son, Robert the Younger, sent at least five vessels to Barbados between 1729 and 1738,[18] whilst his other sons, Joshua and John, traded there with the *Endeavour* around the same time. The family's lengthy associations with colonial trade enabled their members to develop good trading connexions at home and abroad. Robert Lawson's partner in at least two voyages to Barbados during this period was Isaac Moss, a hosier and Quaker from Manchester.[19] This contact was obviously the result of long-standing family ties. Mercy Moss, sister to Isaac, had married Robert Lawson of Sunderland Point in 1716 and Isaac himself had married Robert's sister four years later.[20] This link more than likely facilitated the Lawson merchants' access to the more lucrative Lancashire cottons. Robert Lawson's other partners included Miles Townson, George Middleton, Robert Foxcroft, all important merchants in Lancaster at this time, and more frequently Abraham Haworth, another Manchester merchant.[21]

Another prominent firm which undoubtedly benefitted from good trading links at home and in the colonies comprised the Quakers John Dillworth, Miles Townson and the Rawlinsons. Members from these families came to dominate the West Indian trade at Lancaster in the eighteenth century. The partnership was bound together by strong personal ties. For instance, in 1734 Thomas Hutton Rawlinson had married Mary Dillworth.[22] This merchant group also joined hands with Isaac Moss, a connexion they presumably acquired from their fellow Friends, the Lawsons, and he, in turn, perhaps introduced them to the Unitarian, Thomas Touchet, an important manufacturer of linen and cotton goods in Manchester,[23] who also became their partner in trade at this time. Their brigantine, the *Industry*, made repeated voyages to Barbados in the 1730s. The inclusion of a Manchester manufacturer in the partnership would again give these Lancaster merchants easier access to the cheap Lancashire cottons they needed for export, whilst Thomas Touchet's share in the imports would provide him with a ready source of raw cotton. The Rawlinson brothers had further useful connexions in Yorkshire by 1743, if not earlier. During this year they took on an apprentice, Joseph Farrar, son of Isaac, a broad-cloth maker from near Halifax.[24] In addition, the Rawlinsons, as chief ironmasters in the Backbarrow Company, had long-standing interests in Furness ore, which no doubt proved useful in terms of exports and the outfitting of ships.[25] Meanwhile, the firm had their ready supply of juniors to assist them on board ship and overseas in the islands. Thomas Hutton Rawlinson captained the *Industry* in 1735 whilst, as mentioned earlier, his brother Abraham was a resident factor in Barbados.

Thomas Touchet also took shares in a vessel with two more Lancaster merchants at this time. They were George Chippendale and John Middleton who sent their snow, the *Mary*, to Barbados throughout the 1730s. They were to set up its captain, William Wayles, as their resident factor in Barbados to buy and sell the vessel's cargoes.[26] Other important figures to appear in the Barbados records during the 1730s include Miles Birkett, a rival Quaker who traded with Robert Peel and Henry Sergeant, himself captain of their West-Indiaman, the *Hope*; also John Bowes who sent out the *Ann* with Ambrose Gillison.

In contrast, there were the small, casual traders whose names maybe appear just once in the shipping records, often in large partnerships or sometimes alongside the bigger names. These were most likely new names to transatlantic trade and they would have had few of the privileged contacts mentioned in connexion with the larger merchants. These men presumably failed to make sufficient returns to establish themselves as prominent merchants in their own right, in part at least because Lancaster lacked a ready export. If they wished to transcend these limitations and become serious colonial merchants, they needed a means to improve on the returns they received from their investments in colonial trade. Under such circumstances these Lancaster entrepreneurs no doubt looked with interest at a particular branch of transatlantic trade that was being explored and developed close by at Liverpool. It concerned the enforced shipment of African slaves across the Atlantic to the New World where they were required for work on the plantations in large field gangs. A brief account of the trade to date is important in appreciating its potentials for individual investors at this time. Slave trafficking had been recently won over to private enterprise and had a reputation not only for extraordinary rewards which might benefit people from all walks of life but also for respectability. John Newton, a Liverpool Guinea captain in the 1750s, remarked some years later, "It is, indeed accounted a genteel employment and is usually very profitable ..."[27]

This form of Atlantic commerce had been initiated by the Portuguese and in 1562 it was introduced to Britain by John Hawkins. It was developed by many other nations in the seventeenth century and was stepped up to unprecedented levels during the eighteenth to keep pace with insatiable demand. Climatic and social conditions had meant European labour was both unwilling and inappropriate for plantation work and, even when many of the colonies had been fully developed, the short life expectancy of a field slave kept the demand for blacks in the New World buoyant. By the early eighteenth century England had come to lead the field in this Atlantic bonanza, notably after the signing of the Treaty of Utrecht in 1713 whereby the British gained the coveted *Asiento*. This gave them the right to supply slaves to Spain's American colonies. Meanwhile, the organization of the English trade had undergone significant changes.

Throughout the seventeenth century the trade to Africa was the preserve of various London-based companies. In 1660 the Company of Royal Adventurers had been founded. In its new charter, obtained in 1663, the slave trade was first mentioned as a specific objective of the Company. After a number of years the Company failed, but it was succeeded by the much stronger Royal African Company which received its charter in 1672. This company continued to represent London interests and held the monopoly rights of the English slave trade for some years. However, as the eighteenth century approached, trade by means of joint-stock companies with monopoly grants declined and the influence of the individual trader increased. By an Act of 1698 the African trade was finally opened up to private merchants as well. These independent traders had to pay a ten per cent duty to the Royal African Company on imports to and exports from Africa, except for redwood which carried a five per cent duty and for three commodities which were exempt of all duty, namely gold, silver and slaves. For a time the two rival systems operated side by side, but it soon became clear that free trade was more efficient than monopoly and by 1712 the last vestiges of monopoly had disappeared from the English slave trade. One important outcome was for the slave trade to rely less and less on London as its sole headquarters. It spread first to Bristol and then to Liverpool, where independent merchants were eager to tap the wealth that was to be gained from the unprecedented demand for black Africans in the colonies.[28]

The purchase and transportation of slaves added an extra, middle stage to the commercial enterprise. The economic argument in favour of this additional undertaking was that it could prove very lucrative and thereby increase the overall returns on investments in colonial trade. Carefully selected, specialist cargoes were shipped out to Africa on the first leg of the voyage where they were exchanged for slaves. On the second leg, infamously known as the "Middle Passage", the slaves were transported to the colonies where they were sold, it was hoped, at a good profit, that is to say for substantially more than the value of the original cargo. The proceeds, or at least some of them, could then be used to purchase colonial produce. This would then be sold back in England or elsewhere as a re-export, again at a profit, if all went well.[29] Slave trafficking therefore added a risky but highly lucrative element to a colonial venture, giving it a triangular structure. Its potential for boosting a merchant's returns must have been attractive. At this time, it should be remembered, the trade's reputation rested on the undisputed profits made in the early decades of the eighteenth century.[30] Being a trade which had already offered opportunities to small nations, such as Denmark and Sweden, when they could find no openings in the West Indian or American trades,[31] the slave trade likewise offered scope, on an individual basis, to the smaller, less experienced private merchants.

Reconstruction of a slave-ship hold at Wilberforce House Museum, Hull.
Courtesy of Hull City Museums & Arts Galleries

It was against this background that Lancaster sent its first slave ship to Africa in 1736. This was the *Prince Frederick*, bound for the Guinea coast. Alas, nothing is known about its ownership, nor about that of Lancaster's second slaver, the *Royal Ann*, which set sail two years later.[32] Therefore, explanations as to why they were sent are made more difficult. What is clear, however, is that these very first slave traders began a trickle, which was to grow into a steady flow, of ships being fitted out for Africa from Lancaster, and it was to last for many years to come. It seems likely that their owners had been tempted by the success of their neighbours at Liverpool. The commercial ties which existed between the two ports undoubtedly promoted Lancaster's awareness of Liverpool's slaving enterprises.[33] Opportunists at Lancaster, having realised the potential for making immense profits from a single slaving venture, should all go well, must have considered how they themselves might use this trade to gain greater security and status within their local merchant society.

Liverpool's example would not, however, appear to be the sole explanation for Lancaster's adoption of the 'black ivory' trade. Other ports in the north west, and indeed elsewhere, would have had a similar view of Liverpool's apparent success in the African trade. Yet they, as will be discussed shortly, did not take up the slave trade when Lancaster did, with the exception of a short spell of activity by one merchant at Whitehaven, nor did they pursue it to the same degree in later years. The explanations must be more complex. Lancaster's particular appraisal of the opportunities offered by the slave trade, as exemplified at Liverpool, surely stemmed from the port's unique balance of two distinct features. On the one hand Lancaster sustained a steady but not exceptional economic growth in transatlantic trade whilst on the other its geographical situation meant some of its merchants, notably the less established ones who lacked easy access to cheap convenient exports, all too frequently experienced low profit margins. The precise interplay of these two features would have lured certain individuals to try the slave trade as a means to improve potential profit margins.

Thus Lancaster's first two slave ships were more than likely sent by relative newcomers to colonial trade, probably by some of the less successful merchants who had tried out direct colonial trade in the early 1730s. These would have been men who appreciated the problems attached to making good returns in the West Indies trade, unless one was well connected, and who considered the slave trade as offering better opportunities than other forms of investment despite its risks. Meanwhile, it is significant that none of the prominent merchants who owned West Indiamen in the 1730s, or their sons, appeared as owners of the slave ships which followed on from the

Prince Frederick and *Royal Ann*. A survey of the less prominent colonial traders of the 1730s reveals some interesting information about subsequent slave traders which lends further support to the notion that Lancaster slave merchants were in fact marginal men, that is to say individuals who came from outside or from the fringes of Lancaster's established merchant community.

A number of these early investors' names recurred some years later, not in duplicate, but in the form of their descendants who, in several instances, turned to the slave trade as a means to make their money and establish themselves as prominent Lancaster merchants. Examples include such names as Butterfield, Hinde, Dodson and Addison.[34] It was presumably their relatives' occasional investments in colonial shipping which prompted them to invest in overseas trade. Yet the necessarily small profit margins experienced by their elders tempted them to try adventures of a slightly more risky, but potentially lucrative, nature.

The argument is given more credibility still when one looks at the situations of Lancaster's north-western neighbours. Only Whitehaven had seen the occasional slaving venture to Africa when Lancaster entered the trade and neither it nor the other north-western ports pursued or developed a slave trade to match Lancaster's in the ensuing years.[35] Reasons for this must now be examined. Chester, to the south, had been unable to sustain its colonial trade in the face of fierce competition from its close neighbour, Liverpool. Thus it had neither the independent colonial contacts nor the necessary economic growth. What colonial ventures it did undertake tended to be under the umbrella of the Merseyside merchants, and at this time it made little or no sense for them to outfit slavers at Chester. Meanwhile Whitehaven, through its tobacco trade with the American colonies, experienced the growth and prosperity which Chester missed. The experience and shipping this generated prompted one merchant, Walter Lutwidge, to send his tobacco ships on three slaving ventures to Angola between 1733 and 1739, at times when alternative commerce was unfavourable.[36] However, as it turned out, these were just isolated ventures, convenient stopgaps for the colonial merchant concerned. Overall, Whitehaven merchants had little need at that time to extend their overseas enterprises into the more risky slave trade. They were content to focus their attention on the tobacco trade with Virginia, especially during the boom years of the 1730s and 1740s, a time when the port was also benefitting from a thriving coal trade with Ireland, the trade having emerged from its depression of the 1720s.[37] Moreover, the size of Whitehaven's merchant community was not large[38] and its growth was probably limited, given the port's thinly-populated hinterland. Existing trading opportunities no doubt provided sufficient openings for aspiring merchants at this time. In contrast, Lancaster had a more rapidly expanding merchant community, the result, in part, of the arrival of young men from the prosperous Furness region.[39] Its overseas opportunities, outside the slave trade, were obviously insufficient to accommodate this expansion. Interestingly, Liverpool, despite its opportunities in direct colonial trade, had a strong need to redeploy its contraband fleet at this time. It had been ousted from its profitable trade in Lancashire textiles centred on Jamaica by the Navigation Laws of 1747, and many of these merchants turned to the African trade, where their commercial connexions and experience served them well.[40] Significantly, this was the time when the Liverpool African trade took off. Nearer to home, Preston and Poulton, although they were later to establish stronger connexions with the West Indies than Chester or Whitehaven, had no colonial trade until 1742 and 1750 respectively.[41] Accordingly, they had no experience in colonial trade on which to base any slave-trading activities at this time. Moreover, when they did start a colonial trade, exporting flax, it proved a good staple which meant they did not, overall, share Lancaster's need for slave trafficking.

Thus Lancaster's unique situation, with its experience in and economic growth from colonial trade, tempered as it was by the limitations of the region's exports, meant that it alone amongst the smaller north-western ports gave impetus to certain aspiring local merchants to try their fortunes in the slave trade from 1736 and to pursue it more doggedly in the years to come. In adopting the trade in black Africans, these opportunists hoped to extract additional profits which would compensate for the difficulties they faced in providing lucrative exports which they could exchange for colonial produce.

Lancaster's initial involvement in the slave trade was clearly experimental and patchy. There is no evidence to show that either the *Prince Frederick* or the *Royal Ann* made more than one slaving voyage each. Furthermore, six years ensued before another Lancaster slaver was sent to Africa. One explanation for this might be that these first two Guineamen experienced substantial losses. The trade was also well known for its disastrous returns should a venture succumb to any of the dangers that might beset it. However, it is more likely that a much less localized factor was responsible for this early abatement in outfitting slavers for Africa. In 1739, immediately after Lancaster had made its initial ventures in the slave trade, the war of Jenkin's Ear broke out between Britain and Spain, and by 1744 France had also joined in against Britain. These years of conflict may well have dampened the enthusiasm of these pioneer slave traders, but more importantly, they afforded them, and other aspiring Lancaster merchants, with the means to make acceptable profits in the direct colonial trade, without the need to pursue more risky and experimental ventures in live cargoes. War had certainly benefitted Lancaster's colonial trade before and it no doubt gave Lancaster merchants another boost now, for reasons similar to those already stated.[42] A safe return from a colonial voyage would usually mean an assured profit. Wartime opportunities are given further emphasis when one looks at Schofield's observations for this period. He notes, from his study of the Register General of Shipping, that there was a significant upsurge in the trade figures at this time. He estimates the tonnage of ships engaged in overseas trade belonging to Lancaster, which would include voyages to Ireland, stood at 451 tons in 1737 whereas by 1744 it had more than doubled to reach a record level of 986 tons.[43] This activity again hints at Lancaster's position, as a small marginal port, eager to prosper from the colonies' expanding markets, whenever opportunity arose.

Two more Lancaster slavers were sent to Africa during the later years of this war, which shows that certain Lancaster entrepreneurs were intent on resuming the pioneering activities of the late 1730s. There is little information about the first, other than it was a vessel of a hundred tons.[44] However, more is known about the 130-ton *Expedition* which made two voyages to the Guinea coast in 1744 and 1746. Information on its ownership is particularly illuminating. Although it was registered in London and made its initial clearance from the Thames, suggesting it had been purchased there, its owner Thomas Butterfield was unmistakeably a Lancastrian. As the son of an apothecary who had been a casual investor in colonial trade,[45] the profile of Lancaster's first identifiable slave trader supports the contention that the trade appealed to those who were seeking a more effective means of participating in the opportunities provided by the rising demand for colonial imports.[46]

When the Peace of Aix-la-Chapelle was signed in 1748 an uneasy balance of power was restored to Europe and, with the war boom over, Lancaster evidently saw fit to develop its slave trade so as to establish a regular pattern of trading to Africa. It was surely no coincidence that Walter Lutwidge at Whitehaven was also contemplating another Guinea voyage in October 1749. His concerns in the Virginia tobacco trade had flourished during the war years but, as Beckett points out, once the peace was signed the port's tobacco trade began a noticeable decline from which it never recovered.[47] In a letter to John Hardman of Liverpool, Lutwidge wrote,

> … it wo'd not be disagreeable to me to be concerned a little in the Guinea Trade from your place as I have ships and no Employm't for them that I am at present fond of (I mean the Virg' Trade).[48]

Whitehaven merchants were beginning to face difficulties which were to prompt them, also, to send slave ships to the African coast on a more regular basis for a time.

Seventeen forty eight marked the beginning of almost thirty-eight years of uninterrupted investment in the slave trade by Lancaster merchants, and it was to be a full seventy years before the last Lancaster-owned slaver returned up the Lune after its last African voyage. Throughout much of this period certain Lancaster entrepreneurs evidently found the trade in African slaves a useful and rewarding branch of commerce. It suited the particular circumstances they found themselves in at Lancaster. Meanwhile, the port's established merchants were in a position to grow and prosper through their direct trade with the colonies and, with the investments in these two distinct branches of transatlantic trade, Lancaster experienced a period of commercial development which is often described as its golden age.

Our next concern is the means and methods by which these slave traders conducted their African ventures. Their mode of operation enabled Lancaster to maintain a remarkable foothold in the trade over a considerable period of time. On balance, not only was Lancaster more attracted to the 'black ivory' trade than other small north-western ports, but its merchants appear to have been more successful in what was becoming an increasingly competitive trade as the eighteenth century progressed.

Notes to Chapter I

1. Schofield, *Economic History of Lancaster*, Part 1, p. 10.
2. Craig and Schofield, 'Lancaster Trade in Stout's Time', p. 26.
3. R. Davis, *The Rise of the English Shipping Industry in the Seventeenth and Eighteenth Centuries* (Newton Abbot, 1962), p. 270.
4. This refers to attacks on English commerce by French privateers during the wars of the League of Augsburg, 1688–1697 and the Spanish Succession, 1702–1704.
5. M. M. Schofield, 'The Letter Book of Benjamin Satterthwaite of Lancaster, 1737–1744', *T.H.S.L.C.*, 113, 1961, p. 139.
6. The Act of Union enabled Scottish merchants to carry tobacco under the Navigation Laws of 1660 and 1671.
7. J. V. Beckett, *Coal and Tobacco: The Lowthers and the Economic Development of West Cumberland, 1660–1760* (Cambridge, 1981), pp.106–7.
8. Craig and Schofield, 'Lancaster Trade in Stout's Time', p. 26.
9 . Marshall, ed., *William Stout*, p. 111.
10. Craig and Schofield, 'Lancaster Trade in Stout's Time', pp. 41, 45 and 46. The American Trade was to Virginia for tobacco.

11. Marshall, ed., *William Stout, passim*. Also see Schofield, 'Benjamin Satterthwaite', pp. 139–141.

12. Marshall, ed., *William Stout*, p. 114. Stout criticized Lawson for overspending on land and buildings. This was, however, a common practice for merchants wanting security in an uncertain occupation; see Beckett, *Coal and Tobacco*, p. 114.

13. Schofield, *Economic History of Lancaster*, p. 12.

14. Schofield, 'Benjamin Satterthwaite', p. 133.

15. P.R.O., C.O. 33/16, Part II, 2 May 1737.

16. P.R.O., C.O. 33/16, Parts I and II, 1728–1753.

17. N. Morgan, 'The Social and Political Relations of the Lancaster Quaker Community, 1688–1740', in M. Mullett, ed., *Early Lancaster Friends* (Centre for North-West Regional Studies, University of Lancaster, Occasional Paper No. 5, 1978), p. 24.

18. P.R.O., C.O. 33/16, Part I.

19. Isaac Moss became a freeman of Lancaster, F.R. 1727/28.

20. Craig and Schofield, 'Lancaster Trade in Stout's Time', p. 56.

21. Abraham Howarth and his brother John became freemen of Lancaster (F.R. 1735/36), both being described as merchants of Manchester.

22. Lancaster Friends' Meeting House, Monthly Meeting, Marriages, 14 Oct. 1734.

23. Thomas Touchet was made a freeman of Lancaster, F.R.

24. Free/App. Rolls, 18 Nov. 1746.

25. J. D. Marshall, *Furness and the Industrial Revolution* (Barrow-in-Furness, 1958), p. 20.

26. Marshall, ed., *William Stout*, p. 57.

27. B. Martin and M. Spurrell, eds., *The Journal of a Slave Trader* (London, 1962), p. 95.

28. K. G. Davies, *The Royal African Company* (London, 1957), pp. 15, 41–44 and K. G. Davies, *The North Atlantic World in the Seventeenth Century* (Minnesota, 1974), pp. 117–118. Re. import and export duties laid down by Act of 1698, see E. Donnan, *Documents Illustrative of the History of the Slave Trade to America* (Washington, 1935 and New York, 1969), vol. I, pp. 421–429.

29. The triangularity of slaving ventures has not been questioned except for the later period, see below, ch. 2, p. 90ff.

30. The slave trade's profitability prior to its last sixty years, has not been questioned. See D. Richardson, 'The Costs of Survival: The Transport of Slaves in the Middle Passage and Profitability of the Eighteenth-Century British Slave Trade', *Explorations in Economic History*, 24, 1987, p. 178.

31. Davies, *Royal African Company*, p. 12.

32. P.R.O., Adm. 7/80, 13 Jan 1736 and Adm. 7/82, 26 May 1738 [Mediterranean Passes, Adm. 7, 77–122]

33. No evidence has been found to suggest that Lancaster slave traders had participated in Liverpool ventures.

34. These names appear in the naval office shipping lists for Barbados in the 1720s and 1730s, see P.R.O., C.O. 33/16, Parts I and II. As names in the Lancaster slave trade, see below, ch. 3.

35. Whitehaven had sent the *Swift* to Africa as early as 1711, see A. Eaglesham, 'The Growth and Influence of the West Cumberland Shipping Industry 1660–1800', unpublished Ph.D thesis, University of Lancaster, 1977, p. 90. The port's slave trade did reach significant levels later on, but only between 1750 and 1769. See P.R.O., B.T. 6/3, Bundle B from 57 to 118, 'Tonnage Account of Vessels Clearing G.B. to Africa, 1757–1772'.

36. Re. Walter Lutwidge's ventures, see E. Hughes, *North Country Life in the Eighteenth Century*, Volume 2, 'Cumberland and Westmorland 1700–1830' (London, 1965), p. 45.

37. The fact that several Whitehaven vessels entered Virginia from Barbados with a handful of slaves suggests its merchants found a few slaves assisted them in the purchase of their tobacco. See Donnan, ed., *Slave Trade*, vol. 4, index under 'Whitehaven'.

38. Beckett, *Coal and Tobacco*, p. 112.

39. See below, ch. 3, p. 157.

40. B. L. Anderson, 'The Lancashire Bill System and its Liverpool Practitioners', in W. H. Chaloner and B. M. Ratcliffe, eds., *Trade and Transport: Essays in Economic History in honour of T. S. Willan* (Manchester, 1977), pp.61–62. He suggests William Davenport may have entered the Guinea trade in this way.

41. Schofield, 'Slave Trade', p. 43.

42. See above, p. 13.

43. Craig and Schofield, 'Lancaster Trade in Stout's Time', p. 48.

44. P.R.O., T.64, 26A/273, 'Returns for other Ports in Great Britain', 1734–1754.

45. Christopher Butterfield had been a part-owner in the *Endeavour*, see P.R.O., C.O.33/16, Part I, 29 Nov. 1728.

46. Re. Thomas Butterfield, see below ch. 3, pp. 129–130.

47. Beckett, *Coal and Tobacco*, pp. 107–108.

48. Hughes, *North Country Life*, pp. 47–48.

CHAPTER II

Structure and Operation
of the Lancaster Slave Trade

Available information has provided a reasonable, if at times sketchy, picture of the structure and organization of the Lancaster slave trade, enabling its particular characteristics to be noted and discussed. Comparing and contrasting these with the workings of the African trade elsewhere in the region reveals important explanations, in addition to a simple need for the trade, as to why Lancaster occupied such a prominent position in slave trading amongst the smaller ports. At the same time, regional variations in the structure and organization of the slave trade are indicative of more general commercial conditions and developments of the North West. In terms of the historiography of the slave trade itself, the manner in which the Lancaster merchants conducted their slaving operations is important in its contribution to a greater understanding of the organization of the English trade at large, and in particular in its example of small-scale enterprise within the African trade.

The most effective way to enlarge upon these considerations is to analyse each of the facets of a slaving venture in turn. They will be discussed in much the same order as they would have occurred in a typical slaving venture and can be divided into two broad stages. The first covers the various procedures which culminated in the acquisition of African slaves. The second concerns the disposal of slaves in the colonies, together with a discussion on the forms of remittance. This encompasses an important historiographical issue, namely the triangularity of a slaving enterprise.

Part I   The Quest for Slaves

Partnerships

The first consideration for an entrepreneur contemplating a slave-trading venture would have been how to raise the necessary finance for the enterprise. This was generally a shared undertaking at Lancaster as elsewhere. The capital investment was long-term and this, together with the inherent risks associated with the slave trade, influenced merchants to spread their assets. Investments were complex too. Ralph Davis notes the slave trade distinguished itself from many other eighteenth-century trades in that shipping and trading were "intertwined in a single common venture".[1] This was another reason for sharing the load. The size of partnerships is significant as it tells us something about how important the slave trade was to the investors concerned and thereby alludes both to their individual circumstances and to the more general situation of their port. The evidence shows that the size of partnerships did vary from one port to another.

Comprehensive details of partnerships were not given before the beginning of the statutory registration of all merchant ships in 1786. Various earlier sources, though far from complete, do give a reasonable indication as to the size of Lancaster partnerships before this date. The naval office shipping lists[2] usually quoted the ship's register and, though the list of owners was often a summary, a number of more detailed examples, most frequent for the American colonies of Georgia and South Carolina during the 1750s and 1760s, suggest an average partnership of just four shares per vessel.[3] The largest partnership was that given for the *Antelope*, where seven owners took shares in a voyage to Africa then Georgia in 1766. Meanwhile solo ventures, though uncommon in the slave trade, were not unknown at Lancaster. Miles Barber undertook several African ventures on his own, sending the *Thetis I* to South Carolina in 1759 and the *Dove* to Georgia in 1761 and 1766.[4] One-man investments point to the enthusiasm with which the slave trade was embraced by certain merchants at Lancaster. Another useful source confirms the size of Lancaster slaving partnerships. The Liverpool Plantation Registers, extant from 1743 to 1784 with the exception of the years 1774 to 1778, gave registration details for Lancaster Guineamen which used the Port of Liverpool on their way to Africa. A calculation based on nineteen such registrations, made between 1759 and 1784, gives an average share per vessel of just under one-third. This arises from registrations varying from two single investors to one with six owners.[5] The Statutory Registers for Merchant Ships at Lancaster, extant from 1786, recorded the registrations of nine slaving vessels. They too reveal an average of three to four shareholders in each ship.[6]

The size of Lancaster partnerships evidently remained remarkably constant throughout the port's involvement in the African trade. Table 2.1 summarises the information on the size of these partnerships provided by these three documents. It covers thirty-seven Guineamen.

Table 2.1   *Size of Slave-Trading Partnerships at Lancaster, 1752–1802*

Number of Owners	1	2	3	4	5	6	7
Number of Slavers	4	8	8	8	6	2	1

How did this compare with partnerships in the slave trade elsewhere? In discussing the African ventures of a committed slave merchant at Liverpool, Hyde, Parkinson and Marriner note that "the Davenport records show never less than two, usually six to eight and occasionally as many as ten or twelve venturers participating in one voyage".[7] The contemporary *A General and Descriptive History of the Ancient and Present State of the Town of Liverpool* (1798) provides further insight:

> It is well known that many of the small vessels that import about an hundred slaves, are fitted out by attornies, drapers, ropers, grocers, tallow-chandlers, taylors etc., some have one eighth, some a fifteenth (sixteenth), and some a thirty-second.[8]

Concerning slaving partnerships at the Severn port, MacInnes states, "some of the slave firms at Bristol were small one-man concerns, but more often they were partnerships of two to six or more".[9] At a number of the small ports involved in the African trade the ownership of Guineamen was often divided amongst a large group of partners, meaning individual involvement was limited. At Whitehaven, for example, the slaver *Venus* which entered Barbados in 1763, had a long list of owners, namely "Edward Fletcher, Peter How, William Gilpin, Thomas Hartley and Sons, Walter Wright and Company, Hall and Fletcher, Messrs. Spedding and Company, Coupland and Finley, Griffeths, Kelsirk and Company".[10] Another large partnership was to be found at Chester where ten craftsmen invested in the *St. George* in 1750.[11] Although not all slave-trading partnerships at these two ports were necessarily as large as these examples, it is noteworthy that none of the Lancaster registrations show as many different investors for any one venture.

Such information indicates that Lancaster partnerships were typically small and in contrast to those at Whitehaven and Chester in particular. This would be partly explained by the low tonnage of many Lancaster Guineamen, often less than a hundred tons. However, it also signifies that the Lancaster slave trade comprised more than just casual venturers, except perhaps at the outset. The slave trade must have played a more central role in these merchants' affairs. This is given added weight when one notices the long-standing commitment made by many of the Lancaster slave traders, a feature not so apparent at the other small north-western ports.[12] Given the fact that the slave trade was less likely to attract capital from those who could find satisfactory alternatives for their investments, the commitment and persistence of Lancastrians in the slave trade suggest that opportunities in direct colonial trade continued to be restricted at Lancaster during the middle decades of the eighteenth century. These individuals were apparently of the opinion that the investments they were able to make, in their particular circumstances, could be put to better effect in the slave trade. These men were obviously not without some capital and yet their financial situation was presumably inadequate to compete effectively amidst the more established colonial merchants, and they most likely lacked sufficient contacts to break into this somewhat elitist commercial network. In this respect they may be regarded as marginal men. A discussion on the types of men involved in the Lancaster slave trade, together with their motives and the impact of their efforts, will throw more light on this aspect. It will be pursued more fully in the next chapter.

Slaving Vessels

Obtaining a suitable vessel would be the slave traders' next task. The vessels employed at Lancaster were of various rigs. Ships, sloops, schooners and barques all appear in the records, but by far the most common were the snows and brigs. Concerning these Ralph Davis writes,

> These two ships, the brig and the snow, may be called the typical ships of the middle decades of the eighteenth century. They were almost identical and both were used for all purposes, but the snow was more commonly the ocean voyager while the brig could be found most often in home waters, and particularly those of the North Sea. One of their best-known characteristics was the small crew they required.[13]

Lancaster slave merchants, as marginal men, would be anxious to keep wages down to a minimum and keeping costs low was probably the reason why Lancaster slavers were typically small. Table 2.2 illustrates the range of sizes of Lancaster Guineamen for the 1750s, 1760s, 1770s and 1780s.

Table 2.2   *Distribution of Tonnages in African Trade at Lancaster*[14]

	<20	20–29	30–39	40–49	50–59	60–69	70–79	80–89	90–99	100–110	>110	Total Number of Vessels
1750s	1	4	5	6	4	2	5	1	1	2	0	31
1760s	4	1	3	2	4	1	4	4	2	8	1	34
1770s	0	0	0	3	1	0	7	3	0	1	1	16
1780s	0	0	0	0	0	0	3	0	1	2	0	6

40

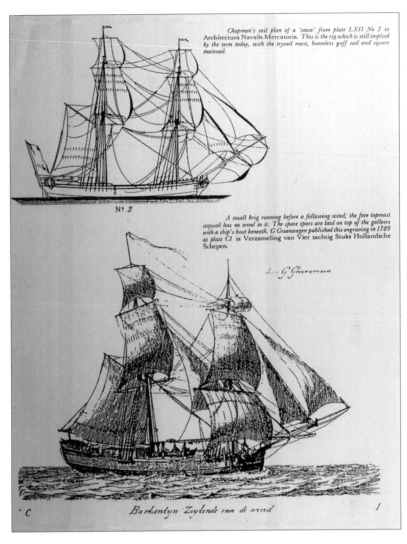

Chapman's sail plan of a 'snow' from plate LXII No 2 in Architectura Navalis Mercatoria. This is the rig which is still implied by the term today, with the trysail mast, boomless gaff sail and square mainsail.

N: 2

A small brig running before a following wind; the fore topmast staysail has no wind in it. The spare spars are laid on top of the gallows with a ship's boat beneath. G Groenwegen published this engraving in 1789 as plate CI in Verzameling van Vier tachtig Stuks Hollandsche Schepen.

d . . . G Groenewegen

Barkentyn Zeylende van de wind

An 18th-century Snow and Brig, typical of the vessels commonly used by Lancaster slave traders. Reproduced by permission from D.R. MacGregor *Merchant Sailing Ships: Sovereignty of Sail, 1775–1815* (London, 1985) p.82

In the 1750s the most popular size for a Lancaster slaver ranged between twenty and seventy tons. The next decade saw a definite increase, with over half the vessels being seventy tons or more, and nine of these were a hundred tons or over. These figures indicate a strong commitment and enthusiasm for the African trade at this time by certain members of the merchant community at Lancaster, and they presumably reflect the successful build-up of capital by some of these opportunists. Schofield suggests, however, that the experimentation with larger vessels was not very successful.[15] This certainly seems to have been the case given the size of slave ships in the 1770s actually fell. Almost two-thirds of these weighed between seventy and eighty tons and only two vessels were a hundred tons or over. The investments in larger vessels had been associated with some of the more dedicated and presumably more successful slave merchants, notably Miles Barber and Thomas Hinde. It is significant that Barber, although continuing to send larger slavers whilst at Lancaster, moved his operations to Liverpool in the mid 1760s, a step Hinde was to take with his son much later on in the 1780s.[16] After the American War of Independence Lancaster slavers, though much fewer in number, did increase in size once more, but tonnages elsewhere were increasing far ahead of these.[17]

How did the size of Lancaster slavers compare with that of slave ships elsewhere before the American War? Lamb has produced figures for Liverpool, London and Bristol and extracts from these are set out below, alongside figures for Lancaster, Whitehaven and Chester.

Table 2.3   *Average Tonnage of Vessels in the West Africa Trade, 1750 to 1775*[18]

	Liverpool	London	Bristol	Lancaster	Whitehaven	Chester
1750–1759	–	142	111	50	104	106
1760–1769	109	159	120	77[19]	110	–
1772–1775	106	108	110	72	–	105

Lancaster vessels were obviously considerably smaller on average than slaving vessels elsewhere. Keeping costs low has already been mentioned as the most probable explanation. Moreover, the small size of ships no doubt afforded them certain advantages in this trade. Schofield notes that small vessels minimised the time it took to slave on the African coast, since only a small cargo of blacks would be needed. This in turn "reduced the length of stay on the coast of Africa where disease might strike crew and slavers, and lessened the risks of disease or food and water shortages on the middle passage to the Americas". Also, "a large number of slaves might flood the markets in some parts of the slave-owning colonies, particularly if other slavers arrived about the same time".[20] These factors were most likely important contributors to Lancaster's relative success in the trade for a time. This view complies with a statement made by a contemporary commentator at Bristol, namely that small vessels "near always get money at the worst of times".[21]

In choosing small outfits for their African ventures, Lancaster traders pursued an individual brand of slaving which set them aside from their large competitors and, as we shall see, may have given them a protected niche in the slave trade. There were certain similarities across the Atlantic. Mannix notes the Yankee traders' preference for small sloops, schooners and brigantines. In 1789 the largest vessel leaving Newport, Rhode Island, was a sloop of sixty tons and the smallest was a schooner of twenty tons. Other vessels included sloops of forty, thirty-five and twenty-two tons and a brig of forty tons. Mannix likens American slaving operations on the African coast to that of retailers in contrast to the wholesalers from Liverpool.[22] Ultimately, as the century progressed and competition grew, the retailers would come to face mounting problems.[23]

So much for the size of Lancaster slavers, but what of their age and construction? Ralph Davis believes that the slave trade called for "strong and well-found vessels" because profitable selling prices of the live cargo were directly related to the speed and care with which the master could accomplish his voyage to the colonies.[24] A study of the age of Lancaster slaving vessels would suggest that Lancaster traders adhered to this maxim. Table 2.4 depicts the relative ages of Lancaster slave ships taken from a sample of forty-three vessels, covering the entire period during which Lancaster took part in the African trade.

Table 2.4   *Distribution of the Age of Lancaster Slavers*[25]

0–1 year	2–6 years	7–15 years	16–22 years
32%	30%	26%	12%

The figures show that nearly a third of Lancaster slavers were new, nearly two-thirds were under seven years old and that the average age of a Lancaster slaver was six years. This is not so different from Liverpool slavers which Jarvis reckons were generally less than five years old. MacInnes, meanwhile, estimates the average age of Bristol slavers selling their cargoes in Virginia between 1727 and 1769 to have been ten years.[26] The Lancaster slave traders were certainly not diverting ships to the slave trade when their best sailing days were over. These opportunists may have had a need to cut costs, but it would have made little sense to risk their investments in unworthy vessels. What is interesting, however, is that one of Lancaster's earliest slave ships, the *Expedition*, was built in London fourteen years before she made her first voyage to Africa in 1744. This, no doubt, denotes the experimental state of Lancaster's slave trade at that time. It is contrasted several years later by the *Jolly Batchelor*, which was not only new when she sailed to Africa in 1748 but was also Lancaster-built, as were the new slavers *Robert*, *Castleton* and *Barlborough* which sailed for the Guinea coast in 1752.[27] The youthfulness of Lancaster vessels does not lend support to Merritt's notion that slave ships were often in a "leaky, worm-eaten condition" and thus unfit to carry a cargo on the home leg of the voyage.[28] Nor does the age of Chester slavers lend such support, where four out of the six Guineamen registered there were new or young vessels. The *St.George*, which made three African voyages between 1750 and 1753, and the *Juno*, which made two trips beween 1773 and 1775, were both new at the outset of their ventures, whilst the *Black Prince* was just two years old when she was registered in 1754, having been built in New England. The exception was the *Duke*, built at Parkgate on the Dee Estuary seventeen years before she made her quest for slaves in 1754.[29] Thus neither Lancaster Guineamen nor those of its neighbours at Chester and Liverpool were generally old, but were they built specifically for the slave trade and what were the implications of their construction? Ralph Davis comments that ships were being specifically designed for the slave trade after 1750 and Mannix writes that Liverpool, being comparatively new to the trade, could build larger and faster ships, especially designed for transporting black cargoes.[30] Although evidence concerning the construction of Lancaster slavers is somewhat patchy, various advertisements in the local Liverpool newspapers show that purpose-built ships were available at Lancaster. For instance, in 1758 an advertisement read,

> To be sold to the highest bidder at the Nag's Head in Lancaster, on Wednesday the 3rd day of January 1759, at six o'clock in the evening, the Schooner *Britannia*, burthen 60 tons or thereabouts just launched off the stocks and intended for the Gambia trade, now lying at Lancaster Quay, with her masts, yards, rigging and other appurtenances, all entirely new. Inventories and further particulars may be had by applying to Mr. William Butterfield and Mr. John Helme merchants in Lancaster.

Another in 1756 read,

> To be sold to the highest bidder at the Sun in Lancaster on Thursday 2nd of September next, the brigantine, *Swallow*, burthen about 70 tons with all her materials as lately arrived from Africa and Barbados. She was built at Lancaster in the year 1751, is well found and of proper dimensions for the slave trade. For particulars apply to Messrs. Satterthwaite and Inman in Lancaster.[31]

However, by no means all Lancaster slave ships were so tailor-made. Other advertisements at Lancaster hint at the flexibility of many of its eighteenth-century vessels. For instance, in 1757 the snow

44

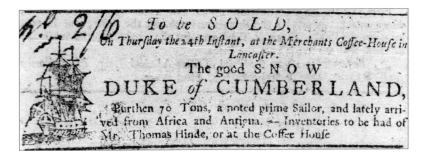

Sale advert in Williamson's 1757 Liverpool Advertiser for the *Duke of Cumberland* which had made two voyages to the River Gambia and Antigua for Thomas Hinde of Lancaster. *Courtesy of Liverpool City Council, Libraries & Arts*

Africa was for sale with all her Guinea materials being described as "suitable for the African or West Indies trade" and in 1765 a public auction was to be held for the good brig *Lively* formerly in the West India trade, a "remarkable fast sailer and very suitable for either the African or American trades".[32] Drake comments on this kind of flexibility stating, "It was convenient to buy ships that were constructed for the slave trade, but West Indiamen could be adapted with facility". In a similar vein Craig writes, "The prevalence of speculative shipbuilding at Chester and elsewhere suggests that most types of vessel were easily transferable from one trade to another". Craig goes on to suggest that such speculative building gave shipbuilders and shipowners certain advantages, such as regular work for the constructors and availability of ships to replace lost vessels for the merchants.[33] The adaptability of Lancaster's eighteenth-century vessels is further demonstrated by the fact that certain of its slavers were sent on direct West Indian voyages in between their slaving ventures. The *Lancaster*, for instance, made at least two voyages straight to Jamaica in 1758 and 1759 between slaving ventures to the same destination in 1756 and 1760. Meanwhile the *Lowther*, after making two slaving voyages to Barbados, sailed direct to Virginia twice in 1758 before being sent there a third time, via Africa, with a cargo of slaves.[34] The registers of later Lancaster Guineamen continued to reflect this tendency to transfer ships from one trade to another. The *Hope II* and the *Tom*, for instance, both purchased by James Sawrey and Company for use in the slave trade in the early 1790s, had been previously employed in the West Indies trade. It may be that some of these later Lancaster vessels, especially if they were old, as were the *Hope II* and the *Tom*, operated at a disadvantage on the slaving leg of a voyage given the abundance of swift, specialised craft at Liverpool by the late decades of the century.[35] These examples are not to suggest that Lancaster ship-builders were not constructing purpose-built slave ships at this time. Both the *Betty* and *Rose* were built on the Lune in 1783, but, as was commonly the case, both were destined for the port of Liverpool.[36] The situation was more indicative of the declining role of the slave trade at Lancaster by the later decades of the eighteenth century.

The fact that many Lancaster slavers were of a general ocean-going construction had other significant consequences for the operation of the trade at Lancaster. Most importantly, it meant such vessels could be more easily adapted for carrying home colonial produce from the West Indies or American mainland. This ties in with Professor Minchinton's observation that, "when the slave vessels had unloaded their slaves they were prepared for the return voyage to their home port. In many cases stages had to be dismantled, to enable the holds to be used for cargo".[37] Such a practice would, for Lancaster at least, quite probably challenge Sheridan and Merritt's argument that slave ships were generally unsuitable for carrying sugar home on the third leg of their journey.[38] Concerning this point Sheridan explains, "Vessels which were specifically constructed for the slave trade were not well suited for the carriage of sugar". Quoting one Guinea captain he writes, "African ships were built for the carriage of a maximum number of slaves. The holds of these vessels were said to be small." In citing another master, he notes, "The West India Merchantmen are built for burthen, full; and in general, I believe, the African ships are built for sailing, sharp built".[39]

It would seem, therefore, that Lancaster slavers, being in the main less specialized than their counterparts sailing from Liverpool, were, in theory at least, more readily adaptable for carrying colonial produce back to Lancaster. One might wonder, however, whether such ships would have been less suited to transporting their slaves than they were to carrying their colonial produce. It seems Lancaster slave traders may well have been keen to procure African cargoes no matter what the conditions were like in the holds of their vessels, if only they could see a return on their investments. Such practices would again denote undertones of marginality within their enterprise. The use of general-purpose craft allegedly meant a lengthier Middle Passage, although the tight schedule operated by most Lancaster slavers does not imply this to have been a significant feature of their trade. This may have helped to offset the effects of probable poor conditions and possible overcrowding on such vessels, circumstances which no doubt made their wretched cargoes more susceptible to misfortune on protracted voyages.[40] As ships at Liverpool became larger and more specialised, it presumably became more difficult for the Lancaster-style slaver to compete, especially when the trade became more cut-throat during the last quarter of the century.

Examples of trading goods used for the purchase of slaves (jar, flagon, manillas and spoon). *Courtesy of Hull City Museums & Art Galleries*

Exports for Africa

In procuring outgoing cargoes for their African adventures, slave merchants would have had to turn to a variety of sources. General accounts suggest supplies came predominantly from the fast developing regions of East Lancashire, Yorkshire and the Midlands. Liverpool's favourable situation, relative to these centres, is well documented. Mannix notes, "She was geographically much closer to the source of goods for the Guinea trade; that is, to the looms, foundries and workshops that produced cheap linens and woolens, iron bars, copper pans, glass beads, cutlery, gunpowder, and muskets".[41] How did Lancaster and the other north-western ports compare? Although the lack of business papers for Lancaster slave traders during the trade's main years of operation makes it difficult to be precise about where they obtained these articles, certain tentative conclusions can be drawn. As yet, nothing has been found in local tradesmen's accounts to suggest Lancaster slave traders made substantial outfits from home-based manufactures. It would seem more likely that they had to go further afield to load their Guinea vessels. No doubt many of their suppliers would have been the same as those used by Liverpool merchants. One document, listing some of the suppliers of a Lancaster slaver, does exist for the later period. This is part of the Package Book for the *Hope II*

Payment for one man slave in the Cameroons in 1792. Extract from James Sawrey's Package Book for the *Hope*. *Courtesy of Lancaster Library*

which is detailed in Appendix A.[42] It features just a handful of Lancaster tradesmen supplying flagons, chests, beans and barley. The two latter items were, most likely, grown locally. In 1774 Thomas Pennant, on his tour of Scotland, commented on Furness farmers growing beans for use as 'food for Negroes' on slave vessels.[43] However, the remaining identified suppliers for the *Hope II's* cargo were based in Liverpool, Manchester, Preston or Kirkham. Other evidence clearly links earlier

Bars of iron, copper or brass were often used when bartering for African slaves. *Courtesy of Hull City Museums & Art Galleries*

Lancaster slave traders with suppliers to their south. William Davenport's Bead Book shows that at least six Lancaster merchants bought their beads from him in Liverpool between 1766 and 1770.[44] Beads formed a crucial part of the African cargo in trade to Gambia, a destination particularly favoured by Lancaster slavers. His general trading accounts also reveal that Richard Millerson bought iron discs in 1768, whilst Miles Barber bought spirits, gunpowder and beef between 1763 and 1765.[45] Other evidence is more speculative. Textiles, the most valuable part of a slave ship's cargo, would most likely have come from Manchester manufacturers or even the Liverpool warehouses which stored imported Indian cottons, although one textile supplier may well have been closer to home. Beckett notes the popularity of Kendal cottons for the Guinea trade.[46] Copper and brass wares were commonly supplied by works at Cheadle in North Staffordshire or Warrington, both of which manufactured goods such as neptunes and manillas (brass pans and copper or brass bracelets) in the 1760s. Iron goods may have come from local production. The Backbarrow Company in Furness, managed by the Rawlinson family and related to the Lancaster West India merchants, was making many items which included Guinea kettles in 1744.[47] These may well have been supplemented by wares from Sheffield, Birmingham and even the Baltic.

This information, though rather tentative, implies that Lancaster slave merchants may well have had to look to the south for a large part of their African cargoes. Indeed, this might be one of the explanations why a number of Lancaster slavers cleared from or via Liverpool. Whilst Lancaster would have been better situated to these manufacturing centres than Whitehaven to its north, it is doubtful it was as well placed as Chester, Preston or Poulton. Its merchants' determination to trade in slaves, despite these cost disadvantages, only adds weight to the notion that they needed the slave trade. The fact that they had no suitable staple exports close to home was the very reason why they had been tempted into the slave trade in the first place. It was hoped that their purchase of a lucrative cargo of slaves would offset the difficulties and expenses of buying an initial cargo from further afield, providing they could conduct other aspects of their trade reasonably effectively. Moreover, even though Lancaster was at a distance from the main supply centres for African cargoes, patience and time were important attributes when making up these complex, assorted cargoes.[48] Lancastrians would be in a better position to compete in a trade where these attributes also played a part rather than in one which relied more exclusively on the availability of local resources.

Captains and Crews

Appointing a suitable captain for an African venture was an important task for the partners concerned. Anstey writes, "It does not seem to have been difficult to recruit masters, mates and even surgeons, for whom there were financial or career inducements".[49] Of course a good Guinea captain needed to be skilled, both as a master mariner and as a business man, given the complex nature and duration of each venture. It is important to ascertain how merchants at Lancaster and the other small ports in the region organized this aspect of their enterprise. A fundamental consideration is whether they recruited local personnel and thereby built up local expertise in the trade, and even created new investors for the future. Table 2.5 (opposite) lists certain relevant findings about some of the captains in the Lancaster slave trade.

It is clear that most, if not all, slaver captains employed by Lancaster merchants originated from the town and its surrounding districts. The Furness region's contribution stands out. The slave trade obviously attracted young and ambitious sons of moderate, middle-income families of this fairly prosperous district, as evident in their fathers' occupations. Quite often it seemed to be a path chosen by one of the junior members of the family, where older brothers had come into their father's trade or land. Their place of apprenticeship is more difficult to identify. A number, including the prominent Guinea captain Robert Dodson, were certainly apprenticed at Lancaster. However, the Lancaster Apprentice Rolls were not comprehensive.

Table 2.5 *Backgrounds of Selected Lancaster Slaver Captains*[50]

Captain's Name	Place of Origin	Father's Occupation	Date of Enrollment as Lancaster Freeman	Date of Lancaster Apprenticeship (where known)	Date & age at first African Command
John Addison	Ulverston	Innkeeper (1739) Clock-maker (1767)	1769/70	–	1763/24 years
John Alman	Aughton (Lune Valley)	Husbandman	1754/55	1742	1754/c.27 years
Samuel Bainbridge	Pennington in Furness (Nr.Ulverston)	–	–	–	1755/c.23 years
Robert Dodson	Stony Cragg (Nr.Ulverston)	Yeoman	1751/52	1744	1753/24 years
Thomas Hinde	Caton	Yeoman	1749/50	–	1748/28 years
John Houseman	Skerton	Maltster	1749/50	–	1750/24 years
Richard Millerson	Ulverston	Mariner	1759/60	–	1752/22 years
John Read	Lancaster	Taylor	1759/60	–	1759/28 years
James Sawrey	Hawkshead	Shopkeeper	1777/78	–	1771/26 years
Samuel Simondson	Urswick	Mariner (Step-father)	–	1739	1751/28 years
John Tallon	Sedbergh	–	1759/60	–	1755/28 years
Henry Tindall	Furness	–	1752/53	–	1751/ –
Thomas Woodburne	Ulverston	–	1769/70	–	1764/ –

They concentrated on those who were able to buy their freedom of the town through their apprenticeships. Those who were apprenticed at Lancaster, yet who were eligible to become freemen through their fathers, for example, were not usually recorded in these rolls. It is, of course, conceivable that some of these young captains had been apprenticed in Liverpool and even filled junior appointments there, enabling them to gain expertise in the African trade. Alternatively, given that a large number originated from Ulverston and its environs, it is also possible some served more general maritime apprenticeships there. Wherever they were trained, Lancaster was evidently not short of local recruits and as the port's involvement in the trade persisted, so the expertise of the slave-trading community grew. This would inevitably have given Lancaster an edge over the other small slave-trading ports in the region, which never matched Lancaster's period of commitment to the trade. Moreover, their use of local recruits to command their African ventures is, at times, in doubt. Walter Lutwidge, writing from Whitehaven in 1749, proposed that the Liverpool merchant, John Hardmen, should nominate "the Capt. and other officers necessary to be skilled in the Trade, people here being strangers to it".[51] Whereas Whitehaven may have provided some of its own captains at a later date when its slave trading became more frequent for a time, it seems unlikely that similar developments took place at Chester. Here none of the masters was a freeman of the town. The captains of slave ships at Preston and Poulton were probably more local, but little experience could have been gained, given none of the four named commanders made more than a single voyage each.[52] In contrast, at Lancaster, a number of the captains who survived the perils of the slave trade persisted and progressed to become African merchants themselves. This had important implications for the development of the slave trade at Lancaster and played a part in distinguishing it from that of the other small ports in the region.[53]

Crew sizes on slavers were generally larger per ton than on other merchant vessels, owing to the need to manage live cargoes on the Middle Passage. Thus a crew of twenty sailed the seventy-ton *Castleton* on five African voyages in the 1750s, whereas one of just thirteen manned her on a direct voyage to Barbados in 1765. Meanwhile, it took fourteen men to crew the smaller forty-ton *Success* on a slaving venture in 1754.[54] These ratios were, no doubt, average for small slavers in England, but at small ports like Lancaster seamen's wages would have been low, giving them a competitive edge. Interestingly, Lancaster crews on slaving vessels were notably larger than those typical for Yankee slavers, as given by Mannix.[55] However, he notes that slave mutinies were not uncommon with small crews, a risk Lancaster merchants presumably did not want to take.

Somewhat patchy evidence concerning the recruitment of Lancaster crews makes it hard to know to what extent seamen on slave ships were predominantly local men or whether they were difficult to entice, as was generally the case elsewhere in the African trade. Anstey describes them as being "Sailors down on their luck and young landsmen with romantic notions of the Guinea trade".[56] Available evidence suggests the use of local recruits, particularly from the outlying districts, during the early period when the trade was at its height. When two seamen were lost on the Guinea Coast in 1755 and 1757, their probate records described them both as being "late of Lancaster". Further evidence makes it clear that the first, John Abraham, originated from North Meols near Southport, whilst

Jonathan Lindall (Lindow) came from Ulverston where he had also been married. A third mariner to die on an African voyage at this time was Thomas Moncaster. He came from Bolton-le-Sands, a few miles to the north of Lancaster.[57] More local recruits can be found in records relating to the payment of relief for seamen's widows and disabled seamen. Amongst these records was Eleanor Kilner of Ulverston whose husband had been 'kill'd on board the *Mary* at Gambia by the Negro's' in 1761 and John Batty of Lancaster, 'late Seaman on board the *Antelope* Thomas Paley Master', who had lost his 'right Arm at Yanamarew on the Coast of Africa' in 1764.[58] In 1791, however, Robert Foster, son of an investor in the Lancaster slave trade, informed Parliament that Lancaster merchants sometimes faced difficulties in their recruitment of men on account of the trade's reputation for ill-treatment and given the small numbers who returned. He went on to say that Lancaster slavers would sometimes clear via Liverpool in order to pick up their full complement of men.[59] Nonetheless, even during the later period, the outlying districts still supplied some of the seamen for slaving voyages as a stone inside Cartmel Priory tells us. It commemorates the death of twenty-three-year-old William Spencer Barrow who had died on the Coast of Guinea in 1793. The slave trade seemingly provided welcome employment, if not a sense of adventure, in the rural districts of North Lancashire and the neighbouring Yorkshire Dales, more particularly when the trade was developing and at its peak. Lancaster slave merchants were conceivably better off in terms of recruiting their seamen than their neighbours, the environs of Whitehaven being more thinly populated and there being more attractive areas of employment further south.

Duration of Slaving Ventures

The time it took a slave ship to complete a venture had important economic ramifications. The optimum duration of a triangular voyage was considered to be no more than twelve months, though, as Minchinton notes, it was "comparatively seldom achieved". At Bristol he estimates that between 1763 and 1767 an average slaving voyage selling at Jamaica took 15.5 months, one selling at Barbados took 12.9 months, whilst one selling at the Mainland colonies took 18.4 months.[60] Meanwhile, the three slavers sent to Jamaica and Barbados by Preston and Poulton merchants just ten years earlier all spent over twenty months on their African ventures, which Schofield sees as being too long.[61] No data has been collected for the duration of ventures from Whitehaven, but at Chester no slave ship left on a second voyage inside nineteen months according to Schofield.[62] At

Lancaster the Seamen's Sixpence Accounts provide valuable information on the duration of slaving ventures. The findings are set out in Table 2.6.

Table 2.6 *Average Duration of Lancaster Slaving Ventures*[63]

	1750s	1760s	1770s
Average Duration of Voyage	12.9 months	12.4 months	12.5 months
Size of Sample	31 vessels	37 vessels	28 vessels

These figures indicate that Lancaster slave traders operated tighter schedules than their competitors at Chester, Preston and Poulton. A speedy return on investments was advantageous and more especially for men who were using the slave trade to establish themselves at Lancaster. The short duration of Lancaster ventures must be an important part of the explanation as to why Lancaster ranked well above these ports in slave-trade statistics. It is important to consider the various factors which could influence the length of a slaving voyage.

A very brief stay in the colonies, restricted to the sale of a slave cargo, does not account for the short duration of Lancaster ventures. Lancaster slavers invariably returned laden and this took time.[64] Rather these voyages reflect speed in the earlier stages of a triangular enterprise. This would presumably have been either in the time spent on the African coast slaving and thereby storing slaves, often known as 'coasting', or in the time spent on their conveyance across the Atlantic, with its hazards related to provisioning and disease, or more likely both. Tight schedules in these two stages would carry further advantages for the Lancaster merchants. Recent research has found some correlation between slave mortality and the duration of the voyage; the longer the voyage the greater the loss of life.[65] Of course the diminutive size of Lancaster slavers, which would require only small cargoes, must be part of the explanation for comparatively quick turn-around times on the coast. However, since Preston and Poulton's three slavers ranged between only fifty and seventy tons, this cannot be the only explanation. Experience and contacts along the African coast, once the trade was established, must have made all the difference, as no doubt did contacts in the colonies when tropical produce was procured. Lancaster's early entry into the slave trade and longer involvement in transatlantic commerce would have stood the port in good stead. Accordingly, William Butterfield was able to send his seventy-ton vessel, the *Castleton*, three times to the River Gambia between 1753 and 1755, whilst Poulton traders had time to apply for only two passes for their seventy-ton *Hothersall*.[66]

54

A discussion on regional preferences and methods of slaving on the African coast is an important part of understanding Lancaster's ability to compete in the slave trade. A variety of sources make it clear that Lancaster merchants favoured certain African destinations. Curtin, in his census of the Atlantic slave trade, distinguishes seven slaving regions in West Africa, namely Senegambia, Sierra Leone, Windward Coast, Gold Coast, Bight of Benin, Bight of Biafra and Angola.[67] These are shown on the map overleaf. Definitions, especially those concerning the boundaries of the Windward and Sierra Leone coasts, are often disputed, but, for clarity, Curtin's definitions will be adhered to. Lancaster slavers clearly favoured the first three of these regions. A survey of just over a hundred voyages shows that these three regions accounted for all Lancaster's intended or realised destinations before 1776,[68] and for 87% of them taking its slave-trading period as a whole. Of these, 26% went to the Gambia, 46% to Sierra Leone and 15% to the Windward Coast.[69] In contrast, Curtin estimates that only 7% of Liverpool slavers in 1751, and the same percentage of all English slavers in 1771, sailed to the Gambia.[70] Schofield argues that the River Gambia, together with the coast southwards which had shallow river estuaries and roadsteads, would have only been suitable for the small, shallow draft vessels, typical of Lancaster, whereas larger vessels could not easily find safe anchorages or large numbers of slaves. He quotes from a letter sent by the authorities at James Fort, Gambia, to the African Company in London in 1761, which criticized the presence of larger ships, saying, "100 and 50 to 70 slaves [were] a sufficient number for the Gambia and generally successful".[71]

Several instances amongst the James Fort letters to the African Company suggest that Lancaster slavers used the services of the African Company settlements. In 1762 the Governor reported to the Committee, "We disposed of Hector to Captain Robert Dodson of Lancaster for eighteen pounds sterling". There is also the occasion, again quoted by Schofield, when the Fort tried to help the ship *Mary*, captained by Samuel Sandys, which was cut off by the slaves in December 1761.[72] The African Committee was also in communication with Captain Henry White at Lancaster, through whom they sent various instructions to slave traders at the port. In 1757 they wrote, "We desire you will acquaint the Merchants of Lancaster therewith [namely their fear of French attacks in the Gambia] that they may order the masters of such ships to send their Boats and Papers to the Fort upon their entering the River".[73] Trade evidently took place with independent traders on the Gambian coast as well. A will written in 1763 by Lancaster merchant Henry Lawrence, formerly of Hertford

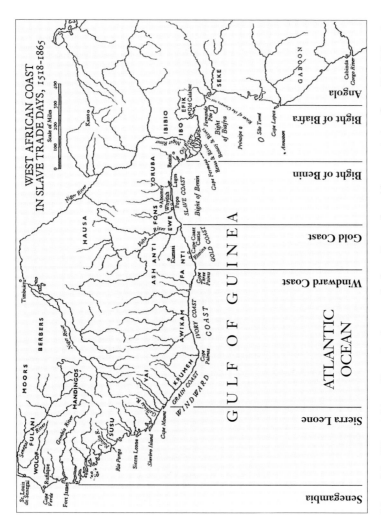

Map of the West African Coast in slave-trade days. Reproduced by permission from D.P. Mannix and M. Cowley, *Black Cargoes: A History of the Atlantic Slave Trade* (London, 1962), frontispiece.

56

and himself partowner of at least one Lancaster slaver, the *Antelope II*, is of particular interest. In it, Lawrence refers to his two children, David and Betsey Lawrence, "which", he wrote, "I believe to be my natural children now residing in Gambia". This points to Lawrence's own residence in the Gambia, presumably as a factor who might have served Lancaster slave ships arriving there. This seems more than likely given Lawrence's appointment of the Lancaster Guinea captain, Robert Dodson, as his first attorney.[74] Captain Dodson made at least nine voyages to Africa aboard four different vessels between 1753 and 1762. The African destination of seven of these ventures is known, and in each case it was to the Gambia.

Clearly, Lancaster captains also bought slaves direct from the natives. In 1756, when the James Fort Governor was trying to starve the Barbazeen people into reason after certain atrocities, "Captain Alman and Dodson's Tender went to their port as if nothing had happened, and traded with them as usual".[75] Several references to tenders suggest that Lancaster captains often sent their mates 'boating', that is "where a longboat or a yawl might be sent several miles inland to obtain two or three slaves from people not living on the coast".[76]

Lancaster traders particularly favoured the Gambia in the 1750s and early 1760s, and then seemed to focus their attention on Sierra Leone and the Windward Coast, where they sent at least forty-seven and sixteeen vessels respectively between 1752 and 1789. Only two vessels destined for the Windward Coast were marked as moving on to the Gold Coast to complete their slave cargoes.[77] There may have been others but this practice seems significantly less common than at Liverpool. This fact again reflects the different needs of the smaller Lancaster slavers and might explain why they managed relatively short ventures, even though slaving at Sierra Leone and the Windward Coast was typically slow. Supply in these two areas was generally organized by "small-scale entrepreneurs, African, European and Afro-European, with limited stocks of slaves and limited capacity to obtain more rapidly".[78] "Captains had to rely mainly on signals made by people on shore, who would make a 'smoke' if they had anything to sell", and each captain made a large number of very small transactions, haggling over the goods to be paid for each slave.[79] John Scovern of Fudda Duggie was, no doubt, one such slaving entrepreneur on the Coast. His will was proved in North-West England in 1761 and with it is a letter dated May 1st 1760 which reads,

> I John Scovern at present on the Windward Coast of Africa, being very sick in body, but of a sound and disposing mind and memory make this my last will and testament … my effects after they are

The River Gambia, West Africa, was ideally suited to the shallow draught of Lancaster slave ships and their tenders. *Courtesy of The Gambian Experience*

valued I leave to the care of Captain John Preston from Lancaster as my sole executor ... I desire Bento, a girl slave to be carried to the West Indies and 4 slaves to be given her out of my stock, I leave William Tydeman 2 slaves, to Sarah Tinder 2 slaves, to my executor Captain John Preston, for his trouble, 8 slaves.[80]

Captain Preston had sailed to Africa three times by this date, once in the *Minerva I* in 1758 and twice in the *Thetis I* in February and December 1759. This latter voyage would have accounted for his presence when John Scovern wrote his letter. No doubt Preston had dealt with him on his earlier voyages. The sale advertisement in the South Carolina Gazette for the sale of the *Thetis I's* first cargo read, "Sale of 212 slaves from Windward and Grain Coast of Guinea".[81] As it turned out Captain Preston's own will was being proved just two years later. He, too, died in Africa on a voyage to Sierra Leone in the *Lancaster* in 1762.[82] Meanwhile, the second probate bondsman for Scovern was Captain Preston's brother-in-law, Miles Houseman, a Lancaster mercer. This strongly suggests Miles was involved in the ownership of the *Thetis I* along with one of his elder brothers, Thomas Houseman. A third brother, John, had skippered three Lancaster slavers during the 1750s.[83] At least one of these, the *Lowther*, had

This item of shipping news in Williamson's 1774 Liverpool Advertiser shows the popularity of Sierra Leone as a destination for Lancaster slave ships. *Courtesy of Liverpool City Council, Libraries and Arts Department*

slaved in the Windward Coast in 1756. A few years later, in 1760, just prior to Scovern's death, another Lancaster slaver, the *Molly I*, carried "200 very likely healthy Negroes from the Windward and Rice Coast of Guinea" to South Carolina.[84] It is quite probable that both these vessels numbered amongst those that Scovern supplied with slaves.

It was, of course, beneficial to receive updated information on trading conditions on the African coast. The advantages of such information could make the difference between profit and loss in a venture. Only regular trade could help to develop good connexions with slave factors on the African coast. Miles Barber, who had started his slave-trading career at Lancaster, received such information from Richard Brew, the Governor of Tantumquerry on the African coast. Brew, in a letter to Barber dated around 1770, wrote,

> … there remains only to tell you that gold commands the trade; there is no buying a slave without one ounce of gold at least on it… the next best article is fine broad striped taffats, flowered cuttanees, Patne Chintz, with small black flowers, fine white grounds, well chose printed linens and cottons, very large brass pans, fine silesias, Danish and birdling gunz, plain taffatys, fine mixed Romauls, sattin stripes, half pint tankards. Goods not in demand as follows, powder, pewter, knives, ells of no kind, halfsays, Negannepauls, Bejutapauls, checks, cherryderries and blue bandanoes; there is at present no Ashantee trade, which is the reason powder and peuter are not called for, however it will not be prudent to send ships, without these articles.[85]

Other interesting evidence concerns Barber's own direct involvement on the African coast. In 1767 he petitioned for permission to carry out his contract to ship slaves on board French vessels in the Gambia River. This implies the factory he set up on the Isle de Los was in existence by then, and it was certainly still in operation in 1779, although it was later destroyed by the Bostonians. Donnan names three merchants who

Slaving practices on the West African Coast. From an oil painting by F-A Biard, c. 1833. *Courtesy of Hull City Museums & Art Galleries*

acted as African agents for Miles Barber.[86] One of these, Thomas Hodgson junior, also a slave trader in Liverpool, was later to return to his native village outside Lancaster.[87] It is quite possible that Barber's factory served other Lancaster ships besides his own.

Throughout their main years of activity, Lancaster slavers kept to these specified regions of the African coast and built up contacts. These were areas where their captains often bought a few slaves at a time, sometimes with the assistance of a tender. It would seem that Lancaster merchants had found themselves a specialist African market which suited their smaller vessels, which in turn suited their pockets. Meanwhile, traders at Chester and Whitehaven sent vessels which would have been too large to compete in the same way in these markets. Thus only one Chester slaver, the *True Blue* in 1773, traded at Sierra Leone, whilst the other eight, all setting sail in the 1750s, slaved at the Bight of Biafra, Angola or the Gold Coast, where they would have been in direct competition with Liverpool wholesalers. At Whitehaven, even three early vessels sent between 1733 and 1739 by Walter Lutwidge had slaved in Angola and his schemes for two more were destined for Angola and the Gold Coast.[88] Once more an interesting comparison can be made between the Lancaster and American slavers. Mannix states that the Yankees avoided Calabar (in the Bight of Biafra) and Angola where "Liverpool captains often bargained with the local monarchs for a whole ship-load. Most of the New England vessels kept northward and looked for cargoes on the Gold Coast or the Windward Coast."[89] It is hard to imagine that the Preston slave traders, or even their captains, had much experience in African or colonial affairs when they sent their three slave ships in 1753, just three years after their first transatlantic ventures.

The way certain Lancastrians operated on the African coast implies they were eager, if not desperate, to procure their cargoes as quickly and conveniently as possible. Certain correspondence, for instance, shows that Lancaster captains, or their mates, did not always handle the natives in the interest of fellow traders. When Captain Alman and Dodson's tender traded with the Barbazeen people in 1756, they undermined Tobias Lisle's efforts to starve these natives to "reason". Thus the James Fort Governor wrote to the Committee, "Whether such conduct is not enough to encourage vilany we must leave to your better judgement, but surely their escaping with impunity after what they were guilty of has been no small instigation to those other rascals". Here he referred to the King and natives of Barsally who "cut off one Fell, in a small sloop belonging to Lancaster and 'tis said the said Captain Fell and 2 men are killed". The Governor also went on to say the murder of whites was rife and "very lately one Harrold, second mate to captain Dodson, and at that time skipper of his tender stabbed a prentice Boy and abused him afterwards in such a manner he died on ye spot".[90] Again, in 1757, a report to the Committee stated,

> very lately Captain Payley of Lancaster, after his trade was done, seized one of ye Head men of Cower and brought him down to ye Fort, alledging twas in order to get satisfaction of ye affairs perpetuated by the King and natives of Barsally on Captain Fell. This affair has set ye Countries all around us in an uproar. Moreover the captains whose business is but begun, clamour loudly against it, adding withal that what's done will be the ruin of trade, and that twill be to no other purpose than setting the natives against ye English.

The Governor went on to express fears that this might enable the French to "cultivate a good harmony with ye Natives".[91] Later indiscretions included incidents of "buckra panyaring" (kidnapping of black Africans by white men). Captain Strangeways, slaving in Sierra Leone aboard the *Juba II* of Lancaster, captured two African traders by getting them drunk and putting them in a sail-case. They were later placed in irons and sold on the slaver's arrival in Antigua.[92] Then there was the alleged incident that a Captain Marshall (Maychel) stole a Guinea King's daughter. Such behaviour by Lancaster captains may well have happened elsewhere, but it did ultimately earn them such a reputation for dealing treacherously with the natives that the abolitionist Thomas Clarkson wrote about it after his visit to the town in 1787.[93] These men must have been both determined and desperate to procure their slave cargoes by any means available, which sometimes put them outside the accepted practices of the trade.

Cargoes from Africa

Lancaster slave cargoes were typically small, not surprising given the size of the vessels which carried them. It has already been mentioned how this resulted in shorter times spent on the African coast, which in turn reduced the danger of disease amongst blacks and whites alike, and avoided possible problems of flooding colonial markets. Mannix comments, "there were two schools of thought among the Guinea captains the 'loose-packers' and the 'tight-packers' ... for many years after 1750 the tight-packers were in the ascendant".[94] Meanwhile, Hyde, Parkinson and Marriner state that "five Negroes for every two tons" was a "ratio said to be normal" for loading a slave vessel.[95] Certain examples would suggest that some Lancaster captains were tight-packers. The hundred-ton *Cato*, with an average capacity for 250 slaves (estimated on 5 slaves per 2 tons), landed '288 Negroes' in South Carolina in 1758, 360 in Jamaica in 1760 and a staggering 560 in Barbados in 1761. Meanwhile, the much smaller forty-ton *Africa I*, with an average carrying capacity of a hundred slaves, had '170 Negroes' for sale in South Carolina on the 9th August in 1753, whereas the fifty-ton *Thetis I*, with a carrying capacity of 125 slaves, brought 212 to South Carolina in 1759.[96] However, the evidence by no means always substantiates this picture. Some vessels arrived at the colonies with considerably less than their estimated capacity, which may have reflected problems of acquisition as well as mortality. The seventy-ton *Castleton* only landed seventy slaves in Virginia in 1752, as against an expected cargo of 150–180, whilst the eighty-ton *Lancaster*, estimated to have a capacity for two hundred slaves brought just eighty-six to Jamaica in 1757.[97] On average, Lancaster slavers carried cargoes just a little below the ratio quoted by Hyde, Parkinson and Marriner, but it should be noted that the carrying capacity would be affected by the layout within each vessel. If Lancaster Guinea captains did pack their cargoes more loosely, it no doubt reflected their purchasing practices on the African coast, namely buying slaves in single or small packages. The extra time needed on the coast to buy more slaves would not have merited the delay and its consequences for the rest of the cargo and crew.

Ship model showing slaves in Middle Passage used by William Wilberforce in the House of Commons during his relentless campaign against the slave trade. *Courtesy of Hull City Museums & Art Galleries*

The emphasis for Lancaster slaving ventures seems to have been more on speed than on the quantity of slaves carried. Meanwhile, slavers from Preston and Poulton never transported human cargoes to match the ratio cited above, nor did they equal Lancaster's speed. The fifty-ton *Betty and Martha* carried just sixty-five slaves to Barbados some twenty months after her pass application at the start of her voyage, whilst the sixty-ton *Blossom* did better in landing 131 slaves there, but only after another lengthy voyage.[98]

Sources indicate that Lancaster slavers would sometimes supplement their human cargoes with 'dead' commodities, particularly elephant teeth and camwood. Hyde, Parkinson and Marriner note that, "In some cases slave trading would hardly be regarded as a predominant feature of the venture".[99] The African produce trade does not seem to have featured strongly at Lancaster, although the *Robert* did enter Barbados in 1752 with four hundred teeth and some wood, in addition to her cargo of sixty slaves, and a Charleston merchant suggested to two Lancaster slave traders that the twelve or fourteen tons of camwood aboard the *Concord* "must be a help to a poor voyage".[100] In contrast, traders at Whitehaven during the early 1760s had strong interests in the gum trade in Senegal, as evident in a memorial sent to their local M.P. at Cockermouth in 1764.[101]

A change of emphasis had occurred at Lancaster by the last quarter of the century, however, when slaving evidently became more difficult for the smaller competitors. In 1781 John Satterthwaite wrote to his brokers, concerning his vessel, the *Sally*, "… she'll have a good deal of dead cargo, and but few slaves". Ten years later James Sawrey was instructing one of his captains to purchase all the ivory and dead cargo he could.[102]

Part II   The Selling of Slaves

Disposing of his human cargo was the Guinea captain's next task. Finding a favourable market was a crucial factor in determining the financial outcome of a slaving venture. In accomplishing this the captain and his employers had to weigh up various considerations. On the one hand they needed to ascertain which colonial markets might be most receptive to their particular slave cargo, taking into account the problems of competition from other slavers. On the other hand they must already have or develop reliable and co-operative business connexions in the colonies, through whom they might not only dispose of their slaves but also acquire a profitable return cargo and/or reliable bills of exchange. They could sail to a different destination for their return cargo, but the transaction could be made much quicker and simpler if both operations were completed in one place with a single factor. This also enabled the vessel to remain in port for repairs and refitment. The relative importance of these various considerations is not altogether clear. No doubt decisions in most cases were based on the complex interplay of the several influences. The two main aspects, namely markets and business contacts, will be discussed in turn, but their interrelatedness should not be forgotten.

Colonial Destinations

Lancaster slave traders definitely showed certain preferences in their selection of colonial markets. In the early days Barbados was evidently the exclusive choice for their African cargoes. Lancaster's first eight or nine slavers are known to have sold there between 1736 and 1752. Although Barbados would certainly have been an attractive market for slaves at this time, it was by no means the only one. However, it is not altogether surprising that these early Lancaster slave traders stayed with this island. One advantage was the shorter passage from Africa, which would help to reduce the risks of the Middle Passage and the

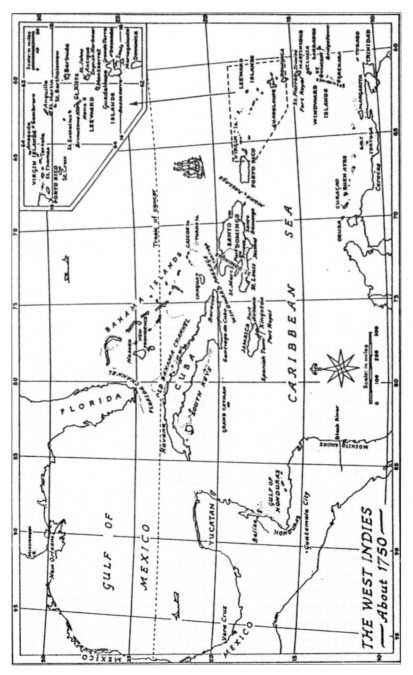

Map of the West Indies. After R. Pares in R. B. Sheridan, *Sugar and Slavery: An Economic History of the British West Indies* (Barbados, 1974), p. xiv. *By permission of Oxford University Press*

period of capital investment. Barbados' geographical location in the Eastern Caribbean tempted many Guinea captains to call there first and try their luck.[103] If the economic climate was unfavourable they could always pass on to other islands such as Jamaica, as indeed the *Expedition* did in 1747, either to sell all or part of their slave cargoes or indeed to fill their vessels' holds with produce for the return journey.

Another advantage of Barbados, for the Lancaster traders, was its familiarity. They would have had an awareness of its produce trade, and would have been able to derive some benefit from the business connexions used in their port's bilateral trade. Consequently, at least eleven more Lancaster slave ships visited the slave markets of Bridgetown between 1753 and 1760, although by this time Barbados was no longer the exclusive port of call for Lancaster captains. By the late 1750s the Barbadian slave population was stabilizing, having sustained noticeable increases since the 1730s.[104] Competition in the island's slave markets would therefore be keener, forcing Lancaster merchants, despite their established trading connexions there, to extend their colonial slave markets. As a result, only two Lancaster vessels visited Barbados in the 1760s, as opposed to the fifteen which sailed there in the previous decade. Jamaica became an important alternative.

The first Lancaster Guineaman to visit Jamaica was probably the *Barlborough*, which arrived in Kingston on its first voyage in the summer of 1753. Its owners must have been satisfied with the results, for the vessel returned there on two subsequent voyages in 1754 and 1756.[105] It is interesting to note that this vessel had sailed via Barbados on its maiden voyage. Presumably its captain, Richard Millerson, had declined to commit its cargo of 101 slaves to that market, despite the fact that his brother, Thomas Millerson, was a resident merchant in Barbados at that time, evidence perhaps that conditions there were changing. In comparison with Barbados, many more Lancaster slaver captains sold their African cargoes in Jamaica during the 1760s, figures which reverse the trend of the previous decade. These developments are evident in Table 2.7 (opposite).

Again, Jamaica was an island where Lancaster merchants had already developed bilateral trading ties and set up a number of resident factors. The Kingston slave market, together with that at Savannah La Mar, remained strong favourites for African slave ships throughout the eighteenth century and the island's long-standing position as a slave entrepôt kept the market buoyant.[106] However, it is significant that William Davenport of Liverpool, who sent a number of his slave ships to Jamaica, seemed to favour its markets when "demand in other important markets had already peaked or was at a low ebb".[107] The Jamaican market evidently provided a reliable, but not always

Table 2.7 *Number of Lancaster Slave Ships Selling at Barbados and Jamaica during the 1750s and 1760s*

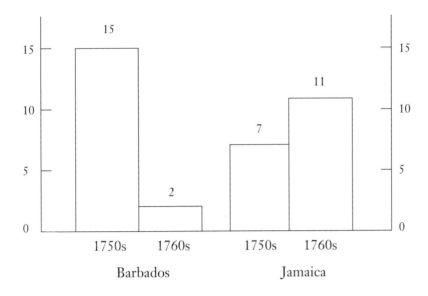

15

15	15
	11
10	10
	7
5	5
2	
0	0

1750s   1760s   1750s   1760s

Barbados   Jamaica

spectacular, market for African slaves. If one studies the colonial destinations of Chester, Poulton and Preston slavers one thing stands out, their captains sold all their cargoes in either the Barbadian or Jamaican slave markets.[108] Lancaster captains did not; they branched out to sell their slaves in other markets. Their employers, as ambitious marginal men, would be eager to seek out the most lucrative markets they could find, and it was probably their sheer determination and enterprise which in turn helped to sustain the Lancaster slave trade over and above that of its north-west neighbours, outside Liverpool. Thus operators at Lancaster, by not staying exclusively with the slave factors of Barbados and Jamaica, shipped their human cargoes to destinations never frequented by the slave ships clearing from the Dee and Ribble. Within the Caribbean this included Antigua, where eight Lancaster slaving voyages were directed between 1755 and 1758. Five of these were made during the first year, between the months of July and October. Lancaster slave merchants were clearly eager to participate in the advantages of the island's expanding plantation economy and perhaps, though there is no evidence to prove it, they came upon reliable business connexions there to facilitate the marketing of their slaves together with the provision of marketable return cargoes. Whatever the reason, Lancaster merchants did not

English Harbour, Antigua. 8 Lancaster slaving voyages were directed to this island between 1755 and 1758. *Photo Andrew Price*

confine themselves to the Caribbean. There were some even more important markets for their slave ships.

It has already been shown that Lancaster slavers generally bought their cargoes in the Gambia and Sierra Leone or on the Windward Coast. Henry Laurens, a prominent slave merchant in Charleston, South Carolina, made it clear that slaves from these regions were especially popular with the local planters. In 1755 he wrote, "There must not be a Callaber among them. Gold Coast or Gambia's are best, next to them the Windward Coast are preferred to Angola's".[109] Accordingly, Laurens' sale advertisement for Lancaster's *Molly I* in 1760 read,

> To be sold, on Wednesday the 15th of this instant October, at Jacksonburgh Ponpon, About Two Hundred very likely healthy Negroes (of the same country as are usually brought from the Gambia) Being the entire Cargo Just arrived in the snow *Molly*, William Denison commander, from the Windward and Rice Coast of Guiney.[110]

Such considerations no doubt explain why one of the most popular destinations for Lancaster slavers was South Carolina. At least twenty-nine Lancaster ventures are known to have been directed there between 1753, the date of its first slave ship's arrival, and December 1774, when the Non-Importation Agreement, resolved by the

68

American Congress on October 20th of that year, came into effect.[111] Indeed, there would have been more if Lancaster merchants had not been advised against sending slave cargoes at certain times. For example, in a letter dated the seventeenth of May 1756, Henry Laurens explained, "We wrote early to our Friends at Bristol, Liverpoole and Lancaster not to have a thought of sending slaves to our Market untill the differences should be adjusted between Great Britain and France".[112] In an earlier letter, Captain Samuel Sandys of the *Duke of Cumberland* had received similar warnings from Henry Laurens, at the request of his employer, Thomas Hinde. He was thereby prompted to sell his cargo of slaves in Antigua instead of the preferred South Carolina market.[113] The sale venue of the *Molly*, and certain other Lancastrian vessels, suggests their owners extracted another advantage from their own particular situation. They evidently utilised the small size and shallow draft of their ships to take their African cargoes to places where larger vessels could not go. In 1760 the *Marlborough* as well as the *Molly* sold at Jacksonburgh, which was a village on the Pon Pon or Edisto River, whilst in 1765 the forty-ton *Antelope II* sold 150 slaves at Beaufort, which was upriver from Port Royal. This same vessel, on a later voyage, visited North Carolina where shallow draft and small size were again crucial.[114]

Lancaster's use of North American slave markets was not emulated in the other small ports of the region. Although Craig, in commenting on Chester shipping, writes, "A more lasting American link was that with South Carolina, which was only severed with the outbreak of the American War of Independence". Schofield remarks that Chester slave traders refrained from sending a single ship there.[115] A probable explanation was the fact that their ships slaved mainly at Calabar and Angola and would therefore have carried the very blacks that Laurens discouraged. Preston and Poulton slavers did not make the American mainland either, despite the fact that their two known African destinations indicate that these slave cargoes would have been well received in the Charleston markets.[116] This may well be explained by the fact that at least two of the three slavers which sailed from Preston or Poulton were employed in the slave trade only amidst a series of direct West India voyages. It is therefore likely that their operators were attracted to the slave trade from their observations of opportunities in the West Indies. Even so, the merchants at Preston and Poulton, notably Langton, Shepherd and Company, were not without contacts in South Carolina, through their direct trade there. This is evident in several letters written in 1756 by Henry Laurens to this firm. Moreover, it seems that either the Kirkham merchants or Henry Laurens sounded out the possibilities of sending slaves to Charleston. However, with the threat of war, conditions in South

Map of British America: Southern Colonies about 1770.

Carolina were not encouraging during the short period Preston and Poulton vessels were involved in the African trade.[117] Thus these Lancashire merchants kept away from a market which might otherwise have proved more profitable and encouraging for them.

Meanwhile, little evidence has been found to suggest that Whitehaven slavers sold in America. The port's connexions in the tobacco trade did not spark off a slave trade with Virginia, and only one vessel has been identified as selling in Charleston, namely the *Betty*, owned by Thomas Hartley and Company, which arrived there in 1760.[118] Henry Laurens, who had taken up the *Betty*'s cargo, had no further contact with Hartley except in May 1764 when he wrote to him suggesting that, should Hartley consign slave cargoes to a new firm, Price and Hest, formed in Charleston in the Spring of 1764, he would give the firm his advice and be responsible for the performance of their obligations.[119] Hartley, however, does not appear to have taken up this invitation, probably for the same reasons as those suggested for slave traders at Chester. The Cumbrian slave ships were also larger than Lancaster's and were therefore more likely to slave amidst the less favoured southern regions of the African coast where the Dee slavers went. This notion would be borne out by the voyage of the 127-ton *Venus*, owned by Thomas Hartley and a large number of other partners, which arrived at Barbados, not Charleston, in 1765 with her cargo of 340 slaves.[120]

The evidence so far discussed illustrates the importance of seeking out markets suited to individual slave-trading practices which determined features such as the size of vessels employed and the type of slave cargo carried. At Lancaster, small vessels encouraged traders to avoid the main areas of competition further south on the African coast. They then found, particularly in South Carolina, markets which were receptive to their type of black African. They even, at times, found a further means of capitalising on their small vessels by reaching less accessible destinations. Above all, these were markets where the size of cargo was probably not all important, or, at least, where the size of cargo could be compensated for by the type of slave carried. This aspect might explain, in part at least, why Lancaster merchants failed to patronize the Virginia slave markets in the same way. They sent only three slavers there altogether.[121] Here the average slave cargo was noticeably larger than that for South Carolina. Klein quotes average figures of 202.6 slaves per vessel for Virginia compared to 155.4 for South Carolina, and he concludes that this perhaps reflected their different African sources of supply.[122] Quite likely the size of a cargo was more important than the type of slave in the Virginia market. Donnan notes that, "Less importance seems to be attached to the section from which the Negroes came in Virginia than was the case with the South Carolina planters".[123] Thus competition with larger slavers from ports like Liverpool would undoubtedly have been too great for Lancaster. Also, according to Klein, South Carolina was importing almost three times as many slaves as Virginia between 1760 and 1769 where imports were declining.[124] Lancaster's ability to market its slaves in South Carolina was evidently another explanation for its relative success in the trade. However, at the same time it may reflect a grim determination on the part of its merchants to succeed, for in travelling to the American mainland their ships were forced to cover extra miles. This was not always seen as popular or desirable. In 1753 the Liverpool captain, John Newton, having landed a cargo of slaves at St. Kitts, wrote in his journal, "And as for Jamaica or America, I should be extremely loth to venture so far". He had, in fact, visited South Carolina in 1749 and lost a lot of his slaves in so doing.[125]

Lancaster traders must always have been susceptible to competition in the slave trade, especially from the Liverpool operators. Their swift adoption of new markets is the most compelling evidence of the marginal character of their trade. It indicates that they were eager, if not obliged, to trade where they might, to seize every opportunity they could. There is no more marked evidence of this than in the Lancastrians' quick response to the territorial exchanges of the Seven Years War. When Martinique and Guadeloupe were taken from the French during the Seven Years War, Lancaster merchants were quick to supply these markets with their African cargoes. Guadeloupe, wrested from the French in 1759, was visited by the *Cato* and its cargo of 560 slaves in 1761, and by the *Eagle* and *Lancaster* the following year. Meanwhile Martinique, seized by the British as late as 1762, was the destination of two Lancaster vessels, the *Juba I* and *Marquis of Granby*, that very same year. There were no subsequent visits to either of these islands for they were restored to France in 1763 by the Treaty of Paris. Likewise, when the Windward Islands of Grenada, St.Vincent and Dominica fell to the British during this war, Lancaster Guinea captains were there selling their cargoes. Grenada proved by far the most popular. It was visited by the *Molly I* with its cargo of 220 slaves in 1764, just one year after it was ceded by the French.[126] The *Molly I* had visited the more popular and competitive Leeward Islands on her previous voyage. Thereafter, at least twenty-three ventures are known to have been sent to Grenada by the Lancaster merchants, and a further three to nearby St.Vincent and Dominica. In having less rigid commitments to established slave factors in the English islands, the Lancaster traders were evidently freer or obliged to trade wherever new opportunities arose. Once again they must, on occasions, have been able to turn their situation to an advantage.

Their adoption of new markets in Georgia, when South Carolina announced its non-importation policy, had certain similarities. Two of their slavers, the *Dove* and *Antelope II*, sailed there in 1766 during the first year of direct sailings between Africa and Georgia.[127] Hitherto slave cargoes to Georgia had been small in number, about eleven per ship, and almost exclusively re-exports from West Indian slave markets. With direct trading from Africa this average rose to 151.3 slaves per ship.[128] The *Dove* returned to Georgia in 1767 along with the *Prince George III* which made a second voyage in 1770.[129] The prohibitive legislation in South Carolina had begun on January 1st, 1766, when an additional duty of £100 was imposed on all slaves imported into South Carolina which was to be paid by the first purchaser. It was to be in operation for three years and it put a stop to the trade until January 1769, when imports were briefly resumed until another Non-Importation Agreement came into effect on January 1st, 1770. This lasted only until December 13th, when the inhabitants of Charleston declared non-importation at an end once more.[130] The opening up of Georgia to cargoes direct from Africa obviously provided Lancaster opportunists with a welcome alternative, especially since its planters likewise preferred slaves from the Senegambia and Sierra Leone,[131] implying quality not quantity was the order of the day.

It is no surprise that Lancastrians resumed trade with South Carolina whenever the prohibitive legislation was lifted. Obviously slave sales were particularly profitable at these times, and South Carolina was, it seems, their overall preference. Thus the *Prince George III*, which had landed its slaves in Georgia in 1767, eagerly returned to South Carolina in 1769, then resumed trade with Georgia the ensuing year. On September 29th, 1770, Laurens, hearing the news that the legislation would again be relaxed, wrote, "You may depend upon it that our Market will be the best in America for fine Negroes".[132] Eight Lancaster Guineamen visited South Carolina before its next Non-Importation Agreement in 1774.

By the early 1770s Grenada had come to match South Carolina as a destination for Lancaster's African cargoes. The island colony was being actively settled by British planters at this time. After 1774, Grenada replaced South Carolina as the already strained relations between England and her mainland colonies deteriorated.

Table 2.8 *Number of Lancaster Slavers Visiting South Carolina and Georgia, 1764 to 1777.*[133]

	1764–1769	1770–1774	1775–1777
South Carolina	8	9	0
Grenada	3	10	8

Table 2.8 shows the changing relationships of these two principal markets for Lancaster slave ships. The *Stanley II* and the *Nelly*, which had taken slaves to South Carolina in 1773, were both selling at Grenada in 1774 and 1775 respectively.[134]

Meanwhile, traders at Chester, Preston and Poulton never developed their slave trade sufficiently to experiment with these different transatlantic markets. There was no African trade out of these ports during the 1760s, the time when Lancastrians sampled these new markets. Only traders at Whitehaven were in a position to test them, and their particular slaving practices evidently kept them away from the mainland colonies.

Modern view of St. George's, Grenada. This island became a popular destination for Lancaster Guineamen afer its capture from the French during the Seven Years War. *Courtesy of Grenada Tourist Board*

Business Connexions in the Colonies: West Indies

Aside from finding markets receptive to their Guinea cargoes, Lancaster slave traders would have had to consider the availability of good reliable business connexions in these colonial venues. The selling of African slaves in the colonies usually receives scant attention. Much of the documentary evidence, such as the naval office shipping lists, ends with the blacks' arrival in the Americas, with no specific details as to how a captain discharged his human cargo or procured goods for the return journey. However, to omit this aspect is to overlook an important and integral part of a triangular enterprise. Relevant sources at Lancaster are unfortunately incomplete, making conclusions somewhat tentative and patchy. Even so, it is possible to build a plausible picture of a trading network with the colonies. It was one which was dominated not only by the interplay of market forces, but also by family connexions and trading partnerships of long and short standing.

In the Caribbean there were several fashions of selling slaves. In some instances they might be sold directly to the West Indian purchasers, but by the 1750s by far the most common method was for a colonial factor to take charge of retail sales for a commission.[135] Merritt, Sheridan and Anderson all argue that the selling of slaves became increasingly controlled by the London West India houses from the Seven Years War onwards, owing to planter indebtedness,

74

although Sheridan concedes that the outports still employed slave factors in the West Indies during the later years of the trade.[136] No evidence has been found to suggest Lancaster merchants employed specific agents to deal with their African cargoes. There surely would not have been sufficient numbers to merit it. At the same time the names of the big London West India houses do not appear in the Lancaster records either, except on one occasion when particular links are evident.[137] Lancaster traders must have used other contacts. Certainly there was a large number of Lancaster merchants and factors living in the West Indies throughout the second half of the eighteenth century. At least some of these are known to have been actively involved in selling slaves, as opposed to just dealing with products sent in direct trade between Lancaster and the colonies. Insufficient evidence makes it difficult to be precise about their numbers or the extent of their operations, but it should be emphasised that Lancaster slave traders would also have drawn important, indirect benefits from the wider network of Lancaster merchants and factors, resident in the West Indies. These indirect benefits will be discussed before looking at the more direct role played by some of the Lancastrians resident in the slave colonies.

Merchants and factors, even if they were not directly involved in dealing with slaves, were in a position to supply Guinea captains and their employers with valuable information. On a general level they would have been able to increase their market awareness. The greater the number of factors in the islands, and of ships plying between Lancaster and the West Indies, the more comprehensive the picture of commercial conditions both sides of the Atlantic. Such information would have been of particular value to Guinea captains, who invariably witnessed very different market conditions towards the end of their enterprise compared with how things had stood at its outset, owing to the lengthy nature of an African undertaking. It is doubtful whether some of the other small north-western ports shared this same advantage in the Caribbean. Craig writes of Chester,

> In an age when so much maritime activity was undertaken by a merchant community having widespread commercial links with the colonial territories, the explanation of Chester's inability to sustain long-standing overseas trade may lie in the apparent absence of such close links, coupled with the fact that Chester's port was not supported by a hinterland manifesting any considerable economic growth.[138]

Whitehaven's involvement in the West Indies trade was small, even after the decline of its tobacco trade to the American mainland during the 1750s.[139] Its merchants' commercial ties must surely have been stronger in Maryland and Virginia, yet Whitehaven ships were not importing slaves to the mainland colonies, rather they opted for West Indian imports and the shorter Caribbean crossing. Meanwhile, Preston and Poulton had better links in the Caribbean owing to the export of flax there during the 1740s and 1750s. Here ties with Lancaster merchants resident overseas are evident. John Birley, a flax merchant of Kirkham, had close trading relations with Inman and Company of Jamaica, and his son, also John, spent three years under the redoubtable Charles Inman,[140] who was himself involved in the slave trade at Lancaster. Indeed, it may well have been these links that inspired the sending of slave ships by the flax merchants. Significantly, the *Hothersall*, which was sent to Africa in 1753 by John Birley, proceeded to Jamaica.[141] Preston's and Poulton's West India links were, however, short-lived. Transatlantic trade from the Wyre ceased after the 1750s, and along with it the slave trade. Thereafter Kirkham flax was more commonly exported from Liverpool and other ports.[142]

Lancaster's slave traders, and presumably those at Preston and Poulton to some extent, surely profited from their ports' West Indian commerce. Meanwhile, some of Lancaster's West Indian factors evidently acted on behalf of the slave merchants and captains in more explicit ways, such as in facilitating or fostering important contacts with local slave dealers for their fellow townsmen or acting as advisers or intermediaries for the two parties. Benjamin Satterthwaite appears to have fulfilled this role on more than one occasion whilst he was factor in Kingston in Jamaica for his Quaker relatives in Lancaster during the mid-1760s.

In one instance, Benjamin Satterthwaite was in correspondence with William Watson, a prominent slave trader in Lancaster, concerning a friend, George Murray, who dealt in slaves in Kingston. At this time William Watson was partowner of the slave ship *Tartar* which had sold 118 blacks in Jamaica in January 1764, with George Murray and his partner James Rowan as the commission agents.[143] On July 10th, 1764, Benjamin wrote to the Lancaster trader,

> Before I conclude I cannot avoid giving you my opinion in regard to the sales of Captain Read's Cargo which is this: that had she gone to any other House here they neither would have made you so good sales nor take[n] the pains these Gentlemen did for your interest.

George Murray was to visit Lancaster and Benjamin went on to request William Watson, as a friend,[144] "to shew all the civility in your power and do him what service you can", in return for many civilities he had received from Murray in Jamaica.[145] Such sentiments testify to the importance of strong personal ties in establishing good business connexions in the eighteenth century.

Ring and staple used by plantation owners and slave traders alike to prevent slaves from escaping. *Courtesy of Hull City Museums & Art Galleries*

Another letter, dated December 10th, 1764, again refers to Benjamin's role in assisting Lancaster slave merchants. This time the letter was addressed to Hugh Wallace of Savannah La Mar in Jamaica. Benjamin wrote,

> Inclosed is a letter for you which I this day received under cover to me from our mutual friend Mr. Miles Barber, the same ship brought me the one for Captain Kendall, which you'll please to give him.[146]

Miles Barber was conveying letters to Benjamin on account of his slaver, the *Dove*.[147] Benjamin obviously acted as a useful intermediary. He was closely acquainted with Barber and his partner Samuel Kilner who were both very active in the Lancaster slave trade at this time. Benjamin had also taken on the job of collecting Samuel Kilner's debts in Jamaica, which was seldom a task undertaken lightly.[148] Meanwhile, Barber and Kilner had sent two slavers to Jamaica the previous year.[149] Quite clearly these Lancaster merchants had found a useful associate in Benjamin Satterthwaite for the colonial stages of their triangular enterprises.

There is further convincing evidence to suggest that Benjamin Satterthwaite played an even more positive role in the West Indies a decade earlier by acting as a commission agent for African slaves himself in the partnership of Satterthwaite and Jones of Barbados. This firm had sold the cargo of slaves aboard the *Charming Nancy* for William Davenport of Liverpool in 1757. At this time it was known as

Law, Satterthwaite and Jones.[150] Two years earlier the firm had shipped fifteen slaves from Barbados to South Carolina aboard the Lancaster slaver *Gambia*, owned by Satterthwaite and Inman.[151] The name Satterthwaite in this latter partnership probably concerned Benjamin's more successful younger brother Thomas Satterthwaite of Lancaster, for Thomas was executor for Charles Inman in 1767, whilst his daughter, Susannah Inman, chose him as her guardian.[152] However, it is possible that the partnership involved Benjamin, since Charles Inman and Benjamin Satterthwaite were named as joint tenants of a house and warehouse with hazardous goods on the north side of Church Street in Lancaster for an insurance policy in 1754.[153] Charles Inman had been apprenticed to the Lancaster slave traders Thomas and William Butterfield, and was factor in the West Indies for many years until his death in 1767. It is quite conceivable that he himself dealt with African cargoes in the Caribbean. The Lancaster connexions of the Barbadian firm which sent the fifteen slaves are clear since Henry Laurens, who dealt with their sale in Charleston, was requested to remit the produce to Samuel Touchet of London; the Touchet family being firm friends of the Lancaster Satterthwaites.[154]

There seems little doubt that the partnership with Jones and Law referred to Benjamin Satterthwaite if one looks at his career in depth. Details of this are given in Appendix B. His involvement in the Barbadian firm would have taken place during the 1750s, at a time when Barbados continued to be a popular venue for Lune slavers. No doubt this partnership dealt with at least some of the fourteen African cargoes carried by ten Lancaster Guineamen which are known to have called at the island in the 1750s and early 1760s. Amongst these were two or three voyages by the *Swallow*, owned by Satterthwaite and Inman.[155] Another slaver which visited Bridgetown in 1756 was the *Bold*, owned by John Heathcote and Company. Heathcote had married Benjamin's younger sister Millicent in 1753, and was apprenticed to Thomas Satterthwaite in 1747.[156] It is also more than likely that Benjamin dealt with African cargoes transported by Liverpool Guineamen. Certainly he had many potential connexions, including men whose families originated, like his own, from Furness, such as the Backhouses, or from the Lune valley, such as the Welches.[157] Moreover, his letter book of the mid-sixties reveals close ties with men such as Captain Samuel Linnecar who had arrived at Barbados with his cargo of Bonny slaves (from the Bight of Biafra) in the Blundell's slaver *Hopewell* in 1756, and may well have called upon the services of Satterthwaite and Jones.[158]

It is also noteworthy that the details of Benjamin's career imply it was again a degree of desperation which drew him, like many of the captains and owners of slave ships, to try and make a living out of selling Guinea cargoes for a time. When his Quaker family denied him employment, after his Anglican marriage, it must have left him in an awkward and embarrassing situation in Lancaster. The pressure or temptation to deal with slave cargoes, in the island he knew well from serving his family as a young factor, would be perfectly comprehensible. It is both significant and ironic that his son John wrote, many years later in 1781, that his partner in St. Kitts, a John Robinson, and therefore indirectly himself, "has got to selling Guineamen because of precaring times".[159]

Interestingly, John Satterthwaite approached John Robinson on his own account at this time, and also another native of North-west England, Richard Hetherington of Tortola, concerning a cargo of slaves aboard his vessel, the *Sally*; but two other Lancastrians before them, who were likewise drawn to do business in the colonial slave markets, merit our attention first. Thomas Millerson of Barbados and Peter Woodhouse of Jamaica both, apparently, acted on behalf of their fellow townsmen during the heyday of Lancaster's trade with Africa.

Thomas Millerson, originally of Ulverston, spent many years in Barbados up to his death in 1768. In 1754 he had received goods from Robert Gillow and ten years later Benjamin Satterthwaite wrote of his still being a merchant there. When Millerson died he left his personal slave, Stephen, to his Barbadian wife and also provided for his natural daughter, Elizabeth Goodwin of Barbados.[160] Meanwhile, his younger brother Richard skippered and owned a large number of Lancaster slave ships. Thomas himself had shares in two of the later ones. Richard Millerson's earlier vessels had sold in Barbados, making it probable that Thomas assisted or even acted as selling agent for their African cargoes and possibly for other Lancaster slave ships as well. Thomas and his younger brother were just two of a number of Ulverston men who played a significant role in the Lancaster slave trade. Their activities in this line of business evidently afforded them with the foothold they needed, as outsiders, to establish themselves as prominent merchants in Lancaster.[161]

Jamaica became the more popular Caribbean destination for the Lune slave ships by the 1760s and here we find another Lancaster family of particular interest. Various members of the Woodhouse family were resident in Jamaica during the middle decades of the eighteenth century. Peter Woodhouse the Elder left an estate in St.George, Jamaica, in his will of 1743,[162] but it was his son, also Peter, who seems to have had more definite connexions in the slave factorage business in this island. He was living in Kingston by 1755, if not earlier. Five years later his will was being proved. Some information contained in this strongly hints at his involvement in slave dealing in Jamaica. He wrote, "I give, devise and bequeath all my slaves to John Seddon (his clerk) on trust he shall sell them for the best advantage and clear proceeds of such sale".[163] His other executors were William Gillison and Thomas Satterthwaite, both Lancaster merchants. Thomas Satterthwaite was actively involved in the Lancaser slave trade at this time, as was one of the witnesses, Richard Millerson, who would have been in Jamaica as master of the slaver *Cato* in the spring of 1760.[164] Slaves were to be mentioned once more in this family's probate records, this time in the will of George Woodhouse, cousin to Peter. Probate was granted in 1782. George was described as being of Kingston, Jamaica and in it he left property, land and slaves on the island which were to be sold.[165]

It could, of course, be argued that Peter and George just left a number of personal slaves in their wills. However, a more detailed look at the evidence indicates otherwise. Both sets of slaves were to be sold for money, which meant they were not following the fate of personal slaves found in other Lancaster wills, where slaves were either made free or left to specified relatives or friends. Thomas Millerson, for example, left his slave Stephen to his wife Sarah, whilst the mariner, John Backhouse, made the following request for his 'two Negro women' and 'one Negro girl' slaves: "I do give and bequeath [them] unto my woman named Betty for her sole use and benefit. And one Negro man named Sama, my slave, I do give him his freedom."[166] It is far more likely that the Woodhouse slaves represented commercial assets, and given no land was mentioned in connexion with the slaves of Peter Woodhouse, they were clearly not working the soil. Besides, Peter was employed as a factor in Kingston, not as a plantation owner. Therefore the legacies of slaves in Peter's will, if not in George's, imply that he, at least, was dealing with imported African slaves in Kingston as a part of his more general commercial enterprises. This would explain why Henry Laurens, in writing to Peter Woodhouse in 1755, informed him that slaves from the Windward Coast and Gambia would serve as better imports to Charleston than West Indian goods.[167] There is in fact no evidence to suggest that Peter Woodhouse exported slaves to South Carolina on this occasion.

Once again the slave trade was evidently helping the ambitious. Peter Woodhouse came from a family of mariners and was employed as a factor in the West Indies, like his father before him. Any slave dealing must be regarded as an important element in his endeavours to upgrade his commercial status. He and his family certainly had potential opportunities in the many Lancaster slave ships which made for Kingston with their human cargoes.

Such ties were not confined to the islands of Barbados and Jamaica either. Richard Hetherington, son of a Kendal yeoman whose family had moved to a village north of Lancaster, was another ambitious young man trying to make his fortune out in the tropics.[168] A careful look at the evidence reveals both his unbridled opportunism and somewhat uncertain status. Although he served as factor in the small island of Tortola for Henry Rawlinson, a member of the Lancaster family who had moved his business operations to Liverpool, when Rawlinson recommended Hetherington for the post of Chief Justice of the island, he was soon forced to relinquish the position on account of his dispute with the authorities over the repayment of some unlawful prize money as well as his inadequate education.[169] His implication in dealing in slave cargoes in Tortola is shown in a letter from John Satterthwaite, written in 1781. Satterthwaite instructed Hetherington as follows:

> I am concerned in a small Guineaman, the *Sally*, Captain Harrison, who may be expected at St. Kitts pretty soon after this letter may reach you, that if it is agreeable to you to take Her up will you be so obliging on receipt here of to drop Mr John Robinson a line acquainting him what you think a small cargo from 100 to 150 slaves might fetch at your island.[170]

Satterthwaite considered John Robinson, his partner in St. Kitts and a native of Broughton-in-Furness, a viable alternative should Hetherington be unable to take up the *Sally's* cargo for any reason. His correspondence also makes it clear that Robinson was selling slave cargoes for some of the big Liverpool merchants, including the Earles and Backhouses; the latter now being related to the Satterthwaites through marriage.[171]

Both Hetherington's and Robinson's marginal status and their involvement in the Caribbean slave markets highlight once more the advantages of slave dealings for those anxious to improve their financial and social standing. It should at the same time be pointed out that none of the individuals aforesaid confined themselves to this one activity, but rather incorporated it as part of a mixed and opportunist portfolio. Robinson ultimately proved himself an unreliable business partner, much to John Satterthwaite's distress, whilst Hetherington became owner of a number of small plantations in Tortola.[172]

It comes as no surprise, meanwhile, to learn that Lancaster's leading slave merchants, the Hindes, came to provide useful links in the Caribbean from within their own family by the later years of the trade. It was, admittedly, a time when their trade was largely centred on Liverpool. Captain Thomas Hinde's son, Thomas junior, acted as guarantor for his Lancaster cousin Joshua who was based in Grenada in the early 1790s and later in Demerara with his brother Robert. John Rawlinson of Lancaster, in letters to Joshua Hinde, commented in 1792, "I was glad to hear you were likely to have so many commissions from Liverpool, that your cousin Thomas offered his Guarantee;

I hope you will soon meet with that success, as to be enabled to return to your native place, with a comfortable competency" and, in the following year, "I hear you are likely to reach handsome commissions on African cargoes."[173]

Lancaster traders developed ties with some of the larger names in slave factorage as well. In Grenada, already cited as an important market for Lancaster's African cargoes in the 1770s and 1780s, there is an interesting connexion between a large London West India House and the port of Lancaster. The Baillie family,[174] formerly of Scotland, who set up this well known House and were large-scale operators in the slave-factorage business in the Caribbean, appear several times amongst Lancaster records both as commission agents for slaves in the West Indies and as partners in two Lancaster West Indiamen. In their role as commission agents, several Lancaster slavers are known to have sold with Messrs. Campbell, Baillie and Company of Grenada in the 1780s and 1790s, a partnership which was clearly selling slaves in Grenada on a big scale. For instance, this firm sold the 205 blacks of the *Molly III*, owned by James Sawrey and John Addison of Lancaster in December 1787, along with the cargoes of three Liverpool slave ships.[175] Then in 1791 Tobias Collins, master of the *Hope II*, was instructed by its owners, again James Sawrey and Company, as follows: "On leaving the Coast you must proceed to the island of Grenada where we shall lodge letters for you with Messrs. Campbell and Bailley and Company".[176]

The firm's involvement in the registry of two Lancaster West Indiamen reveals the important link between the London house and the port of Lancaster. James Baillie and Duncan Campbell, together with Edmund Thornton, all described of St.George's, Grenada, were partners in the *Abbey* registered in 1787, together with John, Edward, George and Thomas Barrow of Lancaster.[177] Edmund Thornton was the link man. A native of Lancaster, he was involved in the Grenada partnership as well, for the signatories of a petition from the island include the Company of Thornton, Baillie and Campbell.[178] The closeness of his connexions with the Baillie family was made explicit when he was requested in 1793 to act for Mrs Baillie in getting in the estate and paying the debts of her late husband James.[179] Meanwhile, the Lancaster Barrow partners were closely related to Edmund Thornton. Edmund's father, William Thornton of Lancaster, and John Barrow were both described as 'uncles' when they were named as executors in the will of John Merrick, who died 'resident in Barbados' in 1774.[180] Edmund Thornton's father, William, had also been involved in slave dealings in Barbados in the earlier period. His partnership with John Thomas there in the 1750s not only served Gillow in 1750, and again in 1752, but also included selling slaves. In 1751 Henry Laurens

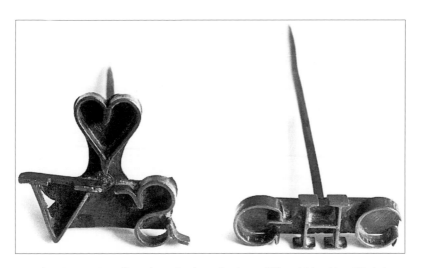

Branding Irons. Branding slaves in the colonies or West Africa identified them as the property of their owners. *Courtesy of Hull City Museums & Art Galleries*

was paying Thomas and Thornton £170 currency for a black woman he had sold for them in Charleston whom he had received from Barbados. Here, then, was another important link for Lancaster Guinea captains.[181] By the time of the second Lancaster registration, namely that of the *Robert* some eleven years later, the Grenada partners had dispersed. Those with shares in this vessel read as George, Thomas and William Barrow of Lancaster, together with James Baillie of London, Edmund Thornton of Whittington Hall, Westmorland and Duncan Campbell of Grenada.[182] However, by this date Lancaster slavers were no longer visiting the island.

From the information so far discussed, certain significant conclusions can be extracted concerning Lancaster's African trade and slave factorage in the West Indies. It is evident that Lancaster slave traders possessed useful personal ties in the Caribbean.[183] These ties, I would argue, must have been especially important to the small-scale operations which typified the slave trade at Lancaster. Without them, many ventures would no doubt have been submerged amidst the practices of impersonal slave auctions run by the big London houses. Lancaster's links served its traders well, affording them certain advantages when it came both to selling their live cargoes and to procuring their return shipments. It was important, if not crucial, to find a commission agent who could be trusted to secure the best slave prices possible and provide good return cargoes or safe bills of exchange, not to mention the tedious and difficult job of collecting debts should they arise. Through their contacts, Lancaster merchants must have gained, once again, a competitive edge over some of their north-western neighbours. Although information concerning the colonial stage of the slave trade at the other small north-western ports has yet to come to light, none of them apparently shared Lancaster's trading network and experience in the Caribbean.

Ironically, the marginality of Lancaster as a port served its slave traders well once more. The paucity of income to be gleaned from Lancaster's exports to the islands meant a number of the West India factors serving the established merchants, especially those who were less secure or simply very ambitious, were tempted, at some time or other, to deal in cargoes of African slaves. Their limited opportunities, therefore, led them to perform a useful, and even vital, role at the colonial apex of a triangular enterprise. Benjamin Satterthwaite made clear the often untenable position of the resident West India factor, when giving his reasons for rejecting an offer to go out to the Caribbean in 1744. He explained, "If I had gone to Barbados they would have engaged me to stay 18 months or 2 years and would engage themselves to send me not more than 2 vessalls which would have done very poorly for me considering the time they would have me stay".[184] In the same vein, K.E. Ingram writes, concerning the Lancaster cabinet-makers, Gillows, "The trade in furniture alone would not have sufficed to provide adequate commissions for the West India merchants or remittances for the English House".[185] Even if their agents had supplemented their incomes with imports of dry goods, as Ingram suggests, some were also tempted into selling shipments of African slaves as well; for amongst Gillow's lists of West India agents appear a number of the Lancastrians cited above, names such as Millerson, Satterthwaite, Thomas and Thornton.[186]

It was the same for some of the employees of the Rawlinson family. Charles Inman and Peter Woodhouse, both Jamaica agents for these West India merchants, evidently dipped into slave factorage from time to time to boost their incomes, as did Richard Hetherington some years later in Tortola. Moreover, it is probable that dealing in slaves assisted these opportunists in establishing themselves as merchants, even planters, in their own right, as opposed to mere factors.[187] Interestingly, Richard Pares comments on how the big business done in slaves in Kingston, Jamaica, and Bridgetown, Barbados, prevented the decline of resident merchants there, as happened elsewhere in the islands.[188]

All these men, with their connexions and experience in the produce trade, would have been well equipped to supply the Lancaster slave ships with return cargoes. Above all, the situation again reflects Lancaster's unique blend of marginality on the one part coupled with some considerable experience in the West Indies by a select body of more established merchants on the other, which together both compelled and enabled its aspiring merchants to pursue a more comprehensive slave trade than their north-western neighbours outside Liverpool.

Business Connexions in the Colonies: North America

By no means all Lancaster slave cargoes were sold in the West Indies. It has already been noted that shiploads of Africans were ferried the extra miles necessary to reach the American mainland. Here the situation was different, but evidently well organized. Lancaster factors were not sent out to the American colonies nor were any transatlantic partnerships formed, as was the case in Bristol.[189] Rather, Lancaster's slave traders, and indeed its bilateral operators, dealt with well-established American merchants. There is, fortunately, far more information available on the selling of slaves by Lancaster traders in the American mainland colonies. This is largely due to the prolific collection of business papers belonging to the South Carolina merchant, Henry Laurens, with whom the Lancaster slave merchants frequently traded.[190] In Laurens, the Lancaster merchants had a reliable and trustworthy business partner. In the first place, he was a regular and diligent correspondent, seeking to enlighten his English traders on current trends and prices. His letters are peppered with examples, sometimes encouraging, as in the following extract from a letter written in July 1755 to Robert and John Thompson, slave traders in Lancaster.

> The Sale of Slaves having continued with us much the same as we advised you last, that is: have hitherto sold mighty well ... 'Tis owing to our success last Year in Indigo and a very good prospect we have the present that People buy with this Spirit. The apparent prospect of a sudden War has not as yet in the least discouraged them and if no declaration is made this Summer we judge Negroes will continue to sell well through the Year [especially] as we are likely to be disappointed of a large part of those that were destin'd here the present Summer.

Laurens referred to the problems of supply in the Gambia where smallpox was rife and whence many vessels were proceeding to the West Indies to avoid South Carolina's quarantine. He concluded, "'Tis our opinion if no war breaks out Slaves will sell as well in October and November as at any time even to Xmas which we think it is our duty to inform you".[191] At other times Laurens warned that prospects were not so auspicious, as was the case almost a year later when he wrote to Captain John Holden of the snow *Anson*, stating,

> The almost certainty of a sudden War with France makes many of our Planters give over the thoughts of buying Slaves this Year and

we have had already a considerable number Imported and several others daily expected to arrive which we fear must bring our Market to a very low Ebb before you could reach us.

Three weeks later Laurens confirmed the situation, informing Holden,

We are now upon a certainty that war was declared in London on the 1st of May and we have had proof how much it affected the price of Slaves at this Market ... Wherefore we cannot by any means wish to see you down here this trip.[192]

Henry Laurens' conditions for selling slaves were clear and generally regarded as fair. When asked by Captain Dodson of the *Gambia* in 1755 on what terms Laurens would take up his slaves, Laurens wrote,

We offered to do it (tho they are come at a very poor time) on the Terms we have ever yet practisd (vizt.) to give the Vessell a Cargo of Our Produce, to pay the Capts. Coast Commission and Mens half Wages etc., and to remit the remainder at the time the payments shall become due. It is our Interest to sell for the shortest Credit possible, because the shorter the payments the less risque of bad debts.[193]

In this instance, Captain Dodson declined Laurens' offer and sold his slaves with the less experienced Charles Mayne in his pursuit of "bills in the bottom for the whole" (the ship to carry home bills of exchange for the entire cargo sold).[194] Laurens strongly suspected these unrealistic terms offered by an inexperienced merchant, and although Charles Mayne described the *Gambia*'s cargo as having "turnd out a fine sale",[195] it is noteworthy that in future concerns Dodson sold his cargoes with either Laurens or his associates, such as Austin and Appleby or Smith, Brewton and Smith.[196]

Careful selection of overseas business associates was crucial, but not all Lancaster merchants were able to sell their slave cargoes with Henry Laurens and his colleagues. By 1763 Laurens was declining offers to sell large slave assignments. Accordingly, in February 1764, he wrote to Smith and Baillies of St. Kitts,

You must know Gentlemen that I have in general declined the African business, altho I have had the most kind and friendly offers from my friends in London, Liverpool, and Bristol, and do believe that I might have sold 1000 or 1500 last Year and more the Year we are now in if I wou'd ask for them but having no Partner I do not choose to embarrass and perhaps involve myself in concerns too unwieldy for a single Man both on his own and his friends Account.[197]

As a consequence, some of the 'second generation' of slave traders, operating from Lancaster at this time, experienced some unfortunate

Lancaster slave traders sold their African cargoes through Henry Laurens, 1724–1792, slave merchant in Charleston, South Carolina. *From a mezzotint by Valentine Green, 1739–1813, after John Singleton Copley. Courtesy of National Portrait Gallery, Smithsonian Institution, Washington, D.C.*

dealings with a new firm named Middleton, Liston and Hope. The Millerson and Watson brothers, together with Robert Dodson, sold various Guinea cargoes in South Carolina with this firm in the mid-sixties as listed in Table 2.9. The American firm failed in Georgia in 1767 and as a result the Lancaster partners faced considerable losses in respect of some of their slave sales.

Table 2.9   *Lancaster Slavers Selling with Middleton, Liston and Hope*[198]

Date	Vessel	Master	Slaves	Owners
27/9/1763	*Marquis of Granby*	John Kitching	200	Robert Dodson and Co.
25/10/1764	*Marquis of Granby*	John Kitching	200	Robert Dodson and Co.
7/5/1765	*Antelope II*	Thomas Paley	150	Richard and John Watson, Thomas and Richard Millerson, Robert Dodson, Henry Lawrence and Thomas Hinde.
3/9/1765	*Prince George II*	John Addison	160	Richard Millerson, William and John Watson, Robert Dodson.
8/10/1765	*King Tom*	John Read	250	William and John Watson, Richard Millerson, Robert Dodson, and John Read.

Henry Laurens, presumably on account of his previous links with Lancaster merchants, was willing to assist and proved himself a useful and loyal associate in such times of adversity. On June 3rd, 1767, he wrote to Richard Millerson criticizing the firm for selling "Negroes to anybody that applied to them without any other consideration than to make a show of high avarages, a fatal mistake both to themselves and their Creditors". In a subsequent letter he added,

> They were as merchants all wrong headed & by no means equal to the scene of business which they engaged in, either in Point of Capital or Experience & with submission I have often wondered at the precipitance of People on your side in ordering large consignments upon them.[199]

Laurens endeavoured to get to the bottom of the affair for the Millersons and was accordingly issued with power of attorney.[200] On October 8th, 1767 he wrote,

> I am now very largely interested on behalf of some English friends about £15,000 Sterling in the affairs of a House which unhappily in the course of about four Years have sunk, totally sunk about 3 times

that amount of Money belonging to London, Bristol, Liverpool and Lancaster.[201]

The Millersons' trust in Laurens is exemplified in a letter written by Laurens to the Lancaster merchants in May 1768. In it he commented that he "shall pay due regard to that absolute confidence you are pleased to repose in me for the management of your unfortunate affairs involved in those of the late Middleton, Liston, and Hope".[202]

In subsequent letters, Laurens commented further on offers made to him by the Lancaster slave traders. On May 25th, 1768 he wrote to Thomas and Richard Millerson proffering his advisory services in the market soon to be opened, adding "I have not resolved upon that Trade again or not". Then in a letter written the following year he addressed Richard Millerson, not only condoling with him on the death of his industrious brother, Thomas, but also clarifying his own situation, stating,

> I am very much obliged to you for the preference intended to me of your African business but I have wholly retired from that branch of Trade & am endeavouring to draw all my commercial concerns within a very narrow compass.[203]

Such information illustrates the importance of reliable and sound-minded business associates in the colonies. Henry Laurens' correspondence with a number of Lancaster slave traders makes it evident that strong bonds of trust and friendship were built up. Such links led to other forms of cooperation between the Lancaster traders and the American merchant. For instance, in September 1768 Henry Laurens corresponded with Robert Dodson, concerning an assistant school teacher. Dodson had requested Laurens to help set up Mr. George Macreth in the colonies, about which Laurens reported to his 'old friend', saying, "In short I shall do anything in my power that you would expect, to serve him on your Account."[204]

No doubt this rapport played its part in enticing Lancaster vessels and their captains across the lengthier Middle Passage. Meanwhile, there is no evidence from Laurens' papers to suggest that merchants from Chester, Whitehaven, Preston and Poulton sold their African cargoes with Laurens, apart from on one isolated occasion with a Whitehaven vessel. If one assumes that the Lancaster merchants' preference for the slave markets of South Carolina was well founded, then traders from the other small north-western ports either failed or were unsuited to share in the spoils of such markets and thereby missed the services of a man like Henry Laurens who, being described as both acute and informed, "took a leading part in the importation of Negroes into Charleston, in the middle decades of the eighteenth century.[205]

Selling the slaves was only part of the function that merchants like Laurens carried out for the English slave traders. There was, in addition, the all-important task of organizing return cargoes and/or bills of exchange as remittance for the sales of black African cargoes. A discussion of this aspect of the slave trade addresses a controversial historiographical issue, namely whether slave ships left the colonies with produce, thereby engendering the prospect of further profits, or whether they sailed in ballast, with bills of exchange as payment for their human imports. Proposers of the latter view have vehemently questioned the 'triangularity' of slaving enterprises in more recent years, primarily in connexion with the trade in the West Indian islands during the second half of the eighteenth century.[206] What needs to be ascertained here is whether Lancaster slavers returned laden or in ballast. The various forms of remittance will be considered first in the mainland colonies and then in the islands on which the historiographical debate is centred.

In the slave trade to the American mainland, which in Lancaster's experience primarily concerned South Carolina, return cargoes were generally available and were usually taken in payment, or part payment for slave imports. Professor Minchinton, on examining Bristol's African trade to America, concludes, "Few if any Bristol slave-vessels appear to have cleared the American mainland colonies for England in ballast". He goes on to say, "American merchants, if Henry Laurens is any example, were ready to find homeward cargoes for slave vessels".[207] Such a policy was evident on numerous occasions for the Lancaster vessels. It is well expressed in Laurens' letter to Robert Dodson in 1755 when he offered to give Dodson's vessel, "a Cargo of Our Produce", and to remit the remainder as payments became due as part of the terms "we have ever yet practisd".[208]

Minchinton lists the normal exports for South Carolina as rice, indigo, skins, turpentine, pitch and tar, but points out that rice, the colony's main product had a market in continental Europe rather than England, which could make it more difficult for the Guinea captains to secure a homeward cargo.[209] However, Bristol slave traders probably faced more difficulties with their imports than their counterparts at Lancaster in that they operated more numerous ventures and generally larger slave ships. In February 1756 Laurens reported, "The Bristol gentlemen have always ships enough with us to carry home as much or more of our produce than their market will take off", and he went on to cite two slave ships destined for Portugal since there was, "no encouragement for them to load for Bristol."[210] It is doubtful that the size and number of vessels employed in the Lancaster trade presented quite the same problems, and no evidence has been found to suggest time-consuming European destinations for its slave vessels departing from Charleston. It is probable that some rice was used on subsequent voyages to Africa. Certainly blacks from the Windward Coast, a popular source for Lancaster slavers, were generally fed on boiled rice and in 1792 the *Hope II* of Lancaster had carried nine casks of rice from Lancaster to Africa. Of course rice was also available on the African coast, for example at Sesthos on the Windward Coast.[211]

Rice was by no means the only option for the returning Lancaster ships. From a study of some of the naval office shipping lists and correspondence of Henry Laurens, it is evident that many Lancaster slave merchants acquired a comprehensive range of produce in return for their African slaves. This is well exemplified by the cargo of the seventy-ton *Molly I*, owned by William Butterfield and Company, which sailed from Charleston for Lancaster in 1760 with 34 barrels of rice, 100 barrels of turpentine, 20 barrels of pitch, 183 barrels of tar, 125 mahogany planks, 60 two-inch pine planks, 2 hogsheads of deerskin, 1 cask of indigo (and some ivory not to be landed in South Carolina). She had sold some 228 slaves from the Windward and Rice Coast of Guinea.[212] Two items in the *Molly I*'s cargo are of particular significance, namely the mahogany and pine planks. A study of the information on return cargoes carried by Lancaster slave ships reveals that lumber was a popular item. In addition to that carried by the *Molly I* in 1760, an entire cargo of timber was imported to Lancaster aboard the *Marquis of Granby* the following year. This consisted of 1,088 planks of Providence mahogany, together with a quantity of Honduras unchipped logwood. Eighteen and a half tons of this latter commodity was also imported by the *Marlborough* in 1760, whilst a year earlier the *Thetis I* had sailed with another 18¼ tons. Logwood was a valuable dye-wood from a tree native to Central America. Its dark brownish-red colour could be changed to produce shades of blue or even black. Alternatively, both the extract and decoction of logwood could be used as astringents in treating diarrhoea and dysentery.[213] The *Molly I* was again transporting wood in 1765 in the form of mahogany and cedar logs.[214] Cabinet-making, most notable under the name of Gillow, had assumed some considerable importance in Lancaster at this time. The Lancaster merchants had evidently found some useful commodities in exchange for their African slaves, alongside the more common imports of rice, indigo, deerskin, pitch and tar.

Of course not all Lancaster slave ships fared so well. On occasions, this reflected poor market conditions in the colonies or simply a poor slaving voyage. In 1756 the forty-ton *Concord* only carried off "a small assorted Cargo", amounting to £1,999.15s.0d currency, including money disbursed for the vessel. This was set against a sale of forty-six surviving slaves from a miserable voyage which amounted to £5,436.4s.2d currency. A further £1,968.10s.1d currency was paid for two bills of exchange (amount £203.3s sterling). This left a balance of £1,467.19s.1d currency which Laurens remitted to Messrs. Thompsons early, explaining to their captain, "We hope that getting your Money quickly home will in some degree help a bad Voyage or forward a better". Laurens also advised the owners, "we have advanced a large proportion of the Produce to help you a little in an unsuccessfull Voyage".[215]

Meanwhile, other vessels advertised for freight rather than conveying imports on their owners' account. A notice in the South Carolina Gazette on April 28th, 1757 read,

For any Port in Great-Britain The Snow ANSON, JOHN HOLDEN Master. Burthen about 300 Barrels of Rice and has very good Accommodation for Passengers. For freight or Passage apply to Austin & Laurens.[216]

Laurens had, in the meantime, contacted James Cowles of Bristol suggesting he might be interested. He wrote, "The master we believe will bring you 3 or 400 barrels of Rice north about if we can but lay in within your limits which we shall endeavour to do".[217] A route 'north about', thereby avoiding the channel coast, would have been advantageous with the disruptions occasioned by the Seven Years War.

Freight-earnings on the third leg of a triangular enterprise, however, appear to have been the exception rather than the rule at Lancaster, the traders evidently preferring to receive cargoes on their own account. Returning 'in ballast' was equally unacceptable. Only two examples from South Carolina have been found. In 1756 the *Gambia*, master Robert Dodson, had, as Laurens put it, sold for "bills in the bottom for the whole", but he did not, apparently, repeat the experience. The only other vessel which is known to have sailed without a cargo was the *King Tom*, on the 31st October 1765, after having landed 230 slaves from the Windward Coast of Africa.[218] Whatever the reasons for this, it is worth noting that the ship failed to make another slaving voyage and that its owners' other Africa-bound vessels generally returned with cargoes.

Voyages by Lancaster slavers to Virginia were few, but again the evidence shows they returned laden rather than in ballast. For example, in 1759 the fifty-ton *Lowther* cleared from Hampton for Lancaster with 18 hogsheads of tobacco, 1 pipe of madeira wine (part of its outward cargo, the slaving voyage was believed to improve it), 2 spars, 6 elephant teeth, 410 barrels of tar and pitch, 115 barrels of turpentine, 246 feet of scantling and 4,250 staves. The quantity of tobacco carried was only small, whereas that carried by the *Juba I* in

1760 was far more consequential. This seventy-ton snow, bound for the Lune from the Virginian port of Hampton, was laden with, "163 hogsheads of tobacco, 4 casks of prize indigo, three dozen oars, one elephant tooth & Co, 60 foot of scantling and planks and 3,000 staves and shingles". Some eight years earlier the *Castleton*, of similar burthen, had cleared from the Upper James River with 102 hogsheads of tobacco and 3,000 staves .[219] An interesting comparison can be made with some average export figures drawn up by Professor Minchinton for slavers clearing from Virginia, as outlined in Table 2.10.

Table 2.10 *Average Export Figures for Slavers clearing from Virginia*[220]

Date	Hogheads of Tobacco	Tons of Iron	Barrels of Pitch	Barrels of Tar	Number of Staves
1749–1755	114	5	6	132	8,279
1756–1763	99	9	–	27	9,426

Clearly, both the *Juba I* and *Castleton* carried sizeable cargoes of tobacco, especially if one considers their small tonnage. Moreover, their figures belie suggestions that slave ships were not at all suitable for the transport of tobacco and in any case the *Castleton* was later employed in direct trade with the colonies.

The information discussed shows that, although no rigid pattern of trade existed for the Lancaster slavers which plied their way across the Atlantic to the American mainland, return cargoes generally played a very important role in the triangular ventures of the Lancaster entrepreneurs. Few ships returned in ballast whilst most appear to have carried cargoes on their owners' account. Indeed, it is probable that the ready availability or nature of these return cargoes, prompted the Lancaster traders to send their ships to these mainland colonies, especially given the market advantages for their slave cargoes, most notably in South Carolina. Maximising returns on each stage of a voyage would be of particular importance to small-scale operators, such as those at Lancaster. In Henry Laurens the merchants were dealing not only with a person who would happily provide them with imports for the third leg of their voyage, but with someone who would even "advance some Produce" in times of adversity. Meanwhile, these American imports came to slave traders at Lancaster alone amongst the small north-western slave ports.

If produce was important on the final leg of voyages made by slave ships leaving America, what was the situation in the Caribbean? The debate as to whether slave ships left the islands with produce or whether they sailed in ballast, with bills of exchange as payment for their African cargoes, needs some amplification before the experience of the Lancaster slavers is examined.[221] The traditional view was that slavers pursued a triangular pattern of slaving, carrying various cargoes on each leg of a voyage. Recent research, however, suggests that slave ships were invariably forced to return from the West Indian colonies, at least, with their holds empty. Both Sheridan and Merritt believe that sugar became very difficult for slavers to obtain. Sheridan argues that after about 1750 the Sugar Trade became largely organized and directed by London agents with the development of the guarantee system, whereby Caribbean planters employed commission agents in England and traded directly with them on their own account.[222] In addition, Merritt suggests that certain planters consigned their sugars to outport merchants who were not directly engaged in the slave trade.[223] As the century progressed, it is argued, the planters sank into greater debt, thereby increasing the subjection of their produce to their English Commission agents, who were supplying much of their needs in the colonies. Thus planters no longer sold a significant proportion of their produce to the slave traders who visited the islands which had hitherto enabled slave ships to transport sugars home. This left African merchants without a viable homeward cargo, or at best with overpriced or inferior sugars. More often than not, captains were compelled to return in ballast, taking discounted bills of exchange as payment for their African slaves.[224] Merritt goes on to point out that this in turn saved the slaving vessels from long, costly delays in the islands and in any case, he adds, "the slave ship was not built to carry hogsheads of sugar and was said to be often in a leaky, worm-eaten condition".[225]

More recently Minchinton, although not denying the trend proposed by Sheridan, Merritt and others, has suggested that their views might need some modification. In his article entitled, "The Triangular Trade Revisited", he cites many instances when produce was acquired by the Guineamen in the islands and goes on to detail statistical evidence showing that many vessels did make lengthy stays at their colonial ports, which must suggest that their masters were loading their ships for the return leg of their voyage. Moreover, Minchinton argues that these vessels were neither worm-eaten nor unsuitable for transporting these dead cargoes and nor were their owners so transitory that they were without contacts in the islands, through whom to secure Caribbean produce. He concludes, "Evidence has been presented to show that although some may have moved from one colonial port to another in ballast, few slave vessels returned to England in ballast. Thus the great majority were able to secure some kind of return cargo." Moreover, if this be the case, he points out, "then the earnings on the return voyage need to be taken into account in any discussion on profitability".[226] This notion of earning on the third leg of an African voyage is seen by Maurice Schofield as a crucial part of a slave-trading enterprise. He suggests that having close colonial connexions in the slave colonies was crucial, not only for assessing the chances of profit in supplying slaves, but also in finding return cargoes to increase that profit.[227] According to B.K. Drake, slavers returning with produce carried another advantage. He suggests that produce provided the slave merchants with "a more immediate return on investment". This would of course be of particular benefit to small, less-established merchants.[228]

What is of importance now is to ascertain how Lancaster traders fitted into this picture, especially since most of their slave ships set sail during the second half of the eighteenth century. That is to say did these Guineamen return to the Lune laden or in ballast?

Although there is not enough information to make a detailed statistical analysis, the naval office shipping lists do provide a reasonable picture. Bearing in mind the limited sources, the overall impression is that Lancaster slave traders preferred their captains to acquire a return cargo of some description from the Caribbean islands they visited. From the data collected, only a handful of Lancaster-registered ships left the islands in ballast. These include the *Bassa* of Ulverston which sailed for Lancaster from Grenada in 1767, the *Molly III* which also cleared Grenada for Liverpool with just its cargo of African produce some twenty years after, and much later still the *Beaver* which arrived in Lancaster from Surinam with one elephant tooth in 1803.[229] There may of course have been others, but as yet they have not been revealed in a study of the shipping lists. Schofield wonders whether the selling of the *Bassa* had resulted from the vessel's return in ballast which thereby denied her owners any extra profit on the final leg of her voyage.

The West Indian produce sent to Lancaster in slaving vessels chiefly consisted of sugar, cotton, rum, mahogany, ginger and the dye-woods fustic and logwood. In Barbados the information concerning clearances of Lancaster Guineamen is confined to just two examples. These voyages took place in the 1750s at a time when Lancaster traders most frequented the island. Here it is useful to make a comparison with a general West Indian vessel sent from Lancaster at a similar date (Table 2.11, overleaf).

The sugar lading per ton for the *Bold* is 0.91 hogsheads, whilst that of the *Exchange* is 1.3 hogsheads. Although this is only one comparison, it is noteworthy that the differences in lading, in this instance, are not as great as often suggested. For these slave traders at any rate, African slaves had enabled them to buy sugar and other West Indian produce. The *Bold*, at least, quite likely sold its slaves and received its return cargo through the Lancaster-connected firm Satterthwaite and Jones. Minchinton specifically mentions that the large size of this firm would have made it easier for them to have produce available.[231]

Table 2.11   *Cargoes of Vessels Clearing Barbados for Lancaster*[230]

Date	Vessel	Tons	Cargo
1753	*Robert*	40	58 hogsheads and 14 tierces rum, 5 tons fustick.
1756	*Bold*	70	64 hogsheads and 19 tierces sugar, 11 puncheons rum, 7 tons logwood, 14 bags cotton.
1757	*Exchange* (non-slaver)	100	130 casks sugar, 3 casks rum, 200 bags ginger, 70mahogany planks, 1 cask coffee.

More information has been found in the naval office shipping lists for Jamaica. Table 2.12 lists cargoes which Lancaster slavers typically brought back to England from Jamaica. They are presumably illustrative of many more return cargoes from the Caribbean.

Table 2.12   *Clearances from Jamaica, Showing Cargoes and Vessel's Length of Stay.*[232]

Date	Vessel	Tons	Length of Stay	Cargo
1747	*Expedition*	100	c.70–80 days	120 hogsheads and 27 tierces sugar, 7 bags cotton, 2,500 feet mahogany, 12 tons wood.
1753	*Barlborough*	40	17 days	10 puncheons rum.
1754	*Barlborough*	40	63 days	62 hogsheads and tierces sugar, 5 tons fustick, 40 bags ginger, 40 tons mahogany, 23 bags cotton.
1755	*Stanley*	70	77 days	37 hogsheads sugar, 18 butts and 76 bags pimento.
1757	*Gambia*	70	110 days	62 casks sugar, 31 puncheons rum, 26 bags cotton, 8 tons logwood, 41 bags ginger.
1765	*Norfolk*	100	105 days	83 hogsheads and 18 tierces sugar, 6 puncheons rum, 413 planks mahogany.
1768	*Thomas and John*	70	86 days	9 hogsheads and 13 tierces sugar, 41 puncheons rum, 34 bags cotton, 36 planks mahogany, 7 bags pimento, 5 tons logwood.
1770s			NO DATA	
1785	*Fenton*	90	—	541 planks of mahogany.
1785	*Hinde*	100	59 days	12 casks sugar, 40 bags cotton, 18 tons logwood and fustick.
1786	*Molly III*	70	32 days	2 casks sugar, 17 puncheons rum, 7 tons logwood and fustick.

In the colonies slaves were exchanged for produce. 'Shipping the Sugar' from W. Clark's Ten Views of Antigua. *Courtesy of British Library*

The fact that all these vessels, with the exception of the *Barlborough* in 1753 and the *Molly III* in 1786, stayed two to three and a half months in Jamaica, a figure comparable with American-bound slavers from the Lune, strongly suggests that their owners were keen to secure homeward cargoes of substance. One wonders why the tiny *Barlborough* stayed only seventeen days in Jamaica to collect a mere ten puncheons of rum as early as 1753 when fuller cargoes were surely available, or what caused the *Bassa* to stay a full sixty-six days in Grenada, only to clear in ballast in 1767. However, such incidents are apparently the exceptions rather than the rule.

There is, indeed, a noticeable decline in the amount of sugar exported from Jamaica in Lancaster slave ships after the mid-1760s, but up to this time levels seem to be of some significance and, interestingly, they seem fairly closely aligned to Minchinton's general figures for the lading of slave vessels from Jamaica. (Table 2.13)

From his figures Minchinton concludes, "Although slave vessels never held more than a modest share of the total trade in sugar, sugar continued to provide a sizeable cargo for the slave vessels until the 1760s".[234]

Table 2.13 *Jamaican Sugar Exports Aboard Guineamen*

Lancaster Samples		Minchinton's Figures[233]	
Date	Lading per Ton (hhds)	Date	Lading per Ton (hhds)
1747	1.2 (*Expedition*)	1744	1.3
1753	– (*Barlborough*)		
1754	1.55 (*Barlborough*)	1754	0.88
1756	0.53 (*Stanley I*)		
1757	0.89 (*Gambia*)		
1765	0.83 (*Norfolk*)	1764	0.53
1768	0.13 (*Thomas and John*)		
1785	– (*Fenton*)	1784	0.22
1785	0.12 (*Hinde*)		
1786	0.03 (*Molly III*)		

The decline in the amount of sugar available in the older colonies after this time, and maybe other produce as well, no doubt propelled Lancaster's African merchants towards Britain's newly acquired islands at this juncture. By 1770 a large proportion of Lancaster slavers destined for the West Indies were making for Grenada. Here it is likely that not only would there have been a good demand for slaves but that the vessels could more readily procure homeward cargoes, including sugar. Unfortunately, there are no surviving naval office shipping lists for the years 1767–1784, the period when seventeen or more Lancaster slavers sailed from Africa for Grenada. However, the island's rapid development at this time supports this supposition. Anderson comments on the rapidity with which the island, along with Dominica, was developed for monoculture after its cession in 1763, and goes on to refer to the boom years of the early 1770s when the island was being actively settled by British planters.[235] Indeed Lancaster's most prominent West India merchants, Thomas Hutton and Abraham Rawlinson, and later their sons, became owners of the Goyave Plantation in Grenada from the mid-1760s.[236]

The thirst of Lancaster slave traders for produce on the return voyage is again illustrated by their activities at the turn of the century. At this time the few remaining Lancaster-owned vessels still carried substantial cargoes, including sugar, back to England. By now they had switched to newer colonies still, such as Trinidad, which was occupied by the British in 1797, and Surinam, which the British captured from the Dutch during the Napoleonic wars. Accordingly, in 1804, the *Johns* of Lancaster left Surinam with 1,555 bags of coffee, 225 bales of cotton, 187 casks of sugar, 7 elephant teeth and 16 'seamersedo'. It made its final voyage to Africa in 1807, returning to Lancaster from

Trinidad in the summer of 1808 with 188 hogsheads and 49 lbs of sugar, 11 casks of coffee, 10 casks of cocoa and 10 bales of cotton.[237]

Sugar, if not always available or of sufficient quality, was clearly not the only valuable produce carried by the Lancaster slave ships returning from the Caribbean; and it would seem wrong to equate triangularity and profitability on the return voyage with sugar imports alone. From table 2.12 above, mahogany was obviously a popular item in the ships leaving Jamaica, as from elsewhere. It has already been noted that this product was particularly welcome in Lancaster, owing to the very successful furniture business of Robert Gillow, and much of this wood, in its finished form, found its way back to the islands in Lancaster West Indiamen. Ingram, in his article on the Gillows, remarks, "Mahogany was naturally a highly desirable form of remittance". In this he was referring to payment in the colonies for Gillow exports. Its value as a form of payment must have benefitted Lancaster slave traders as well. Gillows relied on other merchants to supply them with much of their wood. Their capacious demand for mahogany is evident from the fact that it was sometimes in short supply. On more than one occasion, according to Ingram, Gillows had to "reprove their Jamaican agents for failing to supply them with this commodity to the detriment of their output at home"; and as their business prospered, so their demand for wood expanded.[238] The possibilities of trading slaves for mahogany is best illustrated by the ninety-ton *Fenton*, owned by James Sawrey and Company, which in 1785 brought an entire cargo of the timber, consisting of 541 planks from Jamaica. This amount far surpassed that carried by any slaver just two years later, as listed by Minchinton; the largest amount then being the 232 planks carried by the 274-ton *Antonetta* of London.[239]

From his study of the Gillow Papers, Ingram makes some further observations on West Indian produce, particularly that of Jamaica, which provide useful comments of a broader nature, such as might easily apply to the slave traders as well. For instance, he notes that Gillows requested their agents for dye-woods. These commonly included logwood, which grew in the Caribbean and fustic, a dye-stuff of a large tree also growing in the West Indies. Fustic was sometimes used for inlay work as well as in its more common form in the textile world as a yellow dye.[240] Lancaster had its own dyers, such as Daniel Wane and his son Jeremiah, not to mention its connexions with certain Manchester textile manufacturers. Thus dyewoods gave Lancaster slave ships another useful import, as did cotton, which was requested by Gillows in 1776 from both Jamaica and Grenada. Concerning this, they wrote, "We believe some expect it may get up to 2/- p.lb as the cotton manifacy go's well at this time". Cotton was rarely omitted from the hold of a Lancaster slave ship returning from

Slaves were sold and put to work in large field gangs, producing colonial crops for export. 'Digging the Cane Holes' from W. Clark's Ten Views of Antigua. *Courtesy of British Library*

the West Indies and nor was rum, which was generally regarded as desirable in a homeward cargo. Concerning rum, Gillows suggest strong ones were best and were usually requested to be sent to Dublin or Cork, though weak rums were to be sent to Lancaster.[241]

That slave ships were unsuited to carrying rum, or any other colonial produce for that matter, seems ill-founded in Lancaster's experience. In any case, its Guineamen were neither old nor far removed in design and construction from a West Indiaman. That is to say they were general purpose, all-rounders as opposed to the much larger, more specialised slave ships that have often been quoted from the governmental enquiries, made in the 1780s and 1790s, and on whose evidence much of Sheridan and Merritt's arguments is based.[242] As such, it evidently suited Lancaster slave traders to pursue a triangular trade, wherever possible. The emphasis on sugar undoubtedly became less marked as the eighteenth century progressed and in this respect Lancaster imports, transported by its African vessels, bear some relationship to the developments noted by Sheridan and others. However, to deduce, from the evidence collected, that the Lune slavers returned mainly in ballast appears to be utterly unfounded. Lancaster slave traders, in lacking a firm footing in the port's merchant class, needed to seek out any additional profits that could be accumulated from carrying a cargo on the homeward voyage. Moreover, they probably had the acquisition of these imports in mind when their ships set sail for Africa. Slaves gave them a potentially lucrative and valuable commodity with which to trade in the West Indies. Meanwhile, their home region failed to supply these entrepreneurs with a strongly profitable export that might readily establish them as overseas merchants in a direct trade with the Caribbean islands. In this context, the slave trade at Lancaster might be regarded, for many, as a means into the less risky West India trade rather than as an end in itself. In any case, the scale of their operations at Lancaster probably did not lend itself to the latter. Their African enterprises were seldom, if ever, conducted on the vast scale practised by many Liverpool houses in the second half of the eighteenth century. Lancaster traders were not wholesale operators on the African coast. The retail nature of their captains' business transactions would have been far better suited to exchanging their slaves for produce than bills. Their small enterprises meant smaller profits which in turn called for additional efforts to be made to engender extra earnings on the final leg of the voyage. Furthermore, their vessels being smaller made their holds less daunting and time-consuming to fill, and they had found some useful commodities to import from the colonies to Lancaster which could act as supplements or even substitutes for the more traditional cargo of sugar. Above all, careful and calculated dealings, at each stage of the journey, were a hallmark of these lesser slave traders. They had not followed the crowd in their choice of African or colonial markets and it is therefore likely that they practised careful, individual transactions at the final stage of their operations, in a way that was not altogether necessary for the wholesale operators from the Mersey.

To do this, Lancaster slave traders distanced themselves, to some extent, from the planter-dominated colonies referred to by Sheridan and others; venues where competition for return cargoes became increasingly manifest. Instead, they adopted alternative markets such as South Carolina in the 1750s and 1760s and the ceded islands in the 1760s and 1770s. It is likely that owners of small slave ships at other small north-western ports attempted to return laden as well, in order to boost their profits, and this probably explains, in part, the lengthy voyages of the Preston and Poulton slavers. However, their voyages of twenty months or more duration, despite small slave cargoes, suggest that their captains encountered some difficulty in securing their return produce, as well as experiencing possible delays on the African coast, presumably due to more limited colonial contacts and a lack of expertise. Chester merchants may have faced similar problems in the 1750s, more especially because their vessels tended to be larger and thereby their holds more capacious. Moreover, their last three slaving voyages in the 1770s were directed to Jamaica, where they would not have avoided the difficulties of securing a return cargo. At the same time, it is questionable whether a return cargo would necessarily have been as profitable to investors at Chester, given that they faced such severe competition from their neighbouring West India merchants at Liverpool. Such competition certainly seemed to thwart a direct West India trade at Chester.[243]

Meanwhile at Whitehaven, the slaver *Providence* returned to the Cumberland coast with 41 hogsheads and 12 tierces of sugar in July 1753.[244] Being a brig of just thirty tons, its lading per ton was high and its turn-about time short. It seems likely that Whitehaven's slave merchants, like those at Lancaster, had also found the African slave a useful means to procure colonial produce, since they too lacked a cheap export for the West Indies. More research needs to be done to ascertain whether they continued to secure substantial return cargoes, as competition in the islands increased and their vessels became larger. Certainly, from the evidence so far consulted, the older colonies of Jamaica and Barbados appear as popular destinations for their sizeable African cargoes of the 1760s. It could be that ultimately the problems of securing return shipments, together with the problems of sorting outgoing cargoes, played some part in the slave trade's decline at Whitehaven after the sixties. Unlike Lancaster, the town did not develop any sugar-refining of consequence, which may have caused these merchants difficulties, especially as the quality of sugars exported on slave ships generally declined. Eaglesham suggests that the lack of sugar-refining and of local cotton manufacture may have been of significance in the port's failure to develop a prosperous West India trade,[245] and this in itself is perhaps a significant pointer to the port's lack of enthusiasm and enterprise concerning the West India trade, which presumably stemmed from the merchants' opportunities in alternative commerce. In addition, Whitehaven merchants would not have had such ready access to the buyers of the manufacturing areas of Lancashire as some of their more southerly neighbours, even though coastal shipping no doubt alleviated some of these problems of remoteness. In essence, Cumbrian merchants concentrated more on exports of coal and re-exports of tobacco, which therefore required no local manufactures. In this light, it is possible that slaver captains from Whitehaven, too, may have been encouraged to concentrate their energies on the transportation of large numbers of African slaves across the Atlantic rather than concern themselves with acquiring carefully organized return shipments. Meanwhile, the owners of Lancaster slave ships returning from the Caribbean islands, probably managed to find more accessible and less competitive markets for their produce than the merchants either at Chester or Whitehaven. Thus they experienced an added incentive to return their ships laden and, moreover, this quite likely fired their enthusiasm to enter the slave trade in the first place. Lancaster was not so distant from the Lancashire manufacturing centres as Whitehaven and yet the port enjoyed a greater and more exclusive local demand than its neighbours, with its position at the head of Lunesdale and its connexions through the valleys to Yorkshire and Westmorland and across the sands to Furness and the southern Lakes, areas which experienced more local industry and commerce than is often accredited to them.[246]

From a detailed study of the structure and operation of the slave trade, an attempt had been made to comprehend and explain the particular level and character of slave trading at Lancaster, and at the same time to set this in a regional and national context. In so doing, many passing references have been made to the personnel involved and it is to this more social aspect that the next chapter must be devoted. A discovery of the type of people drawn to slaving should throw more light on the motivations already hinted at for participating in the African trade at Lancaster and elsewhere, and should further help to clarify the complexity of reasons which account for Lancaster's unique stance in the eighteenth-century transatlantic slave-trading statistics.

Notes to Chapter II

1. Davis, *Shipping Industry*, p. 91, and Anderson, 'Lancashire Bill System', p. 73.
2. P.R.O., C.O. 142 Jamaica; C.O. 33 Barbados; C.O. 106 Grenada; C.O. 243 St. Kitts; C.O. 5 Virginia, South Carolina and Georgia.
3. The ship's captain was often one of the owners.
4. P.R.O., C.O. 5/710, *Antelope*, 31 July 1766 and *Dove*, 27 July 1766 and Oct. 1767; C.O. 5/510, *Thetis*, 6 Sept. 1759.
5. Liv.R.O. (Islington), Liverpool Plantation Registers.
6. The Statutory Registers of Merchant Shipping for the Port of Lancaster 1786–1823; now kept at Lancs. C.R.O., (subsequently referred to as Lancaster Shipping Registers).
7. F. E. Hyde, B. B. Parkinson and S. Marriner, 'The Nature and Profitability of the Liverpool Slave Trade', in *Ec.H.R.*, 2nd Series, 5, 1952, p. 371.
8. Quoted in D. P. Mannix, *Black Cargoes* (London, 1962), p. 73.
9. C. M. MacInnes, 'Bristol and the Slave Trade', in P. McGrath, ed., *Bristol in the Eighteenth Century* (Newton Abbot, 1972), p. 172.
10. P.R.O., C.O. 33/17, 21 Mar. 1763.
11. M. Schofield, 'Chester Slave-Trading Partnerships 1750–56', Short Notes in *T.H.S.L.C.*, vol. 130, 1981, p. 187.
12. See below, ch. 3, p. 124.

13. Davis, *Shipping Industry*, pp. 77–8.
14. These tonnage figures are taken from the Mediterranean Passes (P.R.O., Adm. 7, 87–102) and a Board of Trade document entitled, 'An Account of the Tonnage of the several ships cleared from Britain to Africa, 1757–1777' (P.R.O., B.T. 6/3, Bundle B, 57–118). The Tonnage figures in these two documents are not always consistent, in which case the most plausible have been selected. The tonnage measurements are smaller than those employed by the Lancaster Port Commission in their Tonnage Registers; see ch. 4, Table 4.3, p. 177.
15. Schofield, 'Slave Trade', p. 50.
16. Barber's slavers included the *Cato*, *Hamilton*, *Jupiter*, *Rainbow* and *Thetis II*, all of 100 tons; the *Marquis of Granby* of 95 tons; the *Rumbold I* of 140 tons and the *Lion* of 250 tons.
17. A new method of tonnage assessment was enforced after 1786. Tonnage figures after that date need reducing by about a third for comparisons to be made. See D. P. Lamb, 'Volume and Tonnage of Liverpool Slave Trade', in R. Anstey and P. E. H. Hair, eds., *Liverpool, the African Slave Trade and Abolition*, for Historic Society of Lancashire and Cheshire (Liverpool, 1976), p. 99.
18. Re. Liverpool, Bristol and London, see Lamb, 'Volume and Tonnage', pp.98–9. Re. Whitehaven, see P.R.O., B.T. 6/3, Bundle B, 57–118 and Whitehaven Museum's forthcoming booklet on the slave trade by H. Fancy. Re. Chester, see Schofield, 'Slave Trade', p. 40. Re. Lancaster, see P.R.O., Adm. 7, 87–102 and B.T. 6/3, Bundle B, 57–118.
19. Tonnage figures for the 1760s atypically include four very small slaving vessels which were presumably tenders to larger ones. They weighed just 15 to 18 tons each. They have been omitted in these calculations. If they are included, the average becomes 69 tons for this period.
20. Schofield, 'Slave Trade', p. 51.
21. W. E. Minchinton, 'The Slave Trade of Bristol with the British Mainland Colonies in North America 1699–1770', in Anstey and Hair, eds., *Slave Trade*, p. 50.
22. Mannix, *Black Cargoes*, p. 157.
23. See below, ch. 4, pp. 192–3.
24. Davis, *Shipping Industry*, pp 91 and 95.
25. Sources for this table include naval office shipping lists, Liverpool Plantation Registers, Lancaster Registry Book.
26. MacInnes, 'Bristol Slave Trade', p. 173.
27. For *Jolly Batchelor* see E. Kennerley, *The Brockbanks of Lancaster* (Lancaster Museum Monograph, 1981), p.5; for *Barlborough* see P.R.O., C.O. 142/15, 14 Aug. 1754; for *Robert* see P.R.O., C.O. 33/16, Pt. II, 30 Sept. 1752; for *Castleton*, see P.R.O., C.O. 5/1446, 24 Aug. 1752. Between 1752 and 1759, 56% of the new or almost new vessels were built at Lancaster.
28. J. E. Merritt, 'The Triangular Trade', *Business History*, 3, 1960, p. 4.
29. See Schofield, 'Chester Partnerships', p. 189, and Chester Record Office typesheet, 'Evidence about ships sailing in the Slave Trade connected with Chester'.
30. Davis, *Shipping Industry*, p. 295 and Mannix, *Black Cargoes*, p. 70.

31. *W.L.A.*, 27 Aug. 1756 and 15 Dec. 1758.

32. *W.L.A.*, 19 Aug. 1757 and 26 Apr. 1765.

33. B. K. Drake, 'The Liverpool-African Voyage c.1790–1807: Commercial Problems', in Anstey and Hair, eds., *Slave Trade*, pp.128–129. R. Craig, 'Shipping and Shipbuilding in the Port of Chester in the Eighteenth and early Nineteenth Centuries', *T.H.S.L.C.*, 116, 1964, pp. 59–61.

34. Re. *Lancaster*, see P.R.O., Adm. 68/200, London Seamen's Sixpences, 25 Oct. 1758 and 8 Dec. 1759. Crews for these voyages were 14 and 11 men, respectively, compared to the 20 and 30 on her slaving ventures. Re. *Lowther*, see Lancaster Port Commission Tonnage Book, 1756–67, 21 Mar. 1758 and 27 Dec. 1755, kept at Lancaster Maritime Museum.

35. See Lancaster Shipping Register, *Hope II*, 24 Feb. 1787 and *Tom*, 12 Nov. 1792.

36. P.R.O.,B.T. 6/7, Dimensions of Ships of Port of Liverpool in African Slave Trade.

37. Minchinton, 'Bristol Slave Trade', p. 51.

38. See below, p. 94.

39. R. B. Sheridan, 'The Commercial and Financial Organization of the British Slave Trade', *Ec.H.R.*, 2nd Series, 11, 1958, pp. 252–253.

40. See below, p. 54.

41. Mannix, *Black Cargoes*, p.70.

42. L.P.L., MS 3738, *Hope*'s Package Book, 1792.

43. Marshall, *Furness*, p. 32n.

44. Davies-Davenport Papers, Raymond Richards collection, University of Keele, Bead Book 1766–70.

45. Davies-Davenport Papers, Trade Accounts 1768 and Waste Book, 1745–66.

46. Manchester cottons were especially important in the 1750s when the break up of the Moghul Empire cut off the more popular Indian supplies. See A. P. Wadsworth and J. de L. Mann, *The Cotton Trade and Industrial Lancashire*, (Manchester, 1931), p. 160. Re. Kendal Cottons, see Beckett, *Coal and Tobacco*, p. 143.

47. Marshall, *Furness*, p. 31.

48. See D. Richardson, 'West African Consumption Patterns and their Influence on the Eighteenth-Century English Slave Trade', in H. A. Gemery and J. S. Hogendorn, eds., *The Uncommon Market: Essays in the Economic History of the Atlantic Slave Trade* (New York, 1979), p. 309.

49. R. Anstey, *The Atlantic Slave Trade and British Abolition, 1760–1810* (London, 1975), p. 12.

50. Sources used include Free/App. Rolls and Ulv.P.R.

51. Hughes, *North Country Life*, p. 48.

52. Schofield, 'Slave Trade', pp. 42 and 44.

53. See below, ch. 3, pp. 136–143.

54. Re. *Castleton*, see P.R.O., Adm. 7/88, 13 Mar 1753 and C.O. 33/17, 9 Mar 1765. Re. *Success*, see P.R.O., Adm. 7/89, 10 May 1754.

55. Mannix, *Black Cargoes*, p. 157

56. Anstey, *Atlantic Slave Trade*, pp.12–13.

57. Lancs. C.R.O., Wills of John Abraham, WRW/A, 1755; of Jonathan

Lindall, WRW/A, 1757; of Thomas Moncaster, WRW/K. Admon. 1757. Re. Lindall of Ulverston, see Ulv.P.R., 21 Feb 1729/30.

58. L.P.L., MS. 213, Seamen's Relief Book.

59. Parliamentary Papers, 1791, XXXIV, 745, Accounts and Papers.

60. Minchinton, 'Bristol Slave Trade', p. 49.

61. Schofield, 'Slave Trade', p. 45.

62. *Ibid.*, p. 40.

63. The Lancaster Maritime Museum holds a copy of these Accounts. The document records the dates when crew members entered into and were discharged from pay.

64. See below, p. 90ff.

65. J. Postma, 'Mortality in the Dutch Slave Trade' and H. S. Klein and S. L. Engerman, 'A note on Mortality in the French Slave Trade', in Gemery and Hogendorn, eds., *Uncommon Market*, pp. 239–260 and pp. 261–272. These articles reject overcrowding as a prime independent influence on slave mortality, although it would necessarily add to the ill consequences of a protracted voyage.

66. P.R.O., Adm. 7/88 and 89 and Schofield, 'Slave Trade', p. 44.

67. P. D. Curtin, *Atlantic Slave Trade: A Census* (Madison, Wisconsin, 1969), p. 128.

68. An exception is the *Fortune*, which sailed for Angola in 1750. It may not have been a slaver. Its voyage lasted just eight months and it was recorded as sailing to Lancaster from Angola.

69. The remaining 13 per cent went to the Bight of Biafra, Angola and the Gold Coast.

70. Curtin, *Atlantic Slave Trade*, p. 129.

71. Schofield, 'Slave Trade', p. 52. Lamb, 'Volume and Tonnage', p. 102. Lamb states that the shallow River Gambia made the use of vessels of less than 150 tons imperative.

72. P.R.O., T.70/30, Letters to the African Company from the Coastal Forts, 26 June 1762 and 28 Dec. 1796.

73. P.R.O., T.70/29, Letter to the African Company, 9 June 1757.

74. Lancs. C.R.O., Will of Henry Lawrence, WRW/A 1763. For a letter concerning Dodson's appointment as attorney, see below, ch.3, p. 144.

75. P.R.O., T.70/30, 17 Nov. 1756. Alman was captain of *Antelope I*, see Adm. 7/89, 3 June 1756. Dodson's Tender was *Gambia Tender*, Adm. 7/371, 17 June 1756 (Protection of Vessels).

76. Martin and Spurrel, eds., *Journal of a Slave Trader, passim.*

77. Re. *Africa* (1752) and *Old England* (1784) to Gold Coast, see Donnan, ed., *Slave Trade*, vol. 4, pp. 310 and 475.

78. Drake, 'Liverpool-African Voyage', pp.147–8

79. A. Jones and M. Johnson, 'Slaves from the Windward Coast', *Journal of African History*, 21, 1980 p. 32.

80. Lancs. C.R.O., Will of John Scovern, WRW/A 1761.

81. P.R.O., Adm. 7/90: *Minerva*, 25 Oct. 1757; *Thetis*, 23 Feb. 1759 and 8 Dec.1759. Re. sale of *Thetis I*'s cargo, see P. Hamer, ed., *The Papers of Henry Laurens* (Columbia, 1968), vol.3, p.12.

82. Lancs. C.R.O., Will of John Preston, WRW/A 1763. See *W.L.A.*, 25 Feb 1763 for his death on the *Lancaster*.

83. See below, ch. 3, p. 156.

84. Re. *Lowther*, see Cross Fleury's Journal in L.P.L. Re.*Molly I*, see Donnan, ed., *Slave Trade*, vol.4, p. 377.

85. Donnan, ed., *Slave Trade*, vol. 2, pp. 539–540. A subsequent letter was written to Barber on 15 Oct.1771, see *ibid.*, pp. 542–543.

86. *Ibid.*, pp. xxx, 537n, 656n.

87. See below, ch. 4, pp. 188.

88. Re. Chester, see Schofield, 'Slave Trade', p. 40. Re. Whitehaven, see Hughes, *North Country Life*, pp. 45–47.

89. Mannix, *Black Cargoes*, p. 157.

90. P.R.O., T. 70/30, 17 Nov. 1756. Fell's sloop was probably the *Sally I*. P.R.O., Adm. 7/89, 26 June 1756. Miles Barber, slave merchant, and John Preston, slaver captain, were two of his probate bondsmen. See Lancs. C.R.O., Will of Thomas Fell, WRW/A, Admon, 1757 and 1761.

91. P.R.O., T. 70/30, 1 Feb. 1757.

92. Parliamentary Papers, 1791, XXXIV, 745, Accounts and Papers. Mannix, *Black Cargoes*, p. 93. Captain Strangeways was master of *Juba II* to Sierra Leone, P.R.O., Adm. 7/92, 19 Dec. 1766.

93. Schofield, 'Slave Trade', p. 56.

94. Mannix, *Black Cargoes*, pp. 105–6.

95. Hyde, Parkinson and Marriner, 'Liverpool Slave Trade', p. 372.

96. For *Cato*, see P.R.O., C.O.5/510, 6 Sept. 1758; *W.L.A.*, 18 Apr. 1760 and *L.L.*, 18 Dec 1761. For *Africa I*, see Donnan, ed., *Slave Trade*, vol. 4, p.310. For *Thetis I*, see P.R.O., C.O. 5/510, 6 Sept. 1759.

97. For *Castleton*, see P.R.O., C.O. 5/1446, 24 Aug.1752 and T. 70/29, 28 Feb. 1752, for expected cargo. Disease affected its cargo; see Lancs. C.R.O., D.D.O. 11/57, Letter from Thomas Harrison. For *Lancaster*, see P.R.O., C.O. 142/16, 3 Mar 1757. Her expected cargo was 140, see Cross Fleury, *Time Honoured Lancaster* (Lancaster, 1897)

98. Schofield, 'Slave Trade', p. 45. From the ratio cited above, the average carrying capacity of those vessels would have been 125 and 150 slaves, respectively.

99. Hyde, Parkinson and Marriner, 'Liverpool Slave Trade', p. 372.

100. Re. *Robert*, see P.R.O., C.O. 33/16, Pt. II, 30 Sept. 1752. It would have had a capacity for c. 100 slaves. Re. the *Concord*, see Hamer, ed., *Laurens Papers*, vol. 2, p 270, Letter to Robert and John Thompson.

101. Hughes, *North Country Life*, p. 48.

102. Letter to Bland and Satterthwaite, 10 July 1781, in John Satterthwaite's Letter Book kept at Lancaster University. L.P.L., MS 3738, *Hope's* Package Book, Letter to Tobias Collins, 26 Sept 1791.

103. See below, p. 71.

104. Curtin, *Atlantic Slave Trade*, p. 60.

105. P.R.O., C.O. 142/16, 14 Aug. 1754 and 30 Jan. 1756.

106. After 1763 Jamaica witnessed remarkable expansion of plantations, see R. B. Sheridan, 'Commercial and Financial Organization of the British Slave Trade', *Ec.H.R.*, 2nd Series, 2, 1958, p. 259.

107. Anderson, 'Lancashire Bill System', p. 69.
108. Schofield, 'Slave Trade', pp. 40 and 44.
109. Hamer, ed., *Laurens Papers*, vol. 1, p. 295.
110. Donnan, ed., *Slave Trade*, vol. 4, p. 377.
111. Re. first Lancaster sale in South Carolina, see *ibid.*, p. 310 (*Africa I*, 9 Mar. 1753). Re. Non-Importation Agreement, see *ibid.*, p. 470.
112. Hamer, ed., *Laurens Papers*, vol. 2, p. 186, Letter to Richard Oswald.
113. Re. Laurens to Sandys, 22 Jan 1756, see *ibid.*, vol 2, p. 75. Re. Sandys selling in Antigua, see *W.L.A.*, 18 Feb. 1757.
114. Re. *Molly* and *Marlborough*, see Donnan, ed., *Slave Trade*, vol. 4, p. 377. Re. *Antelope*, see *ibid.*, p. 412 and *L.L.*, 14 Apr. 1772.
115. Craig, 'Chester Shipping', p. 47 and Schofield, 'Slave Trade', p. 41.
116. Schofield, 'Slave Trade', p. 44. In 1753 the *Blossom* sailed to the Windward and Gold Coast, and the *Betty and Martha* to Sierra Leone.
117. Hamer, ed., *Laurens Papers*, vol. 2, pp. 290–91 and 336–337.
118. Eaglesham, 'West Cumberland Shipping', p. 90. Donnan, ed., *Slave Trade*, vol. 3, p. 52. Laurens sold 180 slaves from the Windward and Grain Coast.
119. Donnan, ed., *Slave Trade*, vol. 4, p. 394n.
120. P.R.O., C.O. 33/17, 1764.
121. P.R.O., C.O. 5/1446, 24 Aug. 1752, Upper James River (*Castleton*); C.O. 5/1448, 2 Oct. 1759, Outwards, Hampton (*Lowther*) and 29 May 1760, Upper James River (*Juba I*). Venues suggest they capitalised on small size.
122. H. S. Klein, 'Slaves and Shipping in Eighteenth-Century Virginia', *Journal of Interdisciplinary History*, vol. 3, 1975, p. 392.
123. Donnan, ed., *Slave Trade*, vol. 4, p. 234n.
124. Klein, 'Slaves in Virginia', p. 409.
125. Martin and Spurrell, eds., *Journal of a Slave Trader*, p. 81.
126. *Cato*, *L.L.*, 5 Jan. 1762; *Eagle*, *L.L.*, 2 July 1762; *Lancaster*, *W.L.A.*, 25 Feb. 1763; *Juba I*, *L.L.*, 13 Apr. 1762; *Marquis of Granby*, *L.L.*, 14 Sept. 1762; *Molly I*, *L.L.*, 3 Apr. 1764.
127. P.R.O., C.O. 5/710, 27 June 1766, for *Dove* and 31 July 1766, for *Antelope II*.
128. Klein, 'Slaves in Virginia', p. 392n.
129. P.R.O., C.O. 5/710, 1 Oct. 1767, *Dove* and 14 Sept. 1767, *Prince George III* and L.L., 18 Sept. 1770.
130. Donnan, ed., *Slave Trade*, vol. 4, pp. 415n, 433 and 437n.
131. Curtin, *Atlantic Slave Trade*, p. 158.
132. Donnan, ed., *Slave Trade*, vol. 4, p. 437n.
133. P.R.O., C.O. 5/510–511 and 710. Also various entries in *L.L.*
134. Re. *Stanley II*, see Donnan, ed., *Slave Trade*, vol. 4, p. 453 and *L.L.*, 24 Feb. 1775. Re. *Nelly*, see Donnan, ed., *Slave Trade*, vol. 4, p. 454 and Lloyds Subscription Book, 4 July 1775, kept at Guildhall Library, London.
135. See Hyde, Parkinson and Marriner, 'Liverpool Slave Trade', p. 369n.
136. Merritt, 'Triangular Trade', p. 5; Sheridan, 'Commercial Organization', p. 256; Anderson, 'Lancashire Bill System', p. 61.
137. The exception concerns Campbell and Baillie of Grenada, see below, pp. 82–83. Re. big West India Houses, see Sheridan, 'Commercial

Organization', pp. 254–55 and Anderson, 'Lancashire Bill System', pp. 73–5.

138. Craig, 'Chester Shipping', p. 43.

139. Eaglesham, 'West Cumberland Shipping', pp. 88 and 92.

140. F. J. Singleton, 'The Flax Merchants of Kirkham', *T.H.S.L.C.*, 126, 1977, pp. 85 and 92.

141. Schofield, 'Slave Trade', p. 44.

142. Singleton, 'Flax Merchants', p. 92.

143. P.R.O.,C.O. 142/18, 9 Jan. 1764.

144. William Watson had owned the *Cato* with Benjamin Satterthwaite's brother-in-law, John Heathcote, and the *Marlborough* with his younger brother, Thomas Satterthwaite. See P.R.O., C.O. 5/510, 6 Sept. 1758, 10 July 1759 and 29 Aug. 1760.

145. Benjamin Satterthwaite's Bill and Letter Book, 1764–1765, kept at Lancaster University.

146. Benjamin Satterthwaite's Bill and Letter Book.

147. P.R.O., C.O. 142/18, 15 Dec. 1764.

148. Benjamin Satterthwaite's Bill and Letter Book, letters to Samuel Kilner, 19 July and 10 Dec. 1764.

149. P.R.O., C.O. 142/18, 15 Jan. 1763, *Hamilton* and 14 July 1763, *Rumbold I.*

150. Davies-Davenport Papers, William Davenport's Letter Book, 1748–1761. Letter to Messrs. Law, Satterthwaite and Jones, 15 Dec. 1757. For *Charming Nancy* as a slaver, see Donnan, ed., *Slave Trade*, vol. 2, p. 497.

151. Donnan, ed., *Slave Trade*, vol. 4, p.335n.

152. Schofield, 'Benjamin Satterthwaite', p. 165n.

153. Guildhall Library, London, Sun Fire Office, 11936, vol. 89, 8 May 1754.

154. See above, ch. 1, p. 26.

155. For *Swallow*'s voyages to Barbados, see P.R.O., Adm. 7/88, 24 July 1753; *L.L.*, 14 Feb. 1755; and P.R.O., Adm. 7/89, 3 July 1755.

156. For *Bold*, see P.R.O., C.O. 33/17, 16 Nov. 1756 (outwards). For Heathcote's marriage, see Schofield, 'Benjamin Satterthwaite', p. 161. For his apprenticeship, see Free/App. Rolls, 28 Apr. 1749.

157. Re. Backhouses and Welches in the slave trade at this time, see G. Williams, *History of the Liverpool Privateers and Letters of Marque, with an Account of the Liverpool Slave Trade* (London, 1897), pp. 674–677.

158. Donnan, ed., *Slave Trade*, vol. 4, pp. 348–349 and 364.

159. John Satterthwaite's Letter Book, 1781–82, kept at Lancaster University, letter to Stedman Rawlins, 26 Feb. 1781.

160. For Thomas Millerson's baptism, see Ulv.P.R., 28 July 1728. Re. Gillow's consignment, see Gillow Archives, Lancaster University (microfilm), Invoices and Letters relating to shipped merchandise, 1744–1772 (ref. B44/161). For citation in Benjamin Satterthwaite's Letter and Bill Book, see Letter to Thomas Daniel, 18 Oct. 1764. For his will, see Lancs. C.R.O., WRW/A, 1768.

161. Thomas Millerson was an owner of *Antelope II*, and *Prince George III*, see P.R.O., C.O. 5/710, 31 July 1766 and 14 Sept. 1767. Richard Millerson's *Cato* arrived at Barbados with 560 slaves in 1761, see *L.L.*, 18 Dec. 1761.

162. Lancs. C.R.O., WRW/A, 1743. It was called Woodstock Estate. He left

other property in Kingston and also property in Thornton, near Poulton, Lancashire.

163. Lancs. C.R.O., WRW/A, 1760.
164. See *W.L.A.*, 18 Apr. 1760.
165. Lancs. C.R.O., WRW/A, 1782.
166. Lancs. C.R.O., WRW/A, 1770.
167. Hamer, ed., *Laurens Papers*, vol. 2, p. 16.
168. Cumbria Record Office (Kendal), WPR 38/6, Kendal Parish Register and Tunstall Register, Lancashire Parish Record Society, vol. 40. When Hetherington married, his wife and children remained in North Lancashire, see Thornton-in-Lonsdale Register, *Ibid.*, vol. 67.
169. Rawlinson was appointed Agent of the Virgin Islands in 1783, see L. M. Penson, *The Colonial Agents of the British West Indies* (London 1971), p. 110. Re. Hetherington's appointment and dismissal as Chief Justice, see P.R.O., C.O. 314/1, 15 Feb. 1783, 152/163, 11 Jul. 1783 and 152/64, 4 Dec. 1783. I am most grateful to Elizabeth Dracos for this information.
170. John Satterthwaite's Letter Book, 1781–82, 8 Sep. 1781.
171. See F.R.,1784/5 on Robinson's origins. Re. some of his other dealings with African cargoes, see Satterthwaite's letters to William Earle, 6 Mar. and 4 Dec. 1781 and to Thomas and John Backhouse, 21 Aug. 1781; also a copy of an oath, dated 30th June 1781, by Captain William Brighouse to the Borough of Liverpool concerning his sale of slaves with John Satterthwaite and Co. in St. Kitts. John Satterthwaite's sister Mary married John Backhouse of Liverpool; see G.L.A., 7 Jul. 1780 and Lancs. C.R.O., ARR/11, 1780.
172. P.R.O., C.O. 700, Virgin Island BC 338, 1798, reprinted 1826. Again, I owe thanks to Elizabeth Dracos for this information.
173. L.P.L., MS 3718, Foreign Letter Book of John Rawlinson, 1791–98, 1 Dec. 1792 and 30 Apr. 1793. Re. Hindes see below, ch.3, pp. 140–143.
174. See S. G. Checkland, 'Two Scottish West Indian Liquidations after 1793', *Scottish Journal of Political Economy*, 4, 1957, pp. 135–143.
175. P.R.O., C.O. 106/2, Grenada naval office shipping lists include 'List of slaves sold in Grenada since its Restoration to the English in 1784', 8 Dec. 1787.
176. L.P.L., MS 3738, *Hope*'s Package Book, Letter 26 Sept. 1791.
177. Lancaster Shipping Registers, 1 June 1787.
178. P.R.O., B.T. 6/75, 1786–90: Petition against refusal of foreign ships trading in the West Indies.
179. Checkland, 'Scottish Liquidations', p. 139.
180. Lancs. C.R.O., WRW/A, 1774. For Edmund Thornton's baptism, see L/c.P.R., 30 Sept. 1747.
181. Lancaster University, Gillow Archives, 344/161 (microfilm). Donnan, ed., *Slave Trade*, vol. 4, p. 307, Laurens' Accounts.
182. Lancs. C.R.O., Lancaster Shipping Registers, 1 Feb. 1798.
183. Other commission agents were probably not so familiar. The *Agnes II*'s Captain William Harrison sold with a John Gibson of Barbados in 1770/71, see Lancs. C.R.O., QJB/41/1: Debtors' Insolvency Papers, Matthew Wright 1774/75. The *Barlborough*'s Captain Millerson sold with

John and Alexander Harveys of Jamaica in 1753, see P.R.O., C.O. 142/16.

184. Schofield, 'Benjamin Satterthwaite', p. 149.

185. K. E. Ingram, 'The West India Trade of an English Furniture Firm in the Eighteenth Century', *Jamaican Historical Review*, 3, 1962, p. 29.

186. Gillow Archives, 344/161

187. William Lindow was most probably another example; see below, ch. 3, p. 118.

188. R. Pares, *Merchants and Planters*, Economic History Review Supplement 4 (Cambridge, 1960), p. 33.

189. Minchinton, 'Bristol Slave Trade', p. 52.

190. P. M. Hamer and G. C. Rogers, eds., *The Papers of Henry Laurens*, 6 vols. (S. Carolina, 1968–1976).

191. Hamer, ed., *Laurens Papers*, vol. 1, pp. 288–289, Letter 5 July 1755.

192. Hamer, ed., *Laurens Papers*, vol. 2, pp. 227–228, Letter 19 June 1756.

193. *Ibid.*, p. 37, Letter to Law, Satterthwaite and Jones of Barbados, 14 Dec. 1755.

194. *Ibid.*, pp. 49–50, Letter to Thomas Hinde, 23 Dec. 1755.

195. Sheffield Library, Spencer-Stanhope Collection, Box 60549/170, Letter to Benjamin Spencer from Charles Mayne, 10 July 1756.

196. Hamer, ed., *Laurens Papers*, vol. 2, p. 47n.

197. Donnan, ed., *Slave Trade*, vol. 4, p. 387.

198. Sources: Columns 1–4, *ibid.*, pp. 381, 386 and 412–13; Column 5, P.R.O., C.O.5/710, 31 July 1766, *Antelope II*; C.O.5/511, 3 Sept. 1765, *Prince George II*; and 4 Oct. 1705, *King Tom*. *The Marquis of Granby* was owned by Dodson and Co. in 1766, and probably in 1763 as well. See P.R.O., C.O.142/17, 18 Jan. 1766. His partners were, as with his other vessels, probably the Millersons and Watsons.

199. Rogers, ed., *Laurens Papers*, vol. 5, p. 323n and pp. 396–397, letter, 25 May 1768.

200. *Ibid.*, p. 488, Letters to Millerson Brothers, 2 Dec. 1767.

201. *Ibid.*, p. 336.

202. *Ibid.*, p. 696, 25 May 1768.

203. Rogers, ed., *Laurens Papers*, vol.6, p. 587, 3 June 1769 and Donnan, ed., *Slave Trade*, vol 4, p. 423n.

204. *Ibid.*, pp. 109–110, 13 Sept. 1768.

205. Donnan, ed., *Slave Trade*, vol. 4, p. 241.

206. See Sheridan, 'Commercial Organization' and Merritt, 'Triangular Trade'.

207. Minchinton, 'Bristol Slave Trade', p. 52.

208. Hamer, ed., *Laurens Papers*, vol. 2, p. 37.

209. Minchinton, 'Bristol Slave Trade', pp. 53–54. For more details on these exports see C. D. Clowse, *Economic Beginnings in Colonial South Carolina* (Columbia, 1971), pp. 62–3, 131, 162–3 and E. Sirmans, *Colonial South Carolina, a Political History* (Williamsburg, 1966), pp. 21, 227, 269.

210. Minchinton, 'Bristol Slave Trade', p. 54.

211. Mannix, *Black Cargoes*, p. 113. Re. *Hope II*, see L.P.L., MS 3738, Package. D. Richardson points out that basic slave provisions such as beans, peas, rice and flour normally constituted up to 2.5% of British exports to Africa

during the eighteenth century. See D. Richardson, 'The Costs of Survival: The Transport of Slaves in the Middle Passage and the Profitability of the Eighteenth-Century British Slave Trade', *Explorations in Economic History*, 24, 1987, p. 186.

212. Hamer, ed., *Laurens Papers*, vol. 3, p. 53, Invoice, 28 Nov. 1760.
213. *Encyclopaedia Britannica*, vol. 14, p. 805 and *Encyclopedia Americana*, vol. 17, pp. 705–6.
214. For *Molly I*, see Hamer, ed., *Laurens Papers*, vol. 3, p. 53, Invoice 28 Nov. 1760 and P.R.O., C.O. 5/511, 21 Aug. 1765, outwards (mis-written as *Mary* then *Africa*). For *Marlborough*, *Thetis*, and *Marquis of Granby*, see Hamer, ed., *Laurens Papers*, vol. 3, pp. 47, 13, 78, Invoices, 20 Sept. 1760, 5 Oct. 1759 and 24 Aug. 1761, respectively.
215. Hamer, ed., *Laurens Papers*, vol 2, p. 308, 31 Aug. 1756 and p. 439: Letter to Captain Simondson, 27 Jan. 1757.
216. *Ibid.*, p. 534. The *Anson* had sold only seventy 'thin and ordinary' Gambian slaves.
217. *Ibid.*, p. 528, 22 Apr. 1757.
218. P.R.O., C.O. 5/511, 31 Oct. 1765 (outwards).
219. P.R.O., C.O. 5/1448, Clearances: 2 Oct. 1759, *Lowther*; 14 Aug. 1760, *Juba I* and C.O. 5/1446, Clearances: 3 Nov. 1752, *Castleton*.
220. W. E. Minchinton, 'The Triangular Trade Revisited', in Gemery and Hogendorn, eds., *Uncommon Market*, p. 342.
221. A slaver might carry bills of exchange as well as a cargo. This did not mean that a complete cargo was unavailable. It often meant that the proceeds from the sale of slaves exceeded the cost of purchasing a return cargo to fill the ship's hold. See Minchinton, 'Triangular Trade', p. 335.
222. Sheridan, 'Commercial Organization', p. 252.
223. Merritt, 'Triangular Trade', p. 5.
224. Sheridan, 'Commercial Organization', p. 195.
225. Merritt, 'Triangular Trade', p. 4.
226. Minchinton, 'Triangular Trade', pp. 351–52.
227. Schofield, 'Slave Trade', p. 61.
228. B. K. Drake, 'Continuity and Flexibility in Liverpool's Trade with Africa and the Caribbean', *Business History*, 18, 1976, p. 93. Drake's research shows a lot of 19th-century Liverpool slavers returned with sizeable cargoes, pp. 88–90.
229. For *Bassa*, see P.R.O., C.O. 106/1, 17 Jan. 1767; for *Molly III*, see P.R.O., C.O. 106/2, 12 Jan. 1788; for *Beaver*, see *Lancaster Gazette*, 28 Apr. 1803.
230. P.R.O., C.O. 33/16, Part 2 and C.O. 33/17.
231. Minchinton, 'Triangular Trade', p. 337
232. Source, P.R.O., C.O. 142.
233. Minchinton, 'Triangular Trade', p. 343.
234. *Ibid.*, pp. 341 and 343.
235. Anderson, 'Lancashire Bill System', pp. 68–69.
236. Lancs. C.R.O., WRW/A, 1766 and 1780.
237. P.R.O., C.O. 278/7 Outwards, 10 July 1804 and C.O. 300/16, Outwards, 15 Apr. 1808.
238. Ingram, 'Furniture Firm', p. 32.

239. Minchinton, 'Triangular Trade', pp. 346–347.

240. *Encyclopaedia Britannica*, vol. 9, p. 855. Re. logwood, see above, p. 91.

241. Ingram, 'Furniture Firm', p. 33.

242. See above, p. 46 and see Minchinton, 'Triangular Trade', p. 349, on slavers carrying produce.

243. Craig, 'Chester Shipping', p. 49.

244. P.R.O., C.O. 142/15, inwards, 5 June 1753; outwards 2 July 1753.

245. Eaglesham, 'West Cumberland Shipping', p. 92.

246. Ten Lancaster firms, including the slave trader William Watson, supplied a Kirkby Stephen shopkeeper with sugars in the 1760s. In contrast, Whitehaven supplied him with no colonial imports. See T. S. Willan, *An Eighteenth-Century Shopkeeper, Abraham Dent of Kirkby Stephen* (Manchester 1970), pp. 34–35.

CHAPTER III

The Slave Trade Operators

David Richardson concludes his article on the slave-trading operations of William Davenport of Liverpool with the comment that a typical slave trader probably never existed. He continues, "If the evidence of Bristol is anything to go by, Liverpool slave-traders were almost certainly drawn from a wide variety of social and economic backgrounds, and slave-trading probably engaged their capital and energy in widely varying degrees".[1] More research needs to be conducted in these areas, which have been almost entirely neglected. Indeed, Richardson notes that "detailed reconstruction of career profiles of other slave traders has unfortunately attracted little attention from historians".[2] The far smaller number of people concerned in the trade at Lancaster makes a survey of its participants a less daunting task than at any of the three major slave-trading ports and a variety of shipping documents provides a sufficiently comprehensive, if incomplete, list of names involved in the trade.

It has been argued, as an underlying theme in previous chapters that the participants in the African trade were essentially 'marginal men' in the sense of their being individuals who lacked sufficient opportunities to enter or prosper in the port's bilateral overseas trade at profit levels that matched their ambitions. It should be said that a vast expansion of colonial trades had in general made slave trading, in itself, a less attractive proposition. Colonial exports to Britain and Europe grew rapidly in the eighteenth century[3] and Lancaster undoubtedly grasped the opportunities that presented themselves, from the resulting wealth in the colonies, by supplying them with various luxury goods, manufactures and provisions. The region's limited exports and the trade's domination by established merchant families, however, tempted certain ambitious newcomers to seek an alternative. The triangular trade in black Africans apparently offered them a risky, yet potentially lucrative, means of realising their commercial dreams.

This chapter will be concerned with whether information about individual slave traders supports this view. Such a biographical approach will allow us to establish whether the diverse backgrounds of the traders hide deeper patterns which may have governed which individuals became involved in the slave trade and how deeply they became involved. Such a detailed approach should divulge more, too, about why Lancaster stood out among the smaller ports in the unusual nature of its slave-trade statistics. After all, in a small port individual operators may have had quite a considerable impact on trading methods and connexions. Finally, we may assume that individual biographies of Lancaster slave traders will tell us much about the relationship between the slave trade and other aspects of the port's commerce.

Before examining the slave traders themselves, it is important to consider which sections of Lancaster's merchant community did not take part in the African trade. They explain the context in which the Lancaster slave traders operated. If we assume that insufficient opportunities in other forms of commerce determined or tempted entry into the slave trade, it follows that merchants with good prospects in direct trade with the colonies had no need to participate in the more risky African trade. The evidence which follows would seem to confirm this view. It concerns three types of merchant, firstly those whose families or close associates had already established themselves in colonial trade, secondly those who succeeded in joining them in their well-developed commercial networks at home and abroad, and thirdly a particular family which was fortunate enough to develop a valuable export.

The Established Colonial Merchants

The names of established merchants such as Rawlinson, Dillworth, Birket, Townson and Lawson are noticeably absent amongst the records appertaining to the Lancaster slave trade.[4] These Quakers and their associates, who were not all Quakers, continued to dominate colonial trade at Lancaster in the middle decades of the century. It would be easy to suggest that their religious scruples rather than economic considerations determined their abstinence from the African trade, for they were repeatedly entreated to refrain from participation in such an ugly and unchristian traffic.[5] Yet this is not an entirely satisfactory explanation. Not only did they all deal in colonial imports which were based on slave labour, but, more explicitly, as early as 1752 the vessel *Providence* cleared Barbados for South Carolina with "twenty New Negroes" on account of its owners Abraham and Hutton Rawlinson, Thomas and William Dillworth, John Rowlandson and its captain Jonathan Nicholson. Fifteen years later another Rawlinson West Indiaman cleared Grenada for Cape Fear with a cask of 'lincey' (possibly 'linsey', a coarse linen) and ten slaves, and as late as 1786, Thomas Rawlinson owned the *Abbey* which conveyed 180 "new

Negroes" between St. Vincent and Tobago.[6] Such transportation of blacks, although regarded as secondary slave trafficking, it being confined to intercolonial trading, was still in Quaker terms decidedly unchristian. Moreover, these merchants' Quaker beliefs did not deter them from ownership of Caribbean plantations either.[7] Their reasons for not participating in the slave trade proper apparently stemmed from more pragmatic considerations, backed up no doubt by moral scruples.

Their command over colonial trade had undoubtedly grown. This is confirmed in the Lancaster Apprentice Rolls, where these family names, and more especially those of the Dillworths, Rawlinsons and their partners, clearly outnumber the entries of other merchants who took on apprentices during the second half of the eighteenth century. It follows that they had no need to expand their colonial operations into the African trade unless it offered something very exceptional. Yet it is unlikely that the slave trade would have been regarded by those established merchants as anything other than a highly speculative form of commerce, which, in any case, involved capital for a considerable length of time. Established merchants were more concerned with average earnings than individual bonanzas. Much recent work has suggested its overall levels of profitability when averaged out were not quite as immense as certain historians, most notably Eric Williams, would have people believe.[8] In his article entitled "Costs of Survival", David Richardson comments, "Eighteenth-century merchants were certainly well aware of the highly competitive environment within which slaving activities took place, and clearly appreciated the implications of this for the 'average returns' that they might normally expect from the trade".[9] Consequently, on economic grounds it is not surprising to find that none of these established Quaker West India merchants and their associates chose to soil their hands with the spoils of Africa in this overt way. It made little commercial sense. The same would be true for the better-established non-Quaker merchants at Lancaster such as the Anglican, John Bowes, together with the son who followed on from him, or the Presbyterian-turned-Anglican, Ambrose Gillison, and his son William who partnered, then succeeded him.[10]

Limited Expansion of the Colonial Merchant Elite

In the middle decades of the eighteenth century these established colonial merchants at Lancaster were joined by two rather different groups of investors. Certain circumstances directed both groups to opportunities in the West Indies trade which removed any need or temptation to participate to any extent in the African trade. The first group consisted of various inland tradesmen and craftsmen in and around Lancaster who chose to make investments in overseas trade. Their variety of interest was commonplace in Georgian England. These men were usually of good standing and invariably exhibited close ties with merchants already established in colonial trade at Lancaster. Such was Miles Braithwaite, a stocking-frame knitter, who in 1743 partnered James Richardson, brother-in-law to Benjamin Satterthwaite, together with their father-in-law, John Casson, and Thomas Touchet of Manchester.[11] His dual role is made explicit in 1750 when, being described as a merchant, he took on an apprentice to learn the art of stoker-weaver.[12] Meanwhile William Satterthwaite, an ironmonger, was described as merchant on many occasions including the times when he and his Quaker step-father Miles Townson owned the *Martha* in the 1740s.[13] Other merchants in colonial trade included mercers, drapers, tallow-chandlers, to name but a few, and according to factors such as fortune, contacts and commitment, these entrepreneurs might come to concentrate more on their colonial affairs than on their original trade or craft. Of course their non-maritime interests were undoubtedly of some benefit when provisioning a vessel.

In the second group, there were the trainee merchants and mariners who gradually worked their way up and built up sufficient capital to invest in colonial ventures themselves. In other circumstances, these upstarts might have entered the slave trade but, significantly, they progressed through their ability or good fortune to secure a position in the mercantile network of one of the larger firms.

William Lindow, who ultimately became a partner to the Rawlinsons, was one of Lancaster's most successful examples, though even he was not without some brushings with the slave trade. Born close to the town of Ulverston, he was the son of James Lindow, a fairly prosperous yeoman, whose standing no doubt secured William, and a probable brother, apprenticeships to learn the mariner's art.[14] William was admitted a freeman of Lancaster in 1752/53 and was captain of several West Indiamen including the *Rawlinson*, but not, apparently, of any slave ships. He became a resident factor for the Rawlinsons by the late 1750s, initially in St. Kitts. In 1760 a vessel bearing his name sailed to the conquered islands (of the Seven Years War) and by 1763 he was resident in Grenada, presumably for the Rawlinsons, from whence, interestingly, he registered a fifteen-ton schooner, named *Hobby Horse*, which cleared Grenada for Dominica with seventy-eight slaves in 1766.[15] It is, therefore, conceivable that Lindow himself dealt with African cargoes on occasions, bearing in mind that he seemed ambitious, perhaps unscrupulous, and therefore quite likely to use whatever opportunities came his way.

Whatever his means, he obviously met with Abraham Rawlinson's trust and approval. For in 1771, at the rather mature age of forty-seven, William, now described as gentleman, married his employer's daughter, Abigail Rawlinson, at Lancaster.[16] This may have marked the timing of his partnership with Abraham Rawlinson which, in any case, had come into being before 1775 when William Lindow was named executor for a merchant in St. Vincent, whose will makes reference to "monies that may be in the hands of Mr. Lindow or Messrs. A. Rawlinson and Lindow".[17] Lindow was in a position to subscribe £200 towards the completion of Glasson Dock in 1784, the year before he died. His will, proved in 1787, shows that William Lindow died a very successful and wealthy merchant and landowner both at home and in the Caribbean. His overseas estate included shares in three plantations in Grenada and St. Vincent, parcels of urban and agricultural land in several other islands and personalty in the islands of Grenada, the Grenadines, St. Vincent, Dominica, Tortola and elsewhere. At home he owned properties in the Furness district, and his Lancaster residence in Queen's Square suggests a life of style and substance. His will conveyed to his heir not only the "name and Arms of Lindow" but also several carriages and horses. He would no doubt have been pleased to learn that his name lives on in a square and street in Lancaster today.[18] William Lindow's career owed its success to his involvement in the West India trade as promoted by his connexions with the Rawlinson family. Other merchants clearly experienced similarly fortuitous contacts; amongst them David Dockray and John Rowlandson who were also the relatives of yeomen.

In 1748 John Dockray of Upperby in Cumberland apprenticed his son to another Quaker, Joshua Whalley, who, being described as a merchant and grocer, was evidently connected with Miles Townson, for he acted as one of his executors in 1750. By the 1770s Dockray was in partnership with the prominent Quaker merchants, Thomas and John Dillworth, and together they took on one of the largest numbers of apprentices during the 1770s and 1780s, an undisputed sign of their standing and prosperity. David Dockray's commitment meant that he was elected port commissioner seven times between 1767 and 1800.[19]

Meanwhile John Rowlandson, son and younger brother of yeomen, James of Heaton and Thomas of Langthwaite in Scotforth, was master of the West Indiaman *Tryton* in 1749, a vessel he had some part in with Thomas Hutton Rawlinson.[20] Three years later, he had shares in another vessel, the *Providence*, with the Rawlinsons and Thomas and William Dillworth. This vessel had, on one occasion, transported slaves within the Caribbean, a sign that few were above the odd flutter with slave trafficking. In 1758, being described as Captain Rowlandson in a tenancy on Moor Lane, he both was partner in a brewery with David Dockray and also became a port commissioner for the first time, an office he was to hold again in 1764 and 1770.[21] In

William Lindow's house in Queen's Square, Lancaster.

1769 his esteemed friends Joshua Whalley and David Dockray were named as trustees and executors, and he left his estate, shares in vessels and merchandises to his elder son, John, who was resident in Jamaica.[22]

William Lindow, David Dockray and John Rowlandson, all originating from families which had the means to secure them good apprenticeships and at the same time were able to provide them with some initial financial resources, successfully joined the ranks of Lancaster's more committed West India merchants and ultimately became partners or associated with the prominent Quaker families who had assisted them. They feature amidst a long list of merchant names associated with overseas trade at Lancaster. Of course many of these individuals, although listed as merchants, made only occasional overseas investments, perhaps more on a par with William Stout. Others, no doubt, gradually built up their overseas investments independently of the established merchant families. Nevertheless, it is noticeable that a remarkable number of the successful West India merchants of the mid-eighteenth century benefitted from close associations with merchants who had established themselves during the previous decades, as the three individuals cited already have shown. This confirms the notion that opportunities in direct colonial trade were not as forthcoming as might otherwise be supposed. It suggests good contacts were important passports to success in colonial trade at Lancaster. This situation again reflects the cost disadvantages of operating from a port where many of the more lucrative exports to the colonies were generally not available locally, which made good links outside the region and financial credibility that much more crucial. This would inevitably favour the more established merchants and their associates whilst limiting the opportunities for newcomers, making entry into colonial trade more competitive. Undoubtedly, there were certain individuals whose trade was confined to more locally produced wares such as candles, leather goods and provisions, yet it is hard to see that significant sums of money could be made in this way. Consequently, their profits may have been inadequate for the more ambitious. Lancaster was a place where those who developed good contacts and accrued sufficient capital, as William Lindow managed to do, were able to take advantage of the town as a good trade centre and a favourably located port.

It should not be forgotten, however, that William Lindow's rise to affluence and pre-eminence in Lancaster, although largely due to his employment and later partnership with the Rawlinsons, was certainly tainted with slavery. This is evident in his involvement in transporting slaves from one island to another whilst a merchant in Grenada, which implicates him as a possible dealer in Guinea cargoes,[23] and in his interests in West Indian plantations and his ownership of slaves there.[24] Furthermore, whilst Lindow was certainly not a major participant in Lancaster's African trade, he did not entirely abstain from it. In 1772 he was listed as a registered owner of a brig, *Sarah*, which landed 190 slaves at Grenada in 1773, an island where Lindow is known to have had close ties.[25]

Such marginal activities with black slaves, by William Lindow and others, highlight Lancaster's often hidden dependence on revenue derived from the enslavement of Africans and, most importantly, emphasise still further the problems of entering or prospering in the export trade to the colonies where there was a lack of local exports of value. If viable exports had been more readily available, the experience at Lancaster would have been very different, its need for the slave trade much less. The Gillow family, which entered trade with the colonies first as producers rather than merchants and never established direct ties with the slave trade, illustrate this perfectly.

They came to be overseas traders predominantly through their craft as cabinet-makers. Robert Gillow, son of a joiner from Great Eccleston who had started the business, was perhaps experimenting when he sent his first shipment of mahogany furniture across the Atlantic in the 1740s. It was obviously well received, for the firm's trade reached quite considerable proportions as the century progressed. Clearly, Gillow furniture was popular amongst the planters and other affluent members of Caribbean society alike, and by 1769 the firm was wanting to extend its furniture side to equal, if not surpass, that of the port of London.[26] The firm did not confine its exports to furniture alone. It packed the wooden merchandice with other commodities and on occasions these articles, which included the regular Lancaster exports such as textiles, candles, hats and shoes, formed a considerable part of the cargo. By 1760 Robert Gillow was renting land on the Quay at Lancaster and five years later he had an office on Oxford Street in London, whilst his brother, Richard, remained at Lancaster.[27]

Although some Gillow furniture made its way to the plantations at the hand of other Lancaster merchants, such as the Rawlinsons who bought it direct from the Gillows,[28] it is clear that the Gillows exported large quantities of mahogany pieces on their own account. They sent some of this as freight on other merchants' vessels but they owned several ships as well. One of these, the *Africa*, was an ex-Guineaman. It had just completed its fourth slaving voyage, when it was bought and sent to Antigua in 1756 by Robert Gillow and his partner, Henry Baines. Its captain, William Saul, stayed with the ship in its transfer of ownership and in so doing must have converted the contents of his holds from dark-skinned people to dark-hued furniture. One wonders what modifications the vessel underwent, if any.[29] There is, however, no evidence to show that the Gillows themselves were ever tempted to supplement their furniture exports by participating in the triangular trade, even though a number of their business associates, notably the West Indian agents to whom they consigned their goods, were themselves involved in slave dealings at some point.[30] This is quite understandable since the Gillows are, without doubt, Lancaster's foremost example of local initiative, whereby they succeeded in creating a valuable manufacture which could be exported to the colonies as well as sold at home. As a consequence, descriptions of eighteenth-century Lancaster seldom overlook the firm's achievements, as exemplified by Thomas Pennant who visited Lancaster in 1772 and wrote,

> The inhabitants are also fortunate in having some very ingenious cabinet makers settle here; who fabricate most excellent and neat goods at remarkably cheap rates, which they export to London and the plantations. Mr. Gillow's warehouse of these manufactures merits a visit.[31]

The firm's furniture business, together with its development of an overseas market, assured the family of a considerable position in Lancaster society and an active role in the port's overseas trading community, and therefore with sufficient profit margins to preclude any need to contemplate supplementing this with the African trade. Mahogany furniture provided them, and some of their influential fellow overseas traders who purchased their furniture for export, with a substantial and viable commodity which was otherwise lacking at Lancaster for so many would-be traders.

It is clear, from the evidence cited, that these various upstarts, such as Lindow and Gillow, had created opportunities for themselves in direct trade with the colonies. Similar avenues must have presented themselves to other aspiring merchants at Lancaster. However, the fact that many such merchants, as William Lindow testifies, implicated themselves in slave-related activities in their attempts to establish themselves in transatlantic trade must not be overlooked. The financial rewards of such activities could prove very beneficial, and, as such, it must be appreciated that they played a significant, though often unnoticed, role in the business enterprises of the individuals concerned. More importantly, these activities are clearly indicative, once more, of the problems experienced by new merchants trying to establish themselves in colonial trade at Lancaster. In this context, it is hardly surprising to find that other entrepreneurs, also eager to make their way in colonial commerce, focussed their attention more overtly on the commercial opportunities that New World slavery provided, in the form of the African slave trade. These individuals must have responded to the restricted opportunities in other forms of commerce, having been unable to cultivate openings whereby men like Lindow, Dockray and Gillow had managed to concentrate on the West India trade. The African trade would have been particularly attractive to these entrepreneurs. It was, as R. Davis describes it, a trade renowned for its "open access",[32] and then there was its reputation for spectacular returns. Although the average returns of the slave trade were unlikely to have been as fantastic as has been claimed by Williams,[38] no critic denies that some slaving voyages were immensely profitable, nor that its average returns were unacceptably low.[33] In the context of Lancaster's commercial experience, these were evidently worthy attributes. Thus the port's unestablished merchants, considering alternative investments alone failed to provide them with attractive openings for their eager, yet not immense, sums of capital and who, importantly, experienced no qualms as to its propriety, succumbed to what Hyde, Parkinson and Marriner describe as the "lure of extraordinary gain".[34]

The trade's viability at Lancaster, evident in its detailed analysis in the previous chapter, promoted it as an attractive option for a group of Lancaster's aspiring or dissatisfied merchants during the second half of the eighteenth century. Meanwhile, the fact that it did not captivate their more comfortably established or well-connected neighbours confirms its role as a marginal activity, not in terms of its profits, but in terms of its operators.

Focussing attention on those entrepreneurs who implicated themselves in the slave trade at Lancaster should not only clarify their situations, and therefore their motives, but also highlight certain important characteristics that they shared, as well as providing valuable information as to their handling of the slave trade. The evidence which follows sets out to accomplish these tasks.

Lancaster's Slave-Trading Community

The first thing to note about Lancaster's community of slave traders is that it existed long enough for there to be more than one generation of owners and captains, and, of course, of the more sparsely documented crews who served under them. The main thrust of Lancaster's involvement in the African trade took place over a period of more than thirty years and its total association with it spanned seventy-one years. During this time three generations of slave traders are discernible, though of course there are no sharp divides and certain more committed firms undoubtedly spanned more than one generation. This significantly contrasts the situation at the other small north-western ports, where merchants' involvement in the slave trade was much shorter-lived. Preston and Poulton's participation in the trade lasted just four years, whilst Chester's two bursts of activity were both brief, just seven and three years respectively. The twenty-year gap which separated them precluded any significant development of a slave-trading community. Meanwhile, Whitehaven experienced the longest uninterrupted period of trading after Lancaster, but even this only spanned some nineteen years, together with odd, isolated bursts of activity by one merchant family seventeen years, and more, earlier.[35] This makes Lancaster's slave-trading personnel, outside the big ports, both unique and important. It made possible the evolution of a slave-trading group within Lancaster society which, albeit small, featured certain significant developments. At the same time it lends itself to long-term analysis of its make-up and dynamics.

Another interesting feature of Lancaster's slave-trading community relates to its size. Although it was never large, it remained remarkably constant throughout the port's years of greatest activity in the Guinea trade. It should, of course, be remembered that Lancaster slave-trading partnerships were typically small. This is reflected in the figures below and should be taken into account when making comparisons with the size of communities elsewhere.

Table 3.1   *Size of Lancaster's Slave-Trading Community*[36]

Years	Numbers of Owners	Numbers of Captains	Total
1748–1762	18	34	52
1763–1776	24	26	50

On the right is the Kings Arms Hotel in Market Street, Lancaster, and beyond it the tall Building of the Merchants' Coffee House established in 1750. Both were frequented by leading merchants and captains. They have since been demolished. *Courtesy of Lancaster City Museums*

Slave-trading communities in other small north-western ports were much smaller. Chester had a total of around eleven owners, with five of these just participating in one voyage, and six captains, a number of whom came from Liverpool. At Preston and Poulton just three owners and four captains have been identified.[37] Insufficient information makes it difficult to be precise on the numbers involved at Whitehaven, though they were undoubtedly far more substantial than the figures given for Chester, Preston and Poulton. Twelve owners and five captains have been identified so far and the owners, at least, were local men. Further research would almost certainly reveal more. Lancaster's greater involvement in the African trade, both in terms of its duration and the numbers of participants concerned, together with the information that has been gathered on them, makes a survey of its operators that much more valuable and indicative. It should, furthermore, provide a useful standpoint from which to assess the situation elsewhere.

There were, of course, certain broad differences amongst those who put their money into transporting black Africans across the Atlantic. In the first place, there were the committed merchants who between them undertook the active management of the whole venture. Then there were the casual investors whose part was essentially financial, although certain of them may have made some

125

additional contributions, such as assisting with the outgoing cargoes for Africa. Naturally, changes occurred during Lancaster's fairly lengthy period of slave trading, as a result of both local and international conditions, and the situation at the outset was almost certainly unique. For this reason, it is important to consider the earliest group of African traders on their own, separate from their more experienced successors. The situation of slave traders at neighbouring ports outside Liverpool must have been similar to the extent that their short-lived experiences made them pioneers too. A discussion on their slave-trading activities alongside the early Lancaster traders enables useful comparative judgements to be made, which should again highlight the individual circumstances in which these various north-western merchants found themselves.

Early Slave Traders at Lancaster

The earliest investors in slave ships at Lancaster and the neighbouring ports, taking the period up to 1756/57,[38] were a mixed group, variously described as tradesmen and merchants. They were entering this particular branch of overseas trade at a time when an increasing amount of interest was being shown in western ports' transatlantic trading potentials and when at Liverpool, now that the extraordinary advantages of wartime trading with the colonies had ceased, the slave trade was developing as an alluring branch of overseas commerce. Its notoriously unpredictable nature, if not its exploitation of fellow men, would have attracted certain personalities more than others, but, in any case, it seems, from a variety of accounts, that it was seldom a first option. For example, MacInnes writes of the Severn port, "Loud in her wailing, Bristol nevertheless grew rich on the slave trade which she relinquished when other more profitable and safer fields of investment appeared".[39] The evidence strongly suggests that not only was a port's commitment to the slave trade indicative of its overall situation and development, but that an individual's involvement was a pointer as to his current circumstances or standing in the local merchant community. It should be realised that few merchants directed their investments exclusively into the slave trade. This might well imply that other commercial opportunities were sought where practicable in terms of acceptable returns.

Researching Lancaster's early group of African traders reveals eleven main operators. Their names and particulars, indicative of their individual circumstances at the point of their involvement in the Guinea trade, are set out in Table 3.2. One significant feature is the comparatively young age of many of these investors, especially when one considers that slave traders usually owned shares in the vessels themselves as well as in the cargoes they carried, and that, at Lancaster, shares in slavers were typically large. Over half of these investors were at the dawn of their careers and some were undoubtedly making their very first ventures into overseas commerce by outfitting a vessel for Africa.[40]

Table 3.2   *Profile of Lancaster's Early Slave Traders*[41]

Slave Trader	Year of Entry	Age at Entry	Alternative Occupation
John Helme	1756	24	Linen drapers and
& John Fowler		23	upholsterers
John &	1750/51	25	Grocers and
Robert Thompson		23	apothecaries
Thomas &	1744	41	Grocers, apothecaries,
William Butterfield	1751	43	and ropers
John MacMillan	1752	45	Wine merchant
Thomas Satterthwaite	1753	33	Quaker West India merchant
& Charles Inman		c.25	Merchant in West Indies
Dodgs(h)on Foster	c.1752	21	Son of Quaker merchant of Durham
& John Heathcote		c.22	Quaker apprentice at Lancaster, originating from Derbyshire

Further details on two of them are illuminating.

Dodgson Foster and John Heathcote were Lancaster's youngest entrepreneurs in the African trade. As Quakers, their involvement in the slave trade is particularly interesting, since Friends' consciences were frequently scrutinized, as evident in the Lancaster Meeting House records. They did, however, share more than their religious upbringings. Neither was native to Lancaster. Both became free-men of the town in 1751/52, Heathcote having been apprenticed to Thomas Satterthwaite in 1747. Both married into prominent Quaker merchant families in 1753; Heathcote marrying Thomas Satterthwaite's sister, Millicent, and Foster marrying Elizabeth Birket, daughter of Miles.[42] Their Quaker beliefs, together with their connexions with established merchants, make their joint investments in two Lancaster slavers, the *Barlborough* and the *Bold*, somewhat curious.[43] Yet their interest in the slave trade took place at a time when Heathcote's newly acquired brothers-in-law, also brought up as

Quakers, were themselves embarking on African enterprises. Thomas Satterthwaite was concerned in the ownership of Lancaster slavers, Benjamin was most likely disposing of slave cargoes in the colonies, whilst their elder step-brother, William, had sold some slaves with Henry Laurens in July 1751, which had been shipped from Barbados.[44] Influences such as these on two ambitious young men, eager to make their way in a small western port, go a long way to explain what at first seemed an unlikely interest in African affairs. Their interests were not, however, long-lasting. By April 1758 Dodgson Foster was advertising the *Barlborough* for sale and his fellow Friend had been dead a month.[45] Foster's enthusiasm for slaving may have been dampened by Heathcote's departure, but, in any case, the trade had come to a near stand-still at this time as a result of the Seven Years War, and once the initial panic was over, war-time trade, away from the more vulnerable south, was on offer once more at Lancaster. Foster was by this time concerned in a West Indiaman, the *Hawke*, with his father-in-law, which had sailed between the islands and South Carolina in 1757.[46] He apparently no longer required the resources of live cargoes.

The fact that a large number of early Lancaster slave traders came from established trades is another significant feature of Table 3.2. The linen-drapers and upholsterers, John Helme and John Fowler, and the grocers and apothecaries, John and Robert Thompson, all in their early twenties, almost certainly used the African trade as a means of making exploratory investments in colonial commerce. They do not appear to have invested in transatlantic trade before.[47] Helme and Fowler's interests as wholesalers may well have attracted them to the slave trade in terms of providing certain outgoing goods. Hyde, Parkinson and Marriner note, "Frequently the venturers themselves were wholesalers", and thus these individuals "undoubtedly realised special gains".[48] Meanwhile, the Thompson brothers would have been keen to acquire colonial imports for their business as grocers and apothecaries. In 1755 Henry Laurens referred to his inability to ship some indigo which the Thompsons had specially requested and, a year later, their brig, the *Concord*, brought twelve or fourteen tons of camwood from the African coast.[49] Meanwhile, an insurance record of 1758 refers to a small still of theirs in Pudding Lane.[50] A further important inducement for the Thompsons to slave trade would have stemmed from John Thompson's probable apprenticeship to Thomas Butterfield from 1739, for Butterfield was himself sending his first slave ship to Africa in 1744.[51]

The 'black ivory' trade tempted these young wholesalers of average means and influence into trying their luck in transatlantic trade. However, not all Lancaster slave merchants were drawn to the trade so close to the start of their careers. The grocers and apothecaries Thomas and William Butterfield were in their forties at the outset of their investments in Guineamen (unless of course they were the mysterious owners of the Lancaster slavers of the 1730s), as was the wine merchant, John MacMillan, who originated from Dumfries. MacMillan was clearly more concerned in the wine trade with Oporto. His single recorded African venture of 1752 involved his forty-ton *Robert*, which had sailed to Oporto the previous summer skippered by John Blackow, who also put money into the brig's African voyage.[52] Such a venture confirms the unspecialised nature of Lancaster's slave trade at this time. Procuring rum, with the aid of a human cargo, was the likely attraction for MacMillan. A sizeable complement of the spirit was purchased in Barbados with the proceeds from sixty slaves, from whence it was conveyed to Dublin.[53]

Meanwhile, at forty-one, Thomas Butterfield was Lancaster's first identifiable slave-ship owner and his vessel, the *Expedition*, which cleared for Africa in 1744, was only the third Lancaster Guineaman to do so and the first to sail after a respite of six years.[54] This sets him up as a forerunner in the Lancaster slave trade and makes his situation, and that of his brother, prior to their involvement in the African trade, of particular interest. An exploration of their earlier careers suggests what circumstances tempted these pioneers into slave trafficking.

Thomas Butterfield and his younger brother William, who quite probably joined him on this early slaving venture, were proprietors of a rope-walk in 1740 as well as being described as linen and wine merchants during the 1740s.[55] Their many-sided business pursuits necessarily interested them in overseas trade from Lancaster and earned them, and others like them, the more general title of 'merchant'.[56] Their need for imports took them predominantly in the direction of the Baltic, where they could obtain cargoes of hemp and flax, and possibly to venues in Western Europe for wine. This variously involved them in partnerships with the Lancaster merchants John Bowes, James Hornby and John Chippendale.[57] They were also involved in occasional colonial ventures, probably on the level of their father Christopher Butterfield.[58] All these activities apparently earned them a moderate and respected position amidst Lancaster's trading circles, as did their advantageous marriages into the Hornby and Lawson families.[59] Curiously, the Butterfields seemed to glean little advantage in direct colonial trade from this link with the Lawson family. This may owe its explanation to the Lawsons' apparent withdrawal from Lancaster's colonial trade by the middle decades of the eighteenth century. The Butterfields' decision to open up trade with Africa appears to have been a deliberate attempt to diversify and extend their existing overseas trading operations. Colonial imports would have provided valuable supplies for their grocery and apothecary businesses, not to mention the dye-house they also owned.

The *Expedition* carried a cargo of sugar from Jamaica in 1747 and William Butterfield's *Castleton* and *Lowther* cleared with cargoes of tobacco from Virginia in 1752 and 1759 respectively, whilst his *Molly I* brought two tons of camwood along with 228 slaves from the Windward Coast the following year.[60]

William Butterfield's perseverance in the triangular trade after his brother's premature death in 1747, even before his second slaving venture had ended, suggests that the trade satisfied his commercial aspirations. His near-continuous involvement in slavers over a period of twenty years, until he reached the age of sixty-four, concerned him in at least five vessels, and probably more, which made something in the order of eighteen voyages to Africa and the colonies.[61] Like many of his contemporaries, he did not confine himself to buying colonial imports with African slaves, yet he was seldom without a vessel or two in the triangular trade either, a clear sign of its commercial value. He obviously responded to current trading conditions and acted accordingly. In 1747 he purchased from Samuel Touchet a West Indiaman, the *Reynolds II*, which he shared with the Manchester textile merchants John and Abraham Haworth. This vessel made a number of voyages direct to the colonies but in 1755 it was dispatched on a single slaving voyage to the Gambia and Antigua.[62]

The Butterfields' involvement, and especially William's, in the Lancaster slave trade indicates its attraction to men established in local wholesaling and manufacturing businesses, who wished to benefit from the general expansion in colonial commerce. Although their trades involved them in shipping elsewhere, these men were clearly less assured as far as colonial trade was concerned, especially when years of peace meant that war-time bonuses were unavailable. The Butterfields were most likely searching for a means of making more substantial returns in the transatlantic arena. The slave trade offered them good prospects of achieving this, not to mention any additional possibilities in terms of providing African woods for dyes and medicinal purposes. The Butterfields' ambition to succeed as merchants in Lancaster is well expressed in the elder brother's will of 1747. Thomas stressed that he was very desirous that his eldest son, Robert, should become a merchant and settle in Lancaster. Accordingly, he requested his wife to vest in him their house, shop, warehouses and other appurtenance when he attained the age of twenty-one. Should Robert die or not be interested in merchant trade, then the Lancaster estate was to pass to Thomas's second son and, if not to him, to the next and so on. Meanwhile, each son was to be given money to help them towards becoming merchants.[63]

It is useful at this point to digress from Lancaster briefly to make a comparison with the situation of slave traders at other small ports in the region. Their different circumstances provide a valuable context in which to view the situation of traders at Lancaster and at the same time they help to explain the level of involvement of their ports in the transatlantic slave trade.

The Kirkham flax merchants who invested in the slave trade at Preston and Poulton did share one or two similarities with the Butterfields. They were, for example, of a similar age and were well established in a line of business which involved them in the Baltic trade.[64] However, here the similarities end. They had a viable export trade to the plantations when they made their investments in the slave trade. They exported their own manufactures of sailcloth and twine throughout the 1740s, 1750s and early 1760s. This difference undoubtedly explains their lack of commitment and therefore lack of persistence in the African trade. It must have been their close association, John Birley's in particular, with the Lancastrian slave trader Charles Inman, a resident in the West Indies, which acted as a strong influence in prompting them to direct their vessels towards Africa for a few voyages. Given the trade's reputation, they may have been further encouraged in this direction in the hope of making more spectacular returns than were typically on offer to north-west colonial merchants during peace-time. However, their brief encounter was not very successful and their investments ended when the outbreak of war, in 1756, not only disrupted the slave trade temporarily but also improved returns in direct colonial trade. Thereafter, the Kirkham merchants concentrated on exporting their sailcloth to the colonies from the Wyre and later through London, Liverpool and other neighbouring ports. Their ability to operate successfully in the export trade through the hands of merchants at other ports confirms the viability of their product and distinguishes them from the merchants who participated in the slave trade at Lancaster.[65]

The circumstances of slave traders at Whitehaven were different from those of the Kirkham merchants, even though their mature ages also reflected the years they had spent pursuing other business and commercial interests prior to their investments in African ventures.[66] The difference was that the merchants who invested in the slave trade at Whitehaven were filling a vacuum that had developed in their careers, on account of the decline of the tobacco trade in the Cumbrian port.[67] They were not, like the Kirkham merchants, supplementing their colonial interests, but rather replacing them. Under these circumstances, it is hardly surprising that their commitment to the Guinea trade was much greater. Moreover, these displaced tobacco merchants, despite their different circumstances, are comparable with Lancaster slave merchants, in that they, too, adopted this branch of colonial commerce primarily through force of circumstance. The situation of traders at both ports, therefore, highlights the slave trade as a marginal activity.

Recently constructed model of the *King George* slaver of Whitehaven. Purpose-built, this snow of 150 tons traded with Africa in the 1760s when the Cumbrian slave trade was at its height. *Courtesy of Whitehaven Museum*

The slave traders described so far at Lancaster had not of course, been dislodged from an established position in alternative commerce as had been the case at Whitehaven. This is evident both in the young ages of many of the trade's participants at Lancaster and in the long-standing, land-based business interests of the port's more mature venturers. There is, however, one important exception which is clearly demonstrated in the circumstances of Thomas Satterthwaite, partner in the firm of Satterthwaite and Inman, which participated in the slave trade from 1753 to 1760.[68] This particular example becomes even more interesting on the realisation that Satterthwaite's partner, Charles Inman entered the slave trade from an opposite angle. He evidently adopted this branch of commerce in his efforts to set himself up as a colonial merchant. An analysis of this one firm, therefore, provides a particularly valuable illustration of how the slave trade attracted men who were, for different reasons, on the fringes of Lancaster's merchant society.

At first sight, Thomas Satterthwaite seems an unlikely participant in the 'black ivory' trade, being both a Quaker and well-connected, through his step-father, Miles Townson, with the prominent Rawlinson-Dillworth-Townson merchant group. From being made a Freeman in 1742/43, Thomas' early success and standing as a Lancaster merchant is evident in his frequent appearances in the Lancaster Apprentice Rolls. Furthermore, the esteem in which he must have been held by his step-father and partner-in-trade is clearly demonstrated when he was made chief executor of Townson's substantial estate when he was just twenty-seven years old, alongside such senior associates as John Touchet, William Dillworth and Joshua Whalley.[69] After his step-father's death, Thomas Satterthwaite continued to trade with the Rawlinsons, Dillworths and others into the early 1750s, but by this time a marriage somewhat reminiscent of his brother Benjamin's nine years previously "forfeited his Unity with Friends".[70] This act likewise seemed to jeopardise his commercial standing with his family and associates until 1762 when his name appears once more in the Lancaster Apprentice Rolls in association with Thomas and William Dillworth.[71] Two years later he applied for reinstatement as a Friend and, with no objections forthcoming, he and his wife Hannah "received membership" into the Lancaster Meeting.[72]

It was during, and perhaps because of, his period of disownment that he entered partnership with Charles Inman. Inman had been an apprentice to the Butterfield brothers at the time when Thomas Butterfield sent his slaver, the *Expedition*, on its first voyage to Africa in 1744. He had then gained first-hand experience out in the West Indies, acting for a time in several partnerships as an agent for Gillow.[73] It is not altogether surprising that Inman's experiences, fired by his apparent grit and determination to succeed, compelled him in the direction of the African trade. As a comparatively unprivileged, yet ambitious, young merchant he would easily have been captivated by its promises of quick riches and the improved stature this might engender. Meanwhile Thomas Satterthwaite, his senior by eight years, approached the trade in black Africans from a more assured vantage point, descending from his position as an established West India merchant. His association with Inman in slaving ventures is readily comprehensible given the knowledge of his recent disownment by his fellow Friends and therefore his business associates. Their two families had connexions through marriage and they were to remain close friends and associates until Charles Inman's death out in Jamaica in 1767, when Thomas Satterthwaite was not only named his executor, but also chosen by Inman's daughter Susannah to be her guardian.[74]

The fact that their joint investment in the triangular trade ceased, when Thomas Satterthwaite re-established himself in his former niche in bilateral colonial trade, is convincing evidence that it was his temporary disownment and displacement, along with Inman's relative marginality, which had brought them into the African trade. Inman, meanwhile, no longer continued his need for the slave trade either. He now functioned as a successful resident merchant in Jamaica, dealing with the imports and exports of his former slave-trading partner and his well-established business associates.[75]

133

These men were the main operators in Lancaster's earlier period of slave trading. They were presumably joined by a number of casual investors, who often go unidentified, given the registrations for vessels were generally mere summaries. These individuals were an important source of additional finance and, in a number of instances, they would have assisted in supplying cargoes for Africa. The Manchester textile merchant, John Haworth, no doubt operated in this capacity in his partnership with William Butterfield.[76] One would expect him to have had a particular interest in the colonial imports too, though this cannot have been of paramount importance. Records relating to the return cargoes of slavers in which he had a share, though far from complete, reveal no shipments of cotton.

Although these casual investors would have played a valuable role in terms of financing the slave trade, it is unlikely that they showed much concern in, or knowledge about, its management. If it had not been organized for them, they would no doubt have had to find alternative areas of investment. This aspect makes it both timely and informative to consider the slave trade at Chester at this point, for here a passive involvement seems to have been the hallmark of local investment in ships bound for Africa, its active management being left to outsiders. This sets Chester slave traders apart from traders elsewhere in the region and is important because it goes a long way to explain why Chester's experience in the slave trade was different from that of Lancaster.

Extant registrations of Chester slavers show shareholders consisted of a variety of local tradesmen or wholesalers, together with one or two active organizers who disclose distinct Liverpool or even London connexions. For example, a large number of the ten partners who financed the *St. George* between 1750 and 1753 were local wholesalers or craftsmen, including a number of ironmongers, several wet glovers and a roper. Significantly, one of the ironmongers, John Penkett, had connexions in the Liverpool slave trade through his brother William, who was captain, then owner, of a number of slavers there in the 1730s and 1740s. More importantly, the registration included John Pardoe, a prominent Liverpool merchant and slave trader, and John Bagnall, who was established as a merchant in London between 1749 and 1754, but who had inherited extensive property in Chester from his uncle. Bagnall proceeded to organize two more slave ships at Chester in 1755. There had also been an earlier London slaver, named the *Chester*, which had cleared Kingston for the Dee in 1749. It was registered as the property of John Townson and Company. Townson, another merchant resident in London, had owned another vessel with north-western merchants and was evidently in partnership with Bagnall.[77] This information shows that local initiative was not a feature of the Chester slave trade, and that local merchants, wholesalers and craftsmen did not perform active roles in its operation as they did elsewhere. Instead, the organization of African ventures at Chester represented off-shoots of initiative and expertise from London and Liverpool merchants. They undoubtedly enjoyed good connexions in Chester and presumably benefitted from the finance and local services that the resident entrepreneurs could offer, together with the advantages concurrent with operating out of a small port. The situation was, however, to change.

The interruption of slave trading at Chester in 1757 may well be accounted for by the threat of war. The fact that it was not resumed, except briefly in the 1770s, no doubt reflected certain problems of competition as discussed in previous chapters, but it must also be largely explained by the loss of its active operators. John Penkett died in 1758, whilst John Pardoe had gone bankrupt in 1753 and died later that year. Meanwhile, John Bagnall apparently retired from overseas commerce.[78] The consequences of their withdrawal only underlines the importance of outside initiative at Chester.

Thus it was a lack of local enterprise which strongly contributed to the slave trade's limited development at Chester. Ironically Chester, with its dearth of opportunities in other branches of transatlantic trade, might well have benefitted from the African trade, if its investors had been able to organize themselves along the lines of their neighbours at Lancaster. As it was, once the external initiative was removed, there was insufficient local commitment and expertise to carry on the trade amidst mounting competition from Liverpool. In contrast, at Lancaster, local expertise was being built up as the trade in black Africans was actively embraced by local aspiring entrepreneurs wishing to launch themselves into colonial trade, or by more mature merchants or wholesalers wanting to diversify or replace existing commercial activities.

At Lancaster and elsewhere, the active partners investing in slave ships seemed to share a use or need for the triangular trade, albeit for the variety of reasons already discovered, through which they might enhance or maintain their situation, the alternatives being either impracticable or insufficiently attractive. Meanwhile, the influence certain slave traders had upon their juniors and associates should probably not be underestimated. It is also noticeable, however, that out of the early group of African traders at Lancaster few invested their capital and energies in more than a handful of vessels.[79] For some, such as Dodgson Foster, Thomas Satterthwaite and Charles Inman, it evidently signified that they had satisfied the need that had prompted their initial investment. The outbreak of war probably changed the circumstances for many. For example, potential profits in direct colonial trade improved. Unfortunate experiences must have discouraged others from further forays into African waters. At Lancaster both the Thompson brothers and Helme and Fowler experienced at least one disastrous venture apiece. In 1756 the Thompsons' captain, Samuel Simondson, ill with fever, arrived in Charleston with just forty-nine slaves aboard the *Concord*, having buried twenty-two on passage. Furthermore, he had come, against the advice of Henry Laurens, to a poor market. Helme and Fowler experienced a similar disappointment there the following year. Their captain, John Holden, landed just seventy slaves from the holds of the *Anson* on its second voyage, having lost thirty blacks and three-quarters of his crew of twenty-four. Holden then suffered storm damage on the North American coast and his meagre cargo, "mostly thin and low" meant "a good sum could not be hoped for".[80] His employers did not invest in the African trade again.

In spite of the brevity of these early operations, these entrepreneurs had established the trade at Lancaster in terms of regular sailings and developing expertise. They laid the foundations on which the trade was to operate vigorously for the next twenty years and then more sporadically until it was legally obliterated. Importantly, William Butterfield continued his interest in the slave trade beyond many of his contemporaries, thereby demonstrating that it could be of a more serious and deliberate nature. He was then joined by a more specialised second generation. This evolution of a subsequent generation was not experienced at other north-western ports outside Liverpool.

An examination of Lancaster's slave-trading community after the mid-1750s reveals the African trade's continuance and development at Lancaster as a marginal activity, in terms of the type of investors it attracted. It also shows us how the trade was managed effectively over the next twenty years or more. Throughout this period Lancaster's slave-trading community embodied a group of investors who demonstrated far greater commitment to the trade than their predecessors had done, William Butterfield excepted. For whereas no individual entering the trade before the mid-1750s ever owned shares in more than a total of five or six vessels, in the ensuing period at least eight merchants owned more than five or six vessels and four of these had an interest in a dozen or more.[81] There were other important differences. The group included a new type of investor.

Ex-Guinea Captains

The early slave traders had obviously provided employment for the first generation of Guinea captains and a number of the more ambitious and successful of these were able to retire from active duty and invest their profits in the next generation of slaving vessels, a process which was to continue until the trade was outlawed. This social progression was not in evidence at the other north-western ports outside Liverpool. Chester's, Preston's and Poulton's experiences in the slave trade were too short and, whilst Whitehaven's involvement lasted a little longer, it was seemingly not long enough. Moreover, Whitehaven, like the smaller ports to the south of the Lune, never cultivated the same degree of local initiative at the captaincy level, at least in the first instance, which might otherwise have encouraged a similar pattern of self-fulfilment. Instead, the evidence suggests that these smaller ports borrowed much of their expertise from Liverpool and even London, a phenomenon which is not apparent at Lancaster. These captains-turned-investors imparted a wealth of expertise to the Lancaster slave trade, based on their first-hand experience of the African coast and the colonies. A set of instructions entitled "To go into the Camaroons" written by former Guinea captain James Sawrey for Tobias Collins, the master of his slave ship, the *Hope II*, illustrates the depth of this trader's first-hand knowledge of the African coast.

> Run down the Windward Coast as far as Cape Palmas and take your departure from there by the time you reckon yourself abreast of Cape Formosa. Be sure you look out for Fernandepoo which you must run down in three and five and not as laid down in two and forty to windward of which you will be within one mile of the shore. Before you get soundings in forty-four fathoms run down on the North side to the East end, then steer E.b.S.½S. about eleven Leagues then you will be on hard Ground at the mouth of the Cameroons which is a low point bearing from you N.E. about 4 or 5 Leagues, if not at these bearings you must bring it to bear to steer N.E. Northerly untill you be abreast of the Cape then you will have twelve fathom soft Ground within half a mile of the shore. Then keep E.b.N.½N. for the Clump of Trees at the East Point of Old Mole, you'll carry thirteen or thirteen and a half feet over the Flats, keep about two thirds over to the North shore untill abreast of Monubas Mole then haul over to the Town and come too in five or six fathom water. N.B. From the Cape Camaroons I would advise you to come to anchor when in three fathom, to send your Boat over the Flats and Lay a few Buoys for your more certain guide.

Captain James Sawrey proceeded to give details concerning the make-up of beads for trading in the River Camaroon.

> Bunch of small white Domini contains 59 strings, 40 beads on each. Bunch of fisheyes contains 19 strings, 39 beads on each. Blue and Flat the same.[82]

These former slave-ship masters also had first-hand experience of the slave markets and were personally acquainted with some of the dealers and merchants on the African coast and in the colonies. Such expertise gave the slave trade at Lancaster a considerable boost and provided it with a competitive edge. Indeed, Anderson has noted that "Continuity of operations in the slave-trade normally required that a substantial merchant of experience take on the function of 'ship's husband' to oversee the detailed organization of the venture and to attend to the interests of all those involved".[83] The impact of the former Guinea captains on the organization of the trade at Lancaster would further account for the port's position in slave-trading statistics, ahead of the other small north-western ports. Thus not only did Lancaster demonstrate a greater long-term need or use for the African trade, but in pursuing the spoils of Africa more doggedly it developed an expertise over and above its less independent neighbours. This in turn encouraged Lancaster's further involvement in the trade.

Socially and economically, the Guinea captains stood on the very fringes of Lancaster's commercial society. However, for some, their successful perseverance in the African trade, first as captains and then as investors, provided them with the passport they needed to join the ranks of the merchant community. As captains, they would each begin with a small share in the vessel they commanded and, as they were able to increase their share, so they would eventually reach a point when they could become full-time merchant investors themselves. Their decision to remain with the slave trade as merchants almost certainly stemmed from their familiarity with its operations, together with the opportunities it could still offer them as newcomers to the world of investment and partnership. Even so, its fluctuating fortunes no doubt provided them with some anxious moments as balance sheets were carefully scrutinized.

Amongst the Guinea captains who retired from seafaring to invest in the triangular trade, five stand out as successfully establishing themselves as prominent merchants within the Lancaster slave trade and indeed became respected members of the colonial community at large.[84] Though few in number, their expertise and commitment meant they played a distinctive and influential role in the local slave trade. Their initiation as master mariners has already been discussed, and it is sufficient to restate here that a significant number originated from Furness and became Guinea captains at a young age.[85] Interestingly, Table 3.3 demonstrates that they pursued a remarkably similar path into Lancaster's merchant community, even though they entered the slave trade at different times between 1748 and 1771.

The marked similarity of their experiences in entering into the ownership of Guinea vessels suggests that the Lancaster slave trade offered a particular and assured means of self-improvement for those

Table 3.3 *Lancaster's Guinea Captains-turned-Slave Merchants*

Captains turned investors	No.of voyages as captain	No.of years as captain	Age when retired as captain	Age when elected Port Commissioner	Port Commissioner after how many years as owner	Total no. of years as owner	Age when made last investment (age at death)
Thomas Hinde	5	5	33	35	2	40+	75+ (78)
Richard Millerson	6 or 7	10	32	34	2	14	47 (47)
Robert Dodgson	6 or 7	9	33	35	2	14	48 (50)
John Addison	5 or 6	8	32	34	2	17	49 (49)
James Sawrey	5	6	32	not elected or did not stand		13	49 (85)

masters who were both fortunate enough and determined to respond successfully to the demands of the triangular trade. They all became investors in slave ships in their early thirties after commanding between five and seven ventures. The only slight variation was the number of years they took to accomplish this. Their promotion appears relatively swift, and their election as port commissioners, just two years after they became owners, acknowledges their active involvement in the management of their port. There is further evidence to suggest they soon grew in stature in the eyes of their fellow merchants, and in capital too.[86]

The fact that four of the five captains spent comparable periods as investors in the slave trade is more of a coincidence. Richard Millerson's and Robert Dodson's deaths during the American War of Independence terminated two committed and strangely parallel careers, after fourteen years of investment in the Lancaster slave trade and many more years at sea. The grave also put a stop to John Addison's investments some ten years later.[87] The war, which had interrupted his participation in the trade for four years, delayed the initiation of the youngest of the five captains into the ownership of slavers. Captain James Sawrey was actively engaged in transporting black Africans across the Atlantic for the last time when the fighting began.[88] The war evidently offered him alternative opportunities.[89] Later on in the war, his name appeared on the registration document of his old vessel, and this launched him into a career of slaver ownership, implicating him in some eight vessels.[90] It was not his death, however, which prompted his exit from the slave trade in 1794. By this time the Lancaster slave trade was clearly in decline and the problems it was now experiencing undoubtedly accounted for his leaving the trade.

There were strong personal as well as commercial ties between these four men. Richard Millerson and Robert Dodson, both originating from Ulverston and with just eighteen months between them in age, owned at least six slaving vessels together between 1763 and 1771.[91] John Addison, also of Ulverston and a relative to Robert Dodson by marriage, served as their captain during these years. Meanwhile, Richard Millerson acted as bondsman for his marriage in 1771, by which time Addison, too, had become a land-based merchant.[92] His first partners, not surprisingly, were Robert Dodson and Richard Millerson. Millerson later invited his junior colleague to act as one of his trustees, describing him as his "good friend and partner", and his probate also referred to houses in St. Leonard's Gate now in possession of John Addison.[93] After Robert Dodson's and Richard Millerson's deaths, John Addison was joined by James Sawrey, six years his junior and a native of Hawkshead, not far from Ulverston. Sawrey had not commanded any slavers for these Ulverston men but he had skippered one or two Guineamen for another ex-African captain, Thomas Woodburne, who probably originated from Ulverston too. Woodburne now lived in Overton, the native place of John Addison's wife. Together, Addison and Sawrey were partners in four slaving vessels, and in 1788, just after Addison's death, his share in a West Indiaman, the *Jenny*, now belonging to his widow Mary, was transferred to James Sawrey, merchant of Hornby.[94] James Sawrey's slave-trading partners henceforth were land-based merchants rather than Guinea captains, for whom he undoubtedly served as ship's husband.[95] Thus ended this close-knit series of Furness Guinea captains who, on becoming African merchants, so ruled and characterised the Lancaster slave trade during its heyday and beyond. Between them they had provided captains for the trade for twenty-four years, from 1753 to 1777, and experienced organizers for a full thirty-one years, between 1763 and 1794. Their perseverance and impact on the slave trade could not have been matched elsewhere in the North West outside Liverpool. In return, the triangular trade provided them with both employment and a way into Lancaster's colonial merchant community and the economic, social and political opportunities that encompassed.

Nobody embodied and exuded the successes of the slave trade at Lancaster more than Captain Thomas Hinde. An alderman and twice a mayor, he likewise had found his way up from the decks of a Guinea vessel. He was born in 1720, the fourth child of a Caton yeoman. When his father died in 1727, his elder brother William inherited the family farm leaving Thomas and his younger brother, James, to look elsewhere for their personal fortunes when their time came. In 1735, Thomas and James became beneficiaries of a relative, Richard Hinde, whereby they shared an income with their three sisters from a small estate at Sunderland, near Overton. This, together with a small sum left to them by their father, presumably secured them their apprenticeships, Thomas as a mariner and James as a mercer; and in time it would have given them a small amount of capital.[96]

Although details of his apprenticeship and early career are not known, Thomas Hinde's name was to become associated with the slave trade for nigh on fifty years. The length and depth of his experience in the trade made him a key figure amongst local slave traders. He sent more ships to West Africa and stayed in the trade longer than anyone else at Lancaster. Not surprisingly, he served four times as a port commissioner.[97]

His first captaincy was aboard the *Jolly Batchelor* when it sailed for its cargo of slaves in 1748. The following year, he was made a freeman of Lancaster and proceeded to make three more voyages to Africa, commanding the same forty-ton vessel. He gradually built up a share in the vessel, and this enabled him to retire from the sea and assume the life of a land-based merchant.[98] Thereafter, Hinde's name can be found in the registrations of at least sixteen more Lancaster slave ships up into the 1780s, by which time it was becoming increasingly less practical to operate in the slave trade from Lancaster.[99] However, Hinde's predilection for the trade, and indeed that of three of his sons who had already moved south to Liverpool, lived on as he continued to invest in slavers clearing from the Mersey into his late seventies.[100] His affairs no doubt became increasingly managed by his sons and more especially by the eldest, also Thomas.

Thomas Hinde senior died leaving a well-appointed house and estate in the 'Fryerage' in Lancaster to his elder son, £300 annuity to his wife Ann and five legacies amounting to £40,000 to the rest of his children.[101] Meanwhile, the junior Hindes continued as a formidable force in the African trade at Liverpool right up to the trade's abolition in 1807.[102] Their tenacity is exemplified in their wrangle with the Customs in August 1806. Thomas junior and Samuel Hinde came up against a law prohibiting new slavers from leaving Liverpool for Africa. They argued that their vessel, the *Jane*, launched from the stocks at Lancaster in 1801 and then employed in the West India trade, was ultimately intended as a slaving vessel, and should therefore be permitted to make such a voyage before the date of Abolition.[103]

Mayoral portrait of Captain Thomas Hinde, one of Lancaster's most experienced and prominent slave merchants. *Courtesy of Lancaster City Museums*

When the trade was outlawed, the three sons returned, with their substantial fortunes, to live in their native town where they were already investors in a worsted mill.[104] It comes as no surprise to learn that the Hindes featured in a local political extravaganza entitled, 'Lancaster Preserved or Sterling honour entrusted to the select few',

142

dated 1819, some twenty-one years after Captain Thomas Hinde's death. It included the following extract:

Dolphinholme Hero

('The Devil among the Negroes')

Featuring (amongst others)

William Hinde: Lord Q from St. Stephen's. Son of an African Captain. 'It was an open traffic'.
Samuel Hinde: Sam, a Spotted Negro. 'One at night and two in the morning'.[105]

Captain Thomas Hinde's success and effect upon the slave trade was not, it seems, repeated anywhere else outside Britain's three main slaving ports. As one of the senior participants in the trade, Hinde must have influenced and advised many of its investors and operators. He and the other retired Guinea captains formed the very backbone of Lancaster's slave-trading community, the linchpin on which the trade pivoted. Consequently, few detailed registrations concerning Lancaster slave ships omit the names of these experienced former skippers.

Prominent Land-Based Investors and Organizers

However, their capital alone would have been insufficient for financing the African trade, especially given the necessity to spread assets over several ventures. Additional investment was required. As the example of William Butterfield suggests, an important source of this capital were the ambitious, marginal merchants, who had no sea-faring experience in the African trade. They were joined by casual, more passive, investors. Taken all together, these men provided the necessary balance of capital and expertise. Although many invested in bilateral colonial trade as well, their particular commitment to the slave trade meant it assumed some importance in Lancaster's transatlantic commerce. The pattern of slaver ownership at Lancaster is well portrayed in the registration of the *Antelope II* which made five voyages to Africa, under the command of Thomas Paley, between 1763 and 1772. The naval office shipping lists cite the owners as Richard and John Watson, Thomas and Richard Millerson, Robert Dodson, Henry Lawrence and Thomas Hinde.[106] These included three of the ex-Guinea captains already referred to, together with the elder brother of one of them. This was Thomas Millerson, the retired West India captain, who had been a resident merchant or factor in Barbados for a number of years.[107] Meanwhile, Henry Lawrence was the slave factor on the African coast who had befriended Robert Dodson in the Gambia. His investment in the Lancaster slave trade ended suddenly with his death in 1766, when he was described as being late of Lancaster. Attached to his will is a letter written in March 1763. It clearly expresses his confidence in Dodson's expertise. Addressed to the former captain, whom he described as his friend and agent, it reads:-

> As I've appointed you my lawfull attorney and have left you at power for that: its needless for me to say much here in Regard to my concerns in the Ships in the Gambia Trade. I wold have you to get insurances made as for yourself, in all my transactions at sea youll pleas to act as for yourself.[108]

Finally, there were the Watsons, solid financiers and organizers in the Lancaster slave trade during a period which spanned at least thirty-five years. The first member of this family to make ventures to Africa was William Watson . He was the more usual partner to his younger brother, John, who featured in the registration of the *Antelope*, alongside a Richard Watson, probably an error for William, since in 1770 William Davenport was selling beads to William Watson and his son, James, for their vessel, the *Antelope*.[109] Overall, William Watson was one of the most committed investors in Lancaster slavers and his tenacity was no doubt instrumental in keeping the trade alive at Lancaster. Altogether, he owned at least thirteen slaving vessels and probably quite a few more that have not been identified.[110] His involvement in the triangular trade was interrupted during and in the years immediately following the American War of Independence. He and his brother faced considerable financial problems at this time in connexion with the failure of a Dublin firm. In November 1777 Benjamin Satterthwaite wrote several letters to his son, warning him not to involve himself in their difficulties. William Watson did, however, resume his investments in the slave trade in 1788, owning shares in three more Guinea vessels before his death in 1793, at the age of sixty-two.[111]

William and John Watson originated from the Westmorland village of Crosby Ravensworth where their grandfather was vicar.[112] Their elder brother, James, also became a clergyman and was later headmaster of Lancaster Grammar school for nearly thirty years. Ironically, it was he, who, in his retirement, wrote an elegy to 'Samboo' (see Appendix C), an unfortunate black African wrested from his native country and later the West Indies, who had died on his arrival at Sunderland Point in 1736; the unconsecrated grave is marked to this day.[113] William and John evidently came into some money when their father died, intestate, in 1755, and it was later that year that William, aged twenty three, made his first appearance in the Lancaster records, as freeman. His payment for this suggests he had no formal connexions with the town. Two or three

144

Samboo's Grave at Sunderland Point. This epitaph was written by Rev. James Watson, whose younger brothers made substantial investments in the Lancaster slave trade.

'Am I not a Man and a Brother', the emblem of the Anti-Slavery Movement.
Courtesy of Hull City Museums & Art Galleries

years later he was investing in what appears to be his first slave ship, the
Cato. He was then elected port commissioner whilst his first slaver was at
sea.[114] These facts suggest that he had already been active in the port a
short time when he entered the African trade, assuming he did not have
a share in an earlier vessel that has yet to come to light, although the
level on which he was operating is not clear. Gillow records reveal that
William was purchasing furniture for export in 1758 and again in 1763,
denoting his part in direct trade with the colonies by this date, at least.[115]
What seems most probable is that, in 1755, William decided to set
himself up as a merchant in Lancaster and that very early on, he found

146

the risky, but potentially lucrative spoils of the African trade an attractive option for at least some of his capital. It was not long before his brother joined him, for he, too, was made a freeman of Lancaster in 1760.[116] Both brothers, more particularly William, continued to keep a significant share of their capital in the slave trade for most of their merchant careers. It evidently assisted them, as outsiders to the town, in establishing themselves as successful colonial merchants at Lancaster.

Identifying some of William Watson's early slave-trading partners reveals how he may have been encouraged to participate in the slave trade. One of his partners in the *Cato* was John Heathcote, who was married to Millicent Satterthwaite, who, incidentally, later became Watson's wife. William Watson would have known the Satterthwaites through Thomas Satterthwaite's partner, Charles Inman, with whom Watson already had links.[117] It was probably this connexion which prompted his partnership in a slaving vessel with Heathcote in 1758. The following year, with Heathcote dead, William Watson joined Satterthwaite and Inman in sending the *Marlborough* to the Gambia.[118] A few months later, he invested in a third slaver, the *Juba I*, bound for the Windward Coast, this time with his other partners in the *Cato*, these being Thomas Hinde, Richard Millerson and Miles Barber.[119] Once again former Guinea captains were present to provide first-hand expertise, as indeed they were in all of Watson's slaving partnerships.[120] The remaining shareholder, Miles Barber, another newcomer to the trade, persisted to become not only another prominent investor but a real specialist in the organization of slaving ventures as well.

It is considered important to explore Barber's origins and career in the slave trade in some detail, even though his specialization in the trade ultimately took him away from his native town. This is not only because there is illuminating documentation surrounding this particular slave merchant, but also because his initial circumstances, parallel in some respects with the Watsons, can be taken as representative of other individuals who were drawn to the slave trade at Lancaster, and maybe elsewhere too.

Miles Barber was the son of a yeoman of Skerton, also called Miles, who later became an innkeeper in this village across the river from Lancaster. Miles Barber senior died in 1753, leaving his estate to his son when he should reach the age of twenty-five. In his will he wrote,

> It is my will and desire that my son Myles go into the world to imploy and improve himself till he attain the age of twenty-five years and that the above [mentioned] £10 shall be given him at his first going of[f] – and that my Trustees receive the rents of my said 'Estate' till he is of that age ... And when Miles attains 25 years, the said Trustees to convey to him the said Estate ...[121]

The Family of Miles Barber

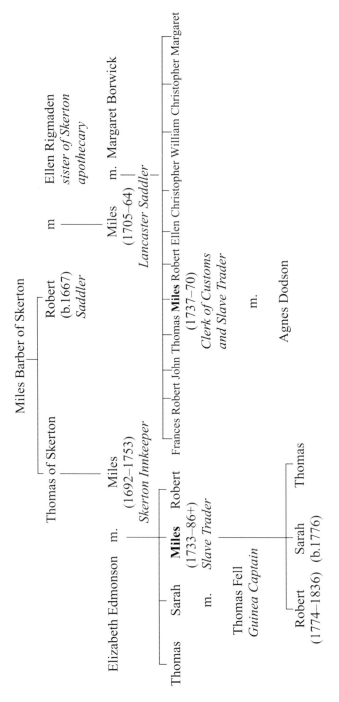

It seems more than a coincidence that Miles Barber junior invested in his first slaver, the *Cato*, in 1758, the year in which he became twenty-five years old.[122] An insurance policy had been taken out in his name, shortly after his father's death, on several buildings in Skerton which were in tenure, together with a brewhouse, all of which amounted to £400.[123] The brewhouse presumably accounted for the fact that the Priory Church was paying Barber for supplying ale in 1754. Two years later, he was described as a wine merchant when he and his second cousin Miles, son of a Lancaster saddler, produced a bond for £200 on the latter's appointment as a Tonnage Officer at Lancaster.[124] Although the wine trade was likely to direct and even confine Barber to European ventures, it was soon the African trade which absorbed his energies and capital. Interestingly, as early as 1752, a vessel registered in Barbados had transported thirty-one slaves, along with butter and bottled ale imported from Lancaster, on a voyage from Bridgetown to South Carolina. Its owners were Miles Barber, John Marsden and James Booth.[125] Miles Barber junior would have been just nineteen years old at this time, making it more likely that this venture concerned his father. The bottled ale suggests this investor was the innkeeper, rather than the saddler. Furthermore, the vessel's master, a Captain Cragg, was one of the tenants of the Skerton property insured for Miles Barber junior in 1754/55. The nature of such a venture most probably gave the young man not just a taste for colonial trade, but demonstrated the potential of trading in African slaves as well. Once he had acquired his moderate inheritance, at the age of twenty-five, the innkeeper's son was ready to launch himself as a merchant in the direction of Africa.

It was the availability of some capital and an awareness of colonial trade, in terms both of its opportunities and limitations, coupled with an ambition to succeed as a prosperous merchant that apparently attracted Miles Barber towards the slave trade. The trade promised riches and was open to all. Similar circumstances and attitudes were more than likely responsible for baiting the other entrepreneurs who likewise decided that the slave trade could offer them the means to establish themselves as colonial merchants.

After the *Cato*, Miles Barber was concerned in at least nine or ten more slave ships at Lancaster in the ensuing seven years. Thomas Hinde continued as his most consistent partner in a large number of these, no doubt injecting the necessary expertise, as well as capital.[126] Meanwhile, Barber was elected a port commissioner in 1761 and two years later he was taking on an apprentice for five years.[127] By this time, however, it is noticeable that Barber's slavers, though described as 'of Lancaster' were operating more from the Mersey than the Lune, and that from 1762 his more usual partner was Samuel Kilner, a native of Ulverston and a Lancaster mariner who was to move to Liverpool.[128]

Barber himself moved to Liverpool around 1765, the year he petitioned to be admitted a freeman of the town on purchase.[129] It cost him £52.10s.0d. He continued his large-scale investments in the African trade, owning something in the order of twenty-five slavers which made frequent voyages to Africa over the next two decades.[130] His move to Liverpool no doubt reflected his decision to specialise in the slave trade to an extent that put him more on a par with William Davenport.[131] His severance with Lancaster, however, was never complete, for almost all his partners originated from north Lancashire. Samuel Kilner was his chief partner until Kilner's death in 1776. Another co-investor was his second cousin, Miles Barber, the former customs clerk at Lancaster. He, too, had moved to Liverpool and in 1769 the two Miles Barbers were admitted simultaneously as freemen to the Company of African Merchants, although the saddler's son died the following year.[132] Thereafter, Barber's partners included Robert MacMillan of Liverpool, son of the Lancaster wine merchant who had himself sent a vessel to Africa, together with James Kendall and William Denison, who had both been Guinea captains at Lancaster and later masters of several Liverpool vessels belonging to Miles Barber.[133] It was almost certainly Barber himself who was responsible for the captains' move to Liverpool, though, as the century progressed, other investors at Lancaster increasingly found some part at least of their operations being channelled through the Mersey. Unfortunately, no probate record had been discovered for Miles Barber. Curiously, he left Liverpool for London in the mid-1780s, where he continued to register ships for Africa. In one at least of these, the *King Jos*, his partner was Josiah Hort, who had commanded Sawrey's and Addison's slaver, the *Molly III*, between 1783 and 1786. Thereafter, Barber disappears from the London directories.[134] Although the whereabouts and time of his death are uncertain, there is a will for his son Robert Barber. He died in 1836 as a merchant in Liverpool, and presumably one of some eminence, given that his bond was for £6,000.[135]

Miles Barber's career has shown that he entered the slave trade as an ambitious young man from a modest family with some knowledge of colonial trade and a moderate inheritance. He was undoubtedly instrumental in introducing larger slave ships for a time at Lancaster and in setting up a slave factory on the African coast. Although his specialization took him away from Lancaster and its slave trade, he never relinquished ties with his native town. Without a doubt, Miles Barber played a crucial and influential role in directing and promoting the slave trade at Lancaster. There was evidently no equivalent entrepreneur at the other small slave-trading ports in the North West, where for reasons already stated, conditions failed to encourage such a commitment to the trade.

Operators like Miles Barber and Thomas Hinde flourished as a result of their long careers in the African trade. Others faced certain financial difficulties, the diverse consequences of which tell us more about slave traders at Lancaster. In 1767 the failure of the North American firm, Middleton, Liston and Hope had meant substantial losses for Thomas and Richard Millerson, together with their chief partners the Watson brothers and Robert Dodson.[136] Interestingly, this experience neither prevented nor deterred the Millersons or their partners from further African ventures. This not only underlines the strength of their commitment to the African trade, but also indicates that their commercial standing had enabled them to weather a financial upset of this order. Moreover, Richard Millerson, in his will proved in 1777, was able to leave a considerable amount of land and property in and around Lancaster, which included his own house on the north side of fashionable St.Leonard's Gate. In addition, there were his investments in merchandise and shipping.[137]

Millerson's fortune may not have been spectacular, but he had succeeded in establishing and maintaining himself as a respected overseas merchant in Lancaster, and this was in spite of his involvement in the bankruptcy of the North American firm, about which Laurens had written to a London merchant, remarking,

> [I] am really so affected from our apprehension of their vast losses that I hardly know to set about a letter to convey such horrible intellegence.[138]

However, not all investors at Lancaster were able to withstand the financial pitfalls of the slave trade. Unprofitable ventures surely dampened the enthusiasm of some of the trade's earliest operators, but, in 1774 one merchant landed himself in Lancaster castle for debt. His foothold in colonial circles must have been far from secure. Matthew Wright, a stocking-frame knitter and hosier from Nottingham, almost certainly entered the African trade at Lancaster with a view to branching out from and even utilising his wholesaling and manufacturing interests. He apparently had some connexions in the locality and he may even have been the Preston Patrick husbandman named Matthew Wright who had married Agnes Yeats of Old Hutton in 1747. This would be compatible not only with the age of his daughter at the time of her marriage in 1769 but also with the names of one or two of his slaving vessels.[139] Either way, he was new to Lancaster's foreign trade and thus once again supports the belief that the Lancaster slave trade attracted, and was in turn promoted by, the existence of marginal operators, men who did not belong to the established elite.

Wright's role in the trade must have been an active one, for he was buying beads from William Davenport alongside Lancaster's chief

Consignment of beads sold to Matthew Wright of Lancaster in 1768 for his slave ship *Agnes*. Extract from William Davenport's Bead Book. *From the Raymond Richards Collection, courtesy of Keele University Library*

operators on at least three different occasions between 1767 and 1769.[140] Furthermore, debtors' insolvency papers reveal he had no less than a half share in the *Agnes II* which made three voyages to Africa between 1769 and 1773. He almost certainly owned shares in another vessel of this name which made two slaving voyages immediately beforehand and which would account for his bead purchases. Both vessels, a sloop and a brig, were commanded by Richard Kendall who married Wright's daughter in 1769, as was the *Molly II* on its initial slaving voyage in which Wright definitely held an eighth share between 1771 and 1774.[141] Wright's assets included money advanced to another of his African captains, William Harrison, payments for slaves sold in Barbados and for rice and slave goods left at Sierra Leone, not to mention the financial returns of two of his slaving vessels. The precise causes of Wright's failure are impossible to unravel without any business papers. However, the fact that his vessel, *Agnes II*, was wrecked off Ireland with only the cargo saved may well have been connected. It is also significant that the assets from his half share in this vessel amounted to just £505, which included the money he had advanced on the brig, whilst the returns alone from his eighth share in the *Molly II* were worth £374.[142]

Clearly, Wright's entry into colonial affairs did not work out. His banishment to Lancaster castle demonstrates the precarious nature of launching oneself into colonial commerce at Lancaster and underlines in particular the uncertain nature of investments in the African trade. It was a trade which worked wonders for many, but one that could turn out to be catastrophic for others, more particularly if a financial setback occurred close to their initiation as merchants, evidence again of their marginal status. It is significant, meanwhile, that Wright's partner did not share the same fate. The explanation for this almost certainly rests with his different circumstances, which imply that his investments in the slave trade were more incidental.

Casual Investors

Edward Salisbury was already a regular participant in the West India trade, with his brother Richard, when he invested in the slave trade with Wright in the late 1760s and early 1770s. This suggests he was well connected.

The son of a Slaidburn lawyer, Edward Salisbury was born in the nearby village of Newton, in the Forest of Bowland, probably on a sheep farm.[143] He came to Lancaster in 1748 as a seven-year apprentice to the mercer John Stout, on completion of which he was admitted a freeman. He then purchased a quay lot and the following year, in 1757, he was described as a wine merchant.[144] He presumably traded overseas in wines and maybe exported woollen manufactures to the colonies at this time too.[145] His involvement in colonial commerce no doubt fuelled his liquor trade, for he certainly imported rum. In 1764, for instance, Benjamin Satterthwaite was dealing with the Salisburys' vessel, the *John*, in Jamaica and shipping rum for them aboard the *Rawlinson*.[146] Three years earlier, Edward Salisbury had been elected a port commissioner for the first time, a position he held again before he invested in the slave trade and then a further three times right up to his sudden death in 1785.[147] All this suggests his investments in transporting African slaves were much more incidental to his overall shipping interests and that they should be viewed as a series of casual financial investments.

The circumstances which directed Edward Salisbury's capital to the slave trade during the late 1760s and early 1770s were probably twofold. He must have considered the Guinea trade an inviting prospect at this time, his investment in slavers presumably aimed at boosting existing colonial revenue. In addition, and perhaps of more importance, his interest was almost certainly promoted by the influence of business associates. His share in the slave ship *Agnes II* with Matthew Wright, and probably in its predecessor of the same name and captaincy, most likely resulted from the two men's acquaintance through their respective connexions in the wool trade. As a wine and spirit merchant, Salisbury was well positioned to provide the outgoing vessels with shipments of rum, an essential component for trading on the African coast. Salisbury's partners in a further vessel, the *Molly II*, featured not only Matthew Wright but seemingly also William Watson and his young stepson, Cornelius Heathcote Rhodes.[148] Such partners make it unlikely that Salisbury's part was other than that of a financial investor and a supplier of trading goods. He would have left the organization to his more experienced partners. Interestingly, his concern in the newly-built *True Blue* in 1772, was with three newcomers to the trade, his brother Richard, Edward Whiteside and Richard Baines. However, it is significant that the vessel sailed under the experienced command of Wright's son-in-law, Richard Kendall, who was also a part-owner. Kendall must have played a crucial part in organizing this African venture, and it is quite plausible that he persuaded Salisbury to take a financial interest in this vessel.[149] After Salisbury's appearance in Wright's bankruptcy papers, it is no surprise to find that he left the slave trade. He did, however, continue in the West India trade right up to his death.

The persuasive powers of personal contacts were most likely responsible for another West India merchant's involvement in the African trade. Samuel Simpson was drawn into the trade alongside experienced operators on more than one occasion. His Furness origins meant that he was well acquainted with two such partners in his first slaver, the *Pitt*, in 1765, namely Robert Dodson and Richard Millerson. Dodson's nephew was later to become Simpson's executor. Simpson's marriage into the Butterfield family may also have been influential.[150]

For Salisbury, Simpson and other West India merchants like them, financial and other interests in the slave trade seem to have been a sideline or at most a temporary distraction from their existing colonial trade. Consequently, they left the organization to the more serious and experienced African merchants and captains, men who, in any case, were probably instrumental in involving these more casual participants in the first place. The success of these active operators relied, to a large extent, on their ability to secure additional capital from family and friends. This enabled them to spread their risks over several vessels, particularly important in the African trade. Thomas Houseman's implication in the slave trade illustrates this means of capital funding as well as anyone.

Although three of the Guineamen that Houseman was concerned in sailed from the Mersey and only one of these was registered at Lancaster, all his partners were fellow townsmen. Houseman's partners in the *Thetis II*, registered in 1761, included Miles Barber, Thomas Hinde and John Preston.[151] Captain Preston, employed as a master in the African trade, was Thomas Houseman's brother-in-law, having married his sister Mary in 1757, and it was their youngest brother, Miles Houseman, who had joined Captain Preston as a probate bondsman for a slave merchant on the Guinea Coast in 1760.[152] Thomas Houseman almost certainly had a share in the vessel's predecessor, also named *Thetis*, as it, too, was owned by Miles Barber and Company and was captained by John Preston on its two African

The Family of Thomas Houseman

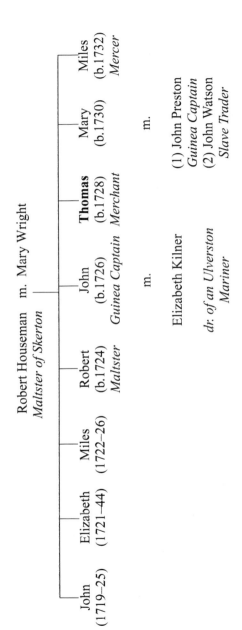

Robert Houseman m. Mary Wright
Maltster of Skerton

John
(1719–25)

Elizabeth
(1721–44)

Miles
(1722–26)

Robert
(b.1724)
Maltster

John
(b.1726)
Guinea Captain

m.

Elizabeth Kilner

*dr. of an Ulverston
Mariner*

Thomas
(b.1728)
Merchant

Mary
(b.1730)

m.

(1) John Preston
Guinea Captain
(2) John Watson
Slave Trader

Miles
(b.1732)
Mercer

voyages in 1759 and 1760. Shortly afterwards, in 1763, Thomas Houseman became a probate bondsman for Preston who had died on a slaving voyage aboard the *Lancaster*.[153] Houseman also had links with his other partners. Both Houseman and Thomas Hinde had brothers engaged as mercers in Lancaster, whilst Houseman and Miles Barber both originated from Skerton. A final connexion between Thomas Houseman and the African trade stemmed from his elder brother John Houseman's captaincy of three slave ships.[154] Thomas Houseman's partners in his next slaver, the *Gambia* of Liverpool, registered in 1764, were Barber once more and Samuel Kilner, who was quite possibly related since Captain John Houseman had married Elizabeth Kilner of Ulverston in 1752.[155] Thomas Houseman's final slaving venture came almost twenty years later when he invested in the *Garnet* of Liverpool with James Garnet, John Watson and John Moore. His obvious connexion here was John Watson, who in 1768 had married his sister Mary, the widow of Captain Preston.[156]

In return for providing his family with the additional capital they needed, Houseman and other casual investors were offered a passive, speculative investment in overseas trade which could prove very lucrative. In addition, the slave trade served as a useful outlet for their other business interests and that of their families, and this in turn assisted those responsible for loading a vessel for Africa. Drake, in commenting on this important function, writes,

> Moreover the nature of 'general trading' often allowed a slave-trader to include commodities for export to Africa which were acquired through an extension of his other interests at primary or wholesale costs.[157]

Certain commodities, such as liquor, have already been mentioned. Textiles were another valuable commodity in outgoing cargoes. This would account for the presence of mercers amongst slave-trading registrations. Thomas Houseman's youngest brother Miles, a probable shareholder in the *Thetis I*, almost certainly contributed to African voyages in this capacity. Another mercer, Miles Mason, also invested in two slavers between 1759 and 1762, again alongside more experienced operators. He must have been exporting goods earlier, given that he had bought three quay lots in 1756 and was elected a port commissioner in 1758. This may well signify an earlier involvement in the slave trade, given that this is the only branch of overseas trade with which his name has been connected. His investments in the Guinea trade ceased, however, and with it his involvement in the port. He evidently did not make a long-term transition from wholesaler to merchant.[158] Mason was, meanwhile, acquainted with a third Lancaster mercer, James Hinde, younger brother to the experienced slaver captain and merchant. James Hinde must have supplied his brother with exports and he may well have invested in some slavers as well. In 1756 he and Miles Mason were both probate bondsmen for George Capstick, a Guinea captain, who had died in command of the *Stanley I*, a slaver owned by William Benison and Company. Benison had married into the Hinde family and his partners quite probably included his brothers-in-law. Capstick, meanwhile, came from Mason's native Yorkshire village, Dent.[159]

Although insufficient registration details make it impossible to calculate the number of passive slave-trade investors at Lancaster, the examples cited show that their contribution to the trade as financiers and wholesalers should not be underestimated, nor, indeed, should the reciprocal benefits of the trade on their business affairs.

A detailed survey of Lancaster's slave-trading community has shown that although some traders were just casual participants and few were true specialists, there developed a small, but solid core of committed investors and organizers of the trade from the mid-1750s. The evidence strongly suggests their level of commitment to the African trade stemmed from their desire to enter colonial commerce or from their need to supplement or replace existing interests within it. The slave trade, with its open access and promises of quick and rich rewards, gave aspiring or dissatisfied merchants a chance to develop their commercial ambitions amidst the competitive world of eighteenth-century transatlantic commerce. Significantly, it was an option not chosen, and presumably not needed, by Lancaster's established merchant families and their associates. In Lancaster a combination of circumstances made entry into this competition especially difficult. The limited value of local exports and the cost of buying in manufactures from elsewhere made it hard for newcomers and small merchants to compete effectively with established merchant groups in direct colonial trade. This situation was intensified given that Lancaster society was expanding at this time. An unprecedented number of ambitious young men were moving into the town, their ambition fuelled by moderate sums of inheritance, resulting from a growing prosperity within the region. It was money they were eager to invest, and existing colonial commerce made them aware of growing wealth in the colonies. Nowhere was this phenomenon more apparent than in Furness, where shipping opportunities were largely confined to coastal trade. Ironically, the prosperity of this region had been promoted by the demands of existing colonial trade in the Lancashire ports for agriculture and iron-ore.[160] From here a considerable number of young men, often younger sons of yeomen and shopkeepers, migrated across Morecambe Bay to Lancaster,[161] or even further south to Liverpool, during the mid-eighteenth century. They went in search of their fortunes, the youngest taking up apprenticeships, and a significant number of their names can be found amongst slave-trading records.[162] Many of these opportunists became investors in the slave trade by working their way up from the decks of Guinea vessels. Their experience in the trade gave them a key role in the management of Lancaster slavers and helped to make it a viable option for many years. Another important component of Lancaster's active slave-trading group were the wholesalers and craftsmen who had prospered on account of their existing business interests, and who were likewise keen to enter the world of transatlantic commerce. Some already had trading links with less distant venues in connexion with their original interests, but they had no secure footing in colonial commerce. These men attracted or were joined by passive, more casual speculators whose financial and other contributions were important to slave-trading operations.

The circumstances of merchants in other small ports in the region did not promote the same dependence on the slave trade. Their trading communities did not experience a similar expansion. Beckett comments on the small size of Whitehaven's merchant community, which reflected the port's more isolated location. The limited nature of Chester's resident merchant group is evident from Craig's observations that many investors in Chester shipping lived a considerable distance from the port. Meanwhile, Schofield shows that the small community at Preston and Poulton remained essentially unchanged, its development being confined to the flax merchants.[163] Smaller merchant communities meant less competition for their members. Chester merchants did face other problems, owing to limited opportunities in overseas trade, and the slave trade might have proved useful, if lack of local experience in colonial trade and competition from Liverpool had not thwarted its development. Meanwhile, Whitehaven merchants were able to invest in the coal and tobacco trades and those at Preston had ample opportunities through their manufacture of flax. The situation at Whitehaven did change with the failure of the tobacco trade, when the displaced merchants moved over to the slave trade, but otherwise there were fewer attractions towards, or needs for, the African trade than there were at Lancaster.

Lancaster's experience shows that, although a variety of people made up the town's slave-trading community, patterns are discernible and that active participants were united by a common need for the trade. This need was present in the ambitious young man, eager to gain access into transatlantic trade, in the dissatisfied merchant or wholesaler who wanted to diversify or extend his existing business interests and in the merchant who had been displaced from existing commerce. Their marginality encouraged a greater involvement in the slave trade and, as a result, these operators gained expertise in the management of their slavers, whilst those elsewhere never progressed much beyond the experimental phase and never developed any real degree of independence from Liverpool.

As the eighteenth century progressed, Lancaster's slave-trading community remained constant and compact as the number of West Indian merchants grew steadily. The more prosperous of these were the established élite and their associates, many of whom had flourished from time spent away in the Caribbean. The slave trade had filled a vacuum in Lancaster's transatlantic trade. However, as the century entered its last quarter, circumstances were changing. The African trade at Lancaster was becoming increasingly less viable and opportunities in direct colonial trade were expanding and developing.

Notes to Chapter III

1. D. Richardson, 'Profits in the Liverpool Slave Trade: the accounts of William Davenport', in Anstey and Hair, eds., *Slave Trade*, p. 81.
2. *Ibid.*, p. 63.
3. See J. F. Shepherd and G. M. Walton, *Shipping, Maritime Trade, and the Economic Development of Colonial North America* (Cambridge, 1972), pp. 38–41.
4. One minor exception concerns John Rawlinson, who owned a share in the *Sarah*, perhaps under the influence of his partner, William Lindow. See Liverpool Plantation Registers, 14 Oct. 1772.
5. Lancaster Friends' Meeting House, Yearly Meeting Papers (1694–1819), 2Ai(a) No.62, 1757.
6. Re. *Providence*, see P.R.O., C.O. 33/16, Part 2, 18 Nov. 1752 and C.O. 5/510, 28 Dec. 1752. For *Sally*, see C.O. 106/1, 7 Mar. 1767. For *Abbey*, see P.R.O., B.T. 6/188, 6 Nov. 1786.
7. John, Thomas, Abraham Rawlinson all had shares in West Indian Plantations. See their respective wills; Lancs. C.R.O., WRW/A, 1793, 1802, 1803. Thomas Rawlinson was criticized for his ownership of slaves. See Lancaster Monthly Meeting, Letters and Papers, Letter 24 Feb. 1792.
8. Eric Williams, *Capitalism and Slavery* (London, 1964, originally published 1944); Anstey, *Atlantic Slave Trade*, ch. 2; R. P. Thomas and R. N. Bean, 'The Fishers of Men: the Profits of the Slave Trade', *Journal of Economic History*, 34, 1974; Richardson, 'Davenport'.
9. Richardson, 'Costs of Survival', pp. 178–96.
10. Bowes and Gillison owned *Castleton*, P.R.O., C.O. 33/17, 9 Mar. 1765. Bowes jr. was executor for William Gillison, Lancs. C.R.O., WRW/A, 1780.
11. Free/App. Rolls, 24 Oct. 1743.
12. Free/App. Rolls, 27 Feb. 1750.

13. Free/App. Rolls, 24 May 1744.

14. William Lindow, Ulv.P.R., 16 Nov. 1724 (or 21 Oct. 1721, 23 Sept. 1734). Brother James Lindow, Ulv.P.R., 28 Dec 1725, F.R., 1751/52. James Lindow captained Lancaster slaver, *Castleton* (P.R.O., Adm. 7/89, 17 Jan. 1756) and West Indiamen and was agent for Rawlinsons (L.P.L., MS 197). A Jonathan Lindow, mariner of Ulverston died on African Coast (Lancs. C.R.O., WRW/F 1757).

15. As freeman, see L.P.L., 1768 Poll Book. Re. *Rawlinson* and *Lindow*, see L.P.L., Rawlinson Papers, MS 197. Re. *Hobby Horse*, see P.R.O., C.O. 106/1, 11 Oct. 1766.

16. Lancs. C.R.O., ARR/11. Abigail Rawlinson was the daughter of Abraham and Ellin Rawlinson, born 20 June 1740, see Lancaster Friends Meeting House, Monthly Meeting (Births).

17. Lancs. C.R.O., WRW/F, Thomas Todd, 1781 (originally of Ulverston). Also see Lancaster University, Gillow Archives, 344/52 (microfilm), Gillows' Ledger, 1776–1780.

18. Lancs. C.R.O., WRW/A, 1787.

19. Re. Dockray's apprenticeship, see Free/App. Rolls, 28 June 1748. Will of Miles Townson, Lancs. C.R.O., WRW/A, 1750. David Dockray as Port Commission, see L.P.L., P/C, Minutes.

20. P.R.O., Adm. 7/86, 22 Sept. 1749 and Free/App. Rolls, 19 Nov. 1746.

21. Guildhall Library, 11936, Sun Fire Office, 1755. P/C, Minutes.

22. Lancs. C.R.O., WRW/A, 1776.

23. David Benson and William Fletcher may also have dealt in slaves. They registered the *King George* in Barbados which ferried 57 slaves from Bridgetown to Tortola (P.R.O., C.O. 33/17, 3 Jan. 1764).

24. A lease made by his trustees specifies the inclusion of 'all Negroes and Slaves, men, women and children and their progeny'. See Manchester Central Library, Lancs. Deeds, L. 248, 1787. Reference supplied by Janet Nelson.

25. Liv. R.O. (Islington), Plantation Registers, 14 Oct. 1772 and *W.L.A.*, 26 Nov. 1773.

26. Gillow Archives, 344/161 (microfilm).

27. Re. Quay Lots, see P/C, 'Accounts on the Reserved Rents on the Quay Lands for 1760'. Re. London office, see Ingram, 'Furniture Firm', p. 22.

28. For example, in 1752 the *Providence* carried a small parcel of mahogany furniture to Barbados for the Rawlinsons (P.R.O., C.O. 33/16, part II). In 1785 the Rawlinsons exported furniture valued at £2,436.5s.8d to the plantations; see Schofield, *Economic History of Lancaster*, Part I, p. 44.

29. Re. Gillow's ownership of *Africa*, see Gillow Archives, 344/161 (microfilm). Re. *Africa* as slaver, see P.R.O., Adm. 7/87–89. The *Africa* was sold by Gillow in 1757 'with all her guinea materials', and as 'suitable for the African or W.I. trade', *W.L.A.*, 19 Aug. 1757.

30. Agents like Charles Inman, Benjamin Satterthwaite and Thomas Millerson.

31. Thomas Pennant, *A Tour of Scotland* (1774).

32. Davis, *Shipping Industry*, p. 19.

33. The volatile nature of the trade has no doubt played a part in fuelling the

debates on profitability which have persisted over many years. More recently J. E. Inikori ('Market Structure and the Profits of the British African Trade in the Late Eighteenth Century', *Journal of Economic History*, 41, 1981) and W. Darity ('The Numbers Game and the Profitability of the British Trade in Slaves', *Journal of Economic History*, 45, 1985) have argued in favour of its profitability.

34. Hyde, Parkinson and Marriner, 'Liverpool Slave Trade', p. 369.

35. Re. Chester, Preston and Poulton, see Schofield, 'Slave Trade', pp. 40 and 44. Re. Whitehaven, see Hughes, *North Country Life*, p. 45 and P.R.O., B.T. 6/7 and B.T. 6/3 (bundle B, 57–118).

36. Sources: various shipping documents cited throughout this book. The figures will be underestimates, given incomplete ownership details of Lancaster slavers. Where captains owned a share in their vessels, they have been counted only once, as captains.

37. See Schofield, 'Slave Trade', pp. 40 and 44 and 'Chester Partnerships', p. 187.

38. This date marks the time when Lancaster's first Guinea captain progressed to become a slave merchant. It also saw the end of a period of peace. By this time Lancaster had experienced twenty years in the trade, and more importantly ten years of continuous trading.

39. MacInnes, 'Bristol Slave Trade', p. 169.

40. At Bristol the age of slave-ship managers was around thirty years, if they had connexions with merchant families, or nearer forty if they were tradesmen, or tradesmen's sons. See D. Richardson, *The Bristol Slave Traders: A Collective Portrait* (Bristol Historical Association pamphlet, 1985), p. 23.

41. Sources: various shipping documents cited throughout this book, also F.R.; Free/App. Rolls; L/c P.R.; Quaker Registers, transcribed by W. G. Howson (1954) at Lancaster University; Guildhall Library, Insurance Policies. The slave merchants exact year of entry is not always clear owing to incomplete ownership details. William Butterfield, for instance, may have entered the trade with his brother in 1744.

42. As freemen, see F.R. On Heathcote's apprenticeship, see Free/App. Rolls, 28 Apr. 1749. Re. his marriage, see Schofield, 'Benjamin Satterthwaite', p. 161. Although Heathcote and his wife were Quakers, they married in an Anglican church, but were reinstated as Quakers the following year. Maybe his slaving activities were responsible. Re. Foster's marriage, see Lancaster Quaker Registers, transcribed Howson, 23 Mar. 1758

43. Re. Foster's ownership of *Barlborough* and *Bold*, see L.P.L., Cross Fleury's Journal and Free/App. Rolls, 2 May 1757. Re. Heathcote's share in *Bold*, see P.R.O., C.O. 33/17, 16 Nov. 1756. Heathcote was registered as an owner of a third slaver the *Cato*, see P.R.O., C.O. 5/510, 6 Sept. 1758. His son was later to invest in the slave trade in 1774.

44. Re. Thomas Satterthwaite, see below, pp. 132–133. Re. Benjamin Satterthwaite, see ch. 2, pp. 93–97. Re. William Satterthwaite, see Donnan, ed., *Slave Trade*, vol. 4, pp. 76–79.

45. Re. *Barlborough's* auction, *W.L.A.*, 21 Apr. 1758. Re. Heathcote's death, see Quaker Registers, 28 Mar. 1758.

46. Hamer, ed., *Laurens Papers*, vol. 2, pp. 496 and 520, Letters to Myles Birket. Re. Foster as part-owner of *Hawke*, see Free/App. Rolls, 2 May 1757.

47. Although Helme was elected a Port Commissioner in 1755, a year prior to his investment in a slaver, and John Thompson was described as a merchant when freeman in 1744, this more likely reflected their involvement in local trade in connexion with supplies for their businesses. See P/C., Minutes and F.R.

48. Hyde, Parkinson and Marriner, 'Liverpool Slave Trade', p. 373.

49. Hamer, ed., *Laurens Papers*, vol. 1, pp. 288–9, Letter to Thompsons, 5 July 1755, and vol. 2, p. 269, Letter to Thompsons, 24 July 1756.

50. Guildhall Library, 11936, Sun Fire Office, 7 Mar. 1758.

51. Free/App. Rolls, 21 Mar. 1739, son of Nicholas Thompson, late of Myerside in Cartmel, yeoman deceased.

52. P/C., Tonnage Book, 1750, 27 July 1751. The vessel was probably named after MacMillan's son Robert, who moved to Liverpool and was himself sending slave ships to Africa by the 1760s.

53. P.R.O., C.O. 33/16, Inwards, 30 Sept. 1752; Outwards, 18 Nov. 1752- cargo: 58 hogshead and 14 tierces rum, 6150 rum and 5 tons fustick.

54. See above, ch. 1, p. 33.

55. For Rope-walk, see Free/App. Rolls, 8 Aug. 1741. As linen and wine merchants, see Gillow Archives.

56. A. Eaglesham notes the frequency with which tradesmen, with different specialities, who were involved in importing raw materials, acquired the vaguer generic term 'merchant', Eaglesham, 'West Cumberland Shipping', p. 317.

57. See Free/App. Rolls.

58. See above, ch. 1, p. 31.

59. Re. William Butterfield's marriage, see L/c P.R., 29 Jan. 1742. Re. Thomas Butterfield's marriage, see Robert Lawson's will, Lancs. C.R.O., WRW/A, 1735.

60. P.R.O., C.O. 142/15, 10 July 1747; C.O. 5/1446, 24 Aug. 1752; C.O. 5/1448, 2 Oct. 1759; C.O. 5/510, 13 Oct. 1760.

61. *Castleton, Lowther, Reynolds II, Norfolk, Molly I.*

62. On Touchet's ownership, see P.R.O., C.O. 142/15, 23 July 1747, outwards. For Butterfield's ownership, see Liverpool Plantation Registers, 7 Dec. 1747. For *Reynold II*'s African voyage, see *L.L.*, 1 July 1755 and 3 Oct. 1755.

63. Lancs. C.R.O., WRW/A, 1747.

64. John Langton was 62 years, John Birley 43 years and William Shepherd 44 years old. See Singleton, 'Flax Merchants', pp. 81, 82, 84 (family trees) and 89 (Baltic trade).

65. They retained some interest in the slave trade at Liverpool in the late 1760s, but left the organization to the experts. See Schofield, 'Slave Trade', p. 45.

66. James Spedding was 36 years old when he invested in *Black Prince*, see Beckett, *Coal and Tobacco*, p. 114.

67. Whitehaven tobacco merchants who invested in the slave trade included

Thomas Hartley, James Spedding, William Gilpin and Peter How. They had probably copied an earlier example, Walter Lutwidge; see above, ch. 1, p. 33.

68. Satterthwaite and Inman owned the *Swallow*, 1753–56 (*W.L.A.*, 27 Aug. 1756); the *Gambia*, 1755–56 (Hamer, ed., *Laurens Papers*, vol. 2, p. 35) and the *Marlborough* (Hamer, ed., *Laurens Papers*, vol. 3, pp. 9–11).

69. As freemen, see F.R.. Re. Miles Townson's will, see Lancs. C.R.O., WRW/A, 1750.

70. For Satterthwaite's partnership with Rawlinsons and Dillworths, see Free/App. Rolls, 15 May 1751. Re. his marriage, see M.B., 5 Oct. 1750. Re. Benjamin Satterthwaite's marriage, see Appendix B.

71. Free/App. Rolls, 16 July 1763. Significantly, there is no mention of Thomas' name in these rolls from 1751 to 1759.

72. Lancaster Friends Meeting House, Preparative Meetings, 2 Dec. and 30 Dec. 1764.

73. For Inman's apprenticeship, see Free/App. Rolls, 1 May 1741. As Gillow's agent, see Gillow Archives, 344/161 (microfilm), letters to Inman, Inman and Peel, Inman and Cort.

74. Charles Inman and Thomas Satterthwaite's elder brother, Benjamin, had both married daughters of John Casson, see Hamer, ed., *Laurens Papers*, vol. 2, p. 35n. Re. Inman's death, see *G.L.A.*, 16 Oct 1767. Concerning Thomas Satterthwaite as executor, see Hamer, ed., *Laurens Papers*, vol. 2, p. 36n; as guardian, see Schofield, 'Benjamin Satterthwaite', p. 165n.

75. Re. Inman as a successful resident merchant in Jamaica, see Benjamin Satterthwaite's Letterbook, 1764–67. Inman may of course have supplemented these business pursuits with an interest in slave cargoes in Jamaica.

76. Haworth owned shares in *Molly I*, see P.R.O., C.O. 5/511, 17 July 1765 (misnamed *Africa* inwards and *Mary* outwards), *Norfolk*, see Liverpool Plantation Registers, 20 June 1769, and possibly in the *Reynolds*, see Plantation Registers, 7 Dec. 1747. He was trustee in Thomas Butterfield's will, Lancs. C.R.O., WRW/A, 1747, and a fellow mortgagee with William Butterfield on a dwelling house in Market Street, Lancaster, see Guildhall Library, 11936, Sun Fire Office Insurance Records, 1758.

77. Schofield, 'Chester Partnerships', pp. 187–188.

78. Bagnall disappeared from London Directories after 1754 and his will of 1766 made no reference to any mercantile activity, see *ibid*.

79. Incomplete data may underplay their total involvement.

80. Hamer, ed., *Laurens Papers*, vol. 2, Letters to Helme and Fowler, 18 Apr. 1757, Thompsons, 20 Apr. 1757 and Augustus and John Boyd, London, 23 Apr. 1757.

81. Active Guinea captains who owned shares in their vessels have not been included. These calculations are necessarily underestimates. The ownership of at least 27 slavers is unknown and partnership details are often summaries. Details of the number of voyages these vessels undertook would reveal more about commitment levels, but insufficient information of the precise dating of registrations makes this difficult. Some Lancastrian slave traders moved to Liverpool and owned more vessels there.

82. L.P.L., MS 378, *Hope*'s Package Book.
83. Anderson, 'Lancashire Bill System', p. 61.
84. Several Lancaster Guinea captains, such as Samuel Kilner and James Kendall moved to Liverpool, to own slave ships there.
85. See above, ch. 2, pp. 50–51.
86. This is evident from a study of local government officers and from insurance and probate records.
87. Re. Dodson's death, see Lancs. C.R.O., WRW/A, 1779 (wills); re. Millerson's burial, see L/c P.R., 13 June 1777; re. Addison's burial, see Lancaster Priory Church, original registers, 13 Jan. 1788.
88. Sawrey commanded *Sally III*, see P.R.O., Adm. 7/100, 10 Aug. 1776 and BT 6/3, 22 Sept. 1776 and *L.L.*, 27 June 1777.
89. See below, ch. 4, pp. 194.
90. *Sally III*, see Liverpool Plantation Registers, 13 Jan. 1781.
91. See Ulv.P.R., 15 Feb. 1728/29 (baptism, Robert Dodson) and 4 Oct. 1730 (baptism, Richard Millerson). Together they were part-owners of *Antelope II* (1763–71), *King Tom* (1764–65), *Prince George II* (1764–65), *Pitt* (1765–66), *Prince George III* (1766–1770) and *Warren* (1770–77).
92. See Ulv.P.R., 9 June 1739 (baptism, John Addison). Re. marriage which linked Dodson and Addison families, see M.B., 28 Apr. 1741 (Thomas Addison to Ann Dodson). John Addison commanded the *Britannia* for Richard Millerson and the *Prince George II* and *III* for Dodson and Millerson. For Millerson as Addison's bondsman, see Lancs. C.R.O., ARR/11, 1771.
93. Millerson, Dodson and Addison owned the *Warren*, 1770–1777, see Davies-Davenport Papers, Bead Book, 4 Jan. 1770, and *G.L.A.*, 7 Nov. 1777.
94. Re. Sawrey's baptism, see H/h.P.R., 28 Feb. 1744–45. Sawrey was master of Woodburne's *Sarah* and *Sally III*. Re. Woodburne in Overton, see Guildhall Library, MS 7253/1, Royal Exchange, 28 Feb. 1774. Addison and Sawrey had shares in *Sally III*, *Old England*, *Molly III* and *Mungo*. Re. *Jenny*, see Lancaster Shipping Registers, 15 Apr. 1788. Woodburne's career was similar to the others. He commanded 5 African voyages over 7 years. He retired from the sea aged ca. 31 years and was elected a port commissioner 4 years later in 1776. However, he left the slave trade permanently during the American War after 5 years of ownership, selling his share in *Sally III* to Sawrey (Lloyds Shipping Register, 1778).
95 They included William Watson, Thomas Willock, a partner of John Addison, and Robert Worswick, a Lancaster banker.
96. For Thomas Hinde as alderman and mayor, see L.P.L., Lancaster Poll Books 1768, 1784 and 1786 and W. O. Roper, 'History of Lancaster, Part 2', *Chetham Society*, New Series, 62, 1907. He was Mayor in 1769 and 1778. Re. his baptism see Lancs. C.R.O., PR 493, Caton Parish Registers. Concerning Hinde and his brothers as beneficiaries, see Lancs. C.R.O., WRW/A, 1727, Thomas Hinde and 1735, Richard Hinde.
97. P/C., Minutes, 1755, 1761, 1764, 1773.
98. As master of *Jolly Batchelor*, see Mediterranean Passes, 1748–1752 (P.R.O., Adm. 7/84–87). Re. share in this vessel, see Hamer, ed., *Laurens Papers*, vol. 2, p. 49.

99. *Duke of Cumberland, Lancaster, Prince George I, Cato, Juba I, Rainbow, Marquis of Granby, Thetis II, Lion, Antelope II, Minerva II, Thomas and John. Betty, Hinde I, Nancy III, Africa II.*

100. Re. Hinde's death, see *G.L.A.*, 8 Feb. 1798. Re. his share in Liverpool slavers, see P.R.O., T 64/286, Slavers from Liverpool, 1789–1795.

101. Lancs. C.R.O., WRW/A, 1798.

102. It has already been mentioned that some members of the Hinde family also served as commission agents for African cargoes in the West Indies. See above ch. 2, pp. 81–82.

103. R. C. Jarvis, 'Customs Letter-Books of the Port of Liverpool', *Chetham Society*, 3rd Series, 6, 1954, p. 151.

104. The Hindes' mill was just south of Lancaster, at Dolphinholme, see J. W. A. Price, *Industrial Archeology of the Lune Valley* (N.W. Regional Studies, University of Lancaster, Occasional Paper, no. 13, 1983), pp. 22–3. When Thomas Hinde junior died, he left extensive land and property (including Undercroft Hall, Ellel) and some coal mines. See Lancs. C.R.O., WRW/A, 1829.

105. L.P.L., loose leaf in political collection.

106. P.R.O., C.O. 5/710, 31 July 1766

107. See ch. 2, p. 79.

108. Lancs. C.R.O.,WRW/A, 1766.

109. William and John Watson were partners in the *Prince George II*, *King Tom* and *Pitt*. Re. bead sale, see Davies-Davenport Papers, Bead Book, 27 May 1750.

110. In addition to those he owned with his brother, he owned *Cato, Marlborough, Juba I, Molly I, II* and *IV, Tartar, Prince George III, Hope II* and *Tom*.

111. Re. financial problems, see Benjamin Satterthwaite Letter Books at Lancaster University, Letters in Nov. 1777 to his son John and to Sargents, Chambers and Co. The Watsons were surety for a Dublin firm for £20,000. Re. Watson's death, see Lancs. C.R.O., Bishops Transcripts (DRB/2/1266), 28 Aug. 1793.

112. Cumbria Record Office (Kendal), WPR/7, Crosby-Ravensworth Parish Register, 1692–1748.

113. As headmaster, see L.P.L., Hewitson's Memoranda, vol. 1, p. 407. Re. 'Samboo's Elegy' see L.P.L., Lonsdale Magazine, vol. 3, 1822, pp. 190–192.

114. Re. father's death, see Cumbria Record Office (Carlisle), Administrative Bond of James Watson, 1755. As freeman, see Free/App. Rolls, 28 Aug. 1756. Re. *Cato*, see P.R.O., C.O. 5/510, 6 Sept. 1758. As Port Commisioner see P/C., Minutes, 1758.

115. Gillow Archives, 344/20 (Day Book, 1756–62) and 344/50 (Ledger, 1763–68).

116. Free/App. Rolls, 7 Oct. 1760.

117. Watson and Inman were both trustees in 1757 for Roger Walshman, a Lancaster tallow-chandler who originated from Preston. Re. William Watson's marriage to Millicent Satterthwaite, see Lancs. C.R.O., ARR/11, 1761 and International Genealogical Index, 14 May 1761, St. Mary's, Lancaster.

118. P.R.O., C.O. 5/510, 10 July 1759.

119. Liverpool Plantation Registers, 16 May 1759.

120. Watson owned vessels with Captains Hinde, Millerson, Dodson and finally Sawrey.

121. Lancs. C.R.O., WRW/A, 1753.

122. See L/c P.R., baptisms, 22 Apr. 1733. Re. ownership of *Cato*, see P.R.O., C.O. 5/510, 6 Sept.1758.

123. Guildhall Library, 11936, Sun Fire Office, 1754/55. One of the tenants was Barber's brother-in-law, Guinea Captain Thomas Fell (M.B., 16 Aug. 1752).

124. W. O. Roper, ed., 'Materials for the History of the Church of Lancaster, Part 3', *Chetham Society*, New Series, 58, 1906, p. 631. P/C., Minutes, 9 June 1756.

125. P.R.O., C.O. 33/16, pt. 2, 17 Nov. 1752 (*Brothers*).

126. They were co-partners in the *Cato*, *Juba I*, *Rainbow*, *Lion* and *Thetis II*, and probably in the *Marquis of Granby*.

127. P/C., Minutes, 1761. P.R.O., Inland Revenue (I.R.) 1/23, 7 Feb. 1763 (Apprenticeship Registers, City).

128. See F.R., 1751/52 and 'Shaw's Liverpool Directory, 1767', in *T.H.S.L.C.*, 78, 1929. Kilner had commanded the Lancaster slaver *Gambia* in 1757, see P.R.O., Adm. 7/90, 9 Sept. 1757.

129. Liv. R.O., Liverpool's Freemen's Committee Book, 1756–95 (ref. 352 CLE/REG 1/1) and Liverpool's Fine for Admitting Freemen, 1746–90 (ref. 352 CLE/REG 1/7).

130. See Liverpool Plantation Registers and William Davenport's Bead Book.

131. Barber's strong commitment is evident from his experimentation with larger vessels, see above, ch. 2, pp. 41–42, his establishment of a slave factory on the Isle de Los, see ch. 2, p. 59, and his sole ownership of a number of slavers.

132. Re. Kilner's death, see Lancs. C.R.O., WCW/Admon, 7 Aug. 1776. Re. the two Miles Barbers in Liverpool, see 'Shaw's Liverpool Directory, 1767'. For their admission to the African Company, see Liv. R.O., Committee Book of African Company, 1 July 1769 (ref. 352/MDi). Re. saddler son's death, see Lancs. C.R.O., WRW/1770. The saddler's son owned *Gannemaras* with his elder cousin, *Friendship* with Robert MacMillan and *Molly* with James Kendall and Andrew White. See Liverpool Plantation Registers, 1769.

133. See Liverpool Plantation Registers. MacMillan became a freeman of the African company at the same time as the Barbers. Kendall was master of Barber's slavers, the *Dove*, and *Thetis II* of Lancaster and later of *Martin*, *Grenada* and *Saville* at Liverpool. He was probably the son of a carpenter of Undermillbeck, Westmorland and apprenticed to Rawlinson (Free/App. Rolls, 1746). Dennison commanded the *Lowther*, *Molly I* and *Sally* of Lancaster, and later at least 5 Barber slavers at Liverpool. Both captains were in 'Shaw's Liverpool Directory, 1767'.

134. Guildhall Library, Lowndes Directory, 1787. Re. London registered vessels, see P.R.O., C.O. 76/5, *Hercules*, 27 Mar. 1786 and R. C. Jarvis and R. Craig, 'Liverpool Registry of Merchant Ships', *Chetham Society*, 3rd Series, 15, 1967, re. *King Jos*, 1786.

135. Lancs. C.R.O., WCW, 1836 (see 1842).

136. See above, ch. 2, pp. 88–89.

137. Lancs. C.R.O., WRW/A, 1778.

138. Rogers, ed., *Laurens Papers*, vol.5, p. 320, Letter to Richard King, 30 Sept. 1767.

139. Re. Wright's bankruptcy, see L.P.L., MS 245, William Hewitson's, 'Memoranda relating to Lancaster and district'. He was freeman of Lancaster in 1762/3, see F.R. Re. his taking on an apprentice, see Free/App. Rolls, 1764. As bondsman to a Preston Patrick couple, see Lancs. C.R.O., ARR/11, 1764. Re. own possible marriage, see M.B., 3 Oct. 1747.

140. Davies-Davenport Papers, William Davenport's Bead Book, 1767–69.

141. See Lancs. C.R.O., Debtors Insolvency Papers, QJB 41/1. Richard Kendall as captain, see P.R.O., Adm. 7/94–96, 1767–1771. Re. Kendall's marriage to Margaret Wright, see Lancs. C.R.O., ARR/11.

142. Both vessels were 70 tons. See Wright's Insolvency Papers. Re. shipwreck of *Agnes II*, see *L.L.*, 8 Jan. 1773.

143. Salisbury left a 90-acre farm with 380 sheep, see Lancs. C.R.O., WRW/A, 1787. I thank Janet Nelson for information about his father.

144. Free/App. Rolls, 1749; as freeman, see Lancaster Poll Book, 1768; re. quay lots and as wine merchant, see P/C., Minutes, 1756 and 1757.

145. Bodleian Library, Oxford, Sherard MS 477. Salisbury supplied the West Indies with hats in 1780s.

146. Benjamin Satterthwaite's Letter Book, 15 June 1764.

147. P/C., Minutes, 1761, 1767, 1773, 1779, 1785. For Salisbury's death, see St. John's Parish Register, 23 May 1785.

148. The *Molly*'s captain, John Read, died at Sierra Leone, see *Cumberland Pacquet*, 9 Feb. 1775. This precipitated the payment of a penal bond of £300 to Read's widow by Heathcote Rhodes of Barlborough, Derbyshire, see L.P.L., bond, 10 Oct. 1775. Salisbury and Heathcote-Rhodes were both John O'Gaunt Bowmen.

149. Liverpool Plantation Registers, 19 Oct. 1772.

150. Re. Simpson's marriage, see *W.L.A.*, 13 Sept. 1765. Re. ownership of *Pitt*, see P.R.O., C.O. 5/511, 26 Nov. 1765. His name does not recur in slaving records until the 1780s and 1790s, when he invested in four more slavers at Liverpool with the Hindes.

151. Liverpool Plantation Registers, 28 Aug. 1761.

152. Re. Preston's marriage, see Lancs. C.R.O., ARR/ 11, his bondsman was Robert Dodson. Re. will of slave merchant, see above, ch. 2, pp. 57–58.

153. Re. *Thetis*, see P.R.O., C.O. 5/510, 6 Sept. 1759 and Adm. 7/90, 18 Dec 1759 and *L.L.*, 3 Mar. 1761. Re. Preston's will, see Lancs. C.R.O., WRW/A, 1763.

154. P.R.O., Adm. 7/87, 9 Nov. 1750 (*Fortune*); /88, 2 Feb. 1753 (*Reynolds I*); /89, 4 July 1754 and 26 June 1758 (*Lowther*).

155. Re. *Gambia*, see Liverpool Plantation Registers, 26 Sept. 1764. Re. John Houseman's marriage, see M.B., 14 Oct. 1752.

156. Re. *Garnet*, see Liverpool Plantation Registers, 7 Aug. 1783. Re. Watson's marriage, see Lancs. C.R.O., ARR/ 11, 1768, the bondsman was John Houseman.

157. Drake, 'Liverpool–African Voyage', p. 129.

158. As mercer, see F.R., 1741/2. For his shares in the *Marlborough* and *Molly*, see P.R.O., C.O. 5/510, 10 July 1759 and 28 Nov. 1760 (outwards). His partners included Robert Dodson, Satterthwaite and Inman, and William Watson. Re. Quay lots and Port Commissioner, see P/C., Minutes, 17 Dec. 1756 and May 1758 and 1761.

159. Re. George Capstick's will, see Lancs. C.R.O., WRW/A, 1756. Re. *Stanley*, see P.R.O., Adm. 7/89, 5 July 1754 and C.O. 142/16, 30 Aug. 1755. For Benison's marriage to Mary Hinde, see M.B., 26 Nov. 1759.

160. Marshall, *Furness*, pp. 31–32.

161. The Dodson family of Ulverston are a good example. When John Dodson, yeoman, died in 1736 all his lands passed to his eldest son, John, whilst Robert Dodson, still a minor, was to go to sea and follow a career in the African trade.

162. Furness men who prospered through the Liverpool slave trade included Moses Benson, son of an Ulverston salt-dealer (see Lancs. C.R.O., WRW/F, John Benson) and John Bolton, son of an Ulverston apothecary (see Sir C. Jones, *John Bolton of Storrs*, Kendal, 1959). Before they entered the slave trade, Benson was a Lancaster West India captain, then factor in Jamaica, whilst Bolton was apprenticed to a West India firm in Liverpool, serving them in St. Vincent. Both died very wealthy men, Bolton retiring to Storrs Hall on Windermere, which is reputedly haunted owing to his part in the alleged murder of a West Indian Negress.

163. Beckett, *Coal and Tobacco*, p. 112, Craig, 'Chester Shipping', p. 53 and Schofield, 'Slave Trade', p. 61.

CHAPTER IV

The Changing Role of the Slave Trade at Lancaster

A study of the Lancaster slave trade would be far from complete if it failed to consider what role the trade played in the local economy. This is not only important to the local and regional history of North-Western England but also raises more general historiographical issues, notably the role of the slave trade in the British economy as a whole. It is also a necessary prelude to an understanding and evaluation of the decline of the trade in African slaves at Lancaster with which this chapter will also be concerned. The trade's impact on the economy will be considered in its broadest sense. The discussion will not be restricted to evaluating the trade in terms of its profitability. The lack of local business papers concerning the Lancaster slave trade, in any case, precludes such an endeavour. Moreover, a significant number of studies have seriously questioned its alleged contributions in terms of capital formation, whilst more recent research has suggested it played a significant role in the British economy, but as part of an interwoven Atlantic system with its effects being at once more modest and complex than Eric Williams has suggested.[1] Thus the aim here will be to assess the slave trade's more general standing at Lancaster, relative to other commerce, and thereby evaluate its overall impact in terms of general economic and commercial developments.

The role of the slave trade in the development of Lancaster has received little serious consideration. Two main factors seem to account for its ready dismissal.

First, the Lancaster slave trade had passed its peak when the trade received its greatest attention, that of its public scrutiny in the face of the abolitionists. There were only a handful of outfits being made when the abolitionist, Thomas Clarkson, visited the port in 1787, and of these he was largely dismissive because of their tendency to clear from Liverpool. Secondly, although Lancaster ranked as Britain's fourth slave-trading port, its share of the national trade was never impressive. This has been highlighted in Bryan Edwards' figures for the number of ships sailing from England in the slave trade together with their cargoes of black Africans in 1771.[2] This must be one of the most widely quoted set of statistics concerning the relative performance of the various ports in the Guinea trade and more especially for Lancaster since it alone is included alongside Britain's three main slave-trading ports. Edwards recorded Lancaster as sending just four slave ships out of a total of 192, which gives it 2.4 per cent of the trade.[3] These figures evoked a dismissive response from Gooderson in his social and economic history of Lancaster. He concluded, "Unlike Liverpool Lancaster derived little direct benefit from the slave trade."[4] This assessment relates to Lancaster's performance in the national slave trade. This is just one aspect. It does not consider the trade's significance in its local context. On the same count it might also be argued that Liverpool's high profile in the national slave trade has caused its role to be overstressed in terms of the local economy and the development of the town.

Lancaster's percentage of the national trade, as worked out from Edwards' figures, is not far removed from its average performance over a longer period of time. A set of statistics compiled by the Board of Trade covering the years 1757 to 1776, a period which encompassed much of Lancaster's activity in the slave trade, has made it possible to estimate Lancaster's share of the national trade in terms of clearances and tonnages. The findings are set out in Table 4.1 below.

Table 4.1   *Clearances and Tonnages of Vessels in African Trade, 1757–1776*[5]

Port	Clearances	Percentage of Total Clearances	Tonnage	Percentage of Total Tonnages
Liverpool	1609	54.2%	172,103	52.2%
London	691	23.3%	85,330	25.9%
Bristol	457	15.4%		
Lancaster	86	2.9%	5,674	1.7%
Whitehaven	46	1.5%	5,462	1.6%
Others	79	2.7%		
Total	2968	100.0%	329,391	100.0%

Lancaster's more meagre share of the total tonnage in the African trade is attributable to the fact that its slave ships were smaller than average.

These figures should be viewed with a certain amount of caution. In some respects they slightly underplay Lancaster's contribution to the national slave trade. This arises out of a complication of the Lancaster trade which poses a particular problem in its evaluation. There was a tendency for Lancaster merchants to clear a number of their vessels from or via Liverpool from time to time, this more commonly in the later decades of the eighteenth century.[6] Although this might indicate problems in the operation of the slave trade at Lancaster, such ventures were still funded by Lancaster–based capital and as such it is felt they should be included in the trade figures for Lancaster in any discussion on the Lancaster economy. Their inclusion gives some idea of Lancaster merchants' total investments in, and returns from, the African trade. Using the same tonnage figures compiled by the Board of Trade, it is possible to adjust the figures in table 4.1, as well as those recorded by Bryan Edwards, to get a more accurate picture of Lancaster merchants' total share of the trade. To do this Lancaster ventures which cleared direct from Liverpool need to be added to the Lancaster figures and removed from those for Liverpool, whilst those which cleared from Lancaster via Liverpool and appear twice in the tonnage figures, once for each of the two ports, need to be removed from the Liverpool figures. Between 1757 and 1776 thirty–seven ventures funded by Lancaster merchants appear in the Board's tonnage figures as clearances from Liverpool. Of these, thirteen are also present in the Lancaster sailings, suggesting these slavers set out from the Lune and proceeded via the Mersey. The remainder presumably embarked from Liverpool direct. Adjustments to the figures give Lancaster 3.5% of the total of African clearances and 2.2% of the total tonnage, whilst Liverpool's share changes to 53.4% and 51.6% respectively.[7] When Edwards' figures are adjusted in this way, as well as allowing for the extra Lancaster clearance given by the Board of Trade, the number of clearances rises from four to six, and in addition there is, according to my research, one further vessel. This not only increases Edwards' total by seventy-five per cent, giving Lancaster 3.6% of the clearances for that year, but also reminds us that even the Board of Trade figures were not fully comprehensive.[8]

Such changes to the Lancaster figures may be regarded as small when set in a national context, but they become of greater significance when assessing the role of the trade locally. Moreover, the readjusted averages and even the revised figures for 1771 do not reveal Lancaster's share of the national slave trade at its peak. This occurred in 1761, a year in which Lancaster merchants invested in ten ventures according to the Board of Trade tonnage figures, two of which sailed from Liverpool. The tonnage book kept by the Lancaster Port Commission adds one further vessel to those clearing from Lancaster, namely the hundred-ton *Eagle*.[9] Lancaster's share of the trade for this year in terms of sailings and tonnage is much more impressive if it is set out alongside the other slaving ports in the following table.

Table 4.2   *Clearances and Tonnages in the African Trade for 1761*

Port	Clearances	Percentage of Total Clearances	Tonnage	Percentage of Total Tonnage
Liverpool	68	55.3%	7,099	50.7%
London	19	15.5%	2,895	20.7%
Bristol	16	13.0%	1,940	13.8%
Lancaster	11	8.9%	1,080	7.7%
Whitehaven	6	4.9%	750	5.3%
Others	3	2.4%	248	1.8%
Total	123	100.0%	14,012	100.0%

These statistics are interesting not only because they depict Lancaster's share of the national trade at its height, but also because they show that this occurred when London and Bristol merchants were holding back in their slaving activities.[10] This presumably owed to the attacks merchant vessels were likely to suffer during the Seven Years War. Their geographical location made the north-west ports much safer centres of operation, and Lancaster's overall performance during this war shows that the merchants utilised the situation to good effect. Another interesting feature of table 4.2 is the disproportionate increase in Lancaster's share of the total tonnage. It was clearly a time when Lancaster slave merchants were trying out larger vessels, which included the 250-ton *Lion* owned by Thomas Hinde and Miles Barber.[11] Although larger vessels were undoubtedly an advantage during years of conflict, this development indicates that Lancaster merchants were both serious and optimistic about their slave trade at this time. If Thomas Clarkson had investigated the trade at this earlier date, his remarks would surely have been very different.

Lancaster slave traders, although they maintained a steady level of operation in the ensuing years, never succeeded in developing their trade along the lines hinted at in 1761. This leaves Lancaster's overall performance in the English slave trade slightly greater than has often been appreciated, but still of limited significance in national terms, except, it might be argued, in peak years like 1761. Meanwhile, Lancaster's unequalled position as a minor port operating in the slave trade cannot be denied. When the same statistics are viewed in the context of its local economy they are surely much harder to dismiss or belittle.

To get Lancaster's percentage of the national slave trade in some sort of perspective in terms of its role in the local economy, it is helpful to make a comparison with Lancaster's part in the national West India trade. The importance of the West India trade in the Lancaster economy and the development of the town has not been, and certainly should not be, questioned. It was undoubtedly the staple trade of Lancaster and its importance increased as the century progressed. It is, however, worth realising that even at its height the West India trade at Lancaster represented a fairly small percentage of the trade nationally. In 1787, a year which represented Lancaster's greatest level of activity to date and when it ranked as Britain's fourth largest port for West India trade, Lancaster merchants' share of the total clearances stood at 8 per cent,[12] whilst their share of the total tonnage was 5.2 per cent.[13] Of course the volume of the West Indies trade was far greater and therefore worth far more to the national and local economies than the slave trade. Even allowing for this, Lancaster's share of the West India trade does provide some sort of standpoint from which to view Lancaster's share of the national slave trade. It surely indicates that the slave trade's influence on the local economy needs more careful consideration. In Lancaster, the slave trade was important in itself, but much more so in its impact on the structure of the local economy.

It is undisputed that overseas trade, primarily that to the American colonies, was crucial to the development of eighteenth-century Lancaster. This gathered momentum during the second half of the century, to which contemporary guide-books lend ample testimony. One anonymous volume, written in 1776, reads:

> Camden says, in his time, the inhabitants were all husbandmen, but it is now more remarkable for commerce than agriculture, being at present a thriving corporation, with a tolerable harbour and custom-house ... Vessels of tolerable burthen go from hence to America, with earthenware and hardware, woollen manufactures etc., and import from thence sugar, rum, cotton-wool etc ...[14]

The slave trade's influence on the development of the port and the local economy would have been as part of this overseas commerce. Interestingly, another account, written at this time, particularised Lancaster's trans-Atlantic trade. In his 'Guide to the Lakes', published just two years later, Thomas West remarked, "the new houses are peculiarly neat and handsome, the streets are well paved and thronged with inhabitants busied in a prosperous trade to Guinea and the West Indies." This desciption, repeated in the British directory of 1799, shows some contemporary commentators, at least, considered the slave trade's impact on Lancaster's new-found prosperity important enough to be specifically mentioned.[15]

Colonial commerce was the life-blood of Lancaster during the second half of the eighteenth century. It had wide-reaching effects on the town and its hinterland. The town changed and grew predominantly

This late 18th-century view of St. George's Quay and the River Lune by
G. Pickering contrasts with Ralph's portrayal of the port some fifty years
earlier. *Courtesy of Lancaster City Museums*

from the effects of this developing commerce. It stimulated the
development of local industries, including ship-building and its allied
trades, furniture-making and a number of other manufactures of trade
goods. It encouraged the supply of certain provisions, especially
alcoholic beverages. Meanwhile, the colonial goods this commerce
brought back to Lancaster included the mahogany on which the town's
most famous manufacturers, the Gillows, depended. Tropical imports
were also responsible for the running of the sugar-house and local dye-
works. The distribution, including re-export, of colonial produce,
together with the collection of goods for outgoing cargoes and the
supply of shipping materials, promoted inland and coastal trade, as well
as commercial ties with Europe.[16] Importantly, overseas trade also
fostered the development of financial institutions, notably in banking
and insurance, together with a valuable, if less tangible, expansion of
commercial know-how, as evident in the growing number of firms in
local trade directories.[17]

What needs to be ascertained here is the strategic place of the
Lancaster slave trade within this commercial development. I would
suggest it played a more significant role than has generally been
appreciated. A useful way to evaluate the slave trade's impact at
Lancaster is to take certain aspects of colonial trade and calculate the

174

slave trade's part. This will give an indication of the slave trade's importance relative to other forms of overseas trade. The obvious aspects to consider are first the volume of ships employed in overseas trade at Lancaster, then the make-up of the local merchant community and finally the type of money involved in overseas trade.

The unpredictable nature of eighteenth-century overseas commerce, made worse in wartime, meant that a significant number of vessels leaving a port never returned. Slave ships, with their detour to Africa, obviously carried additional risks. There were problems with diseases, and slavers could be cut off by the natives. In 1761 the *Mary* of Lancaster was "cut off by the slaves and most of the people murdered". A similar fate befell the *Sally II* in 1774.[18] Slave ships were also particularly vulnerable on their approach to the West Indies in war time. In 1758 the *Minerva I* was taken by the French whilst carrying slaves to Antigua.[19] The dangers of eighteenth-century trade, and that of the African trade in particular, can be seen by comparing data on slaver clearances and returns. Approximately 150 voyages were undertaken by Lancaster-owned slavers in the period 1750 to 1776.[20] In only 110 cases did their crews pay into the local insurance scheme, recorded in the Lancaster Seamen Sixpence Accounts, a payment which was always made at the end of a voyage.[21] Of course misfortune was not the only reason for crews' failing to pay into the Lancaster scheme. A returning ship's captain was sometimes instructed to unlade in a larger port. Captain Saul presumably had such directions when he brought the *Rainbow* back to Liverpool from Antigua in 1761,[22] although this practice does not seem to have been very prevalent. Given the differences between clearances and returns, it would obviously be desirable to consider them separately when assessing the slave trade's representation in Lancaster's colonial commerce. Unfortunately, more research is needed into overseas clearances before this can be done. What will be attempted here is an assessment according to the number of vessels returning to Lancaster, for which there is adequate information. This should give a reasonable indication of the overall trends of the slave trade's relative importance in Lancaster shipping, even though it will tend slightly to underestimate the slave trade's share of investments.

The Lancaster Seamen's Sixpence Accounts serve as a valuable document in making an appraisal of the slave trade's share of colonial commerce. They have been chosen in preference to the more widely quoted Lancaster Port Commission Tonnage Registers because of their clearer and more comprehensive portrayal of colonial trade and in particular that of the African trade.[23] They do, however, have an obvious shortcoming. Their particulars do not include tonnage figures. It would therefore be wise at this point to consider whether

Compensation for the widows of two seamen, killed by slaves aboard the *Mary* of Lancaster on the Coast of Guinea. Extract from Seamen's Relief Book. *Courtesy of Lancaster Library*

the average slaver would have been very different in size from the average colonial merchantman. It has already been seen how the inclusion of tonnage figures coloured the picture of Lancaster's part in the national slave trade. The Port Commission Tonnage Books do provide useful information here. Schofield has used them to work out the number of ships and their tonnage for Lancaster's total overseas trade for the period 1757 to 1800, distinguishing each decade. The figures can be used to calculate the average tonnage of a ship in overseas trade and the results compared with the average size of a Lancaster slaver. The findings are given in Table 4.3.

Table 4.3 *Relative Tonnages* of Vessels in Overseas Trade at Lancaster*[24]

	Average Tonnage of an Overseas Vessel	Average Tonnage of a Slaving Vessel	Slaving Vessel as percentage of Overseas Vessel
1757–1760	91 tons	89 tons	97.8%
1761–1770	110 tons	96 tons	87.2%
1771–1780	114 tons	84 tons	73.7%

* These are *Quay* Tonnages. This measurement is larger than tonnage burthen used in many other shipping records.

These figures imply that, although the Lancaster slave merchants' share of incoming tonnage would have been slightly less than their share of the number of returning vessels, the differences were of limited significance, at least before the slave trade's share of transatlantic trade fell to very low levels, that is after 1776. In other words, whilst these findings should be kept in mind when evaluating the information on incoming ships which follows, they should not alter the impressions given in any dramatic sense.

The two graphs overleaf, which have been constructed from the Seamen's Sixpence Accounts, cover the years 1755 to 1780, a period which encompasses Lancaster's greatest involvement in the slave trade and also the beginnings of its decline. Graph A depicts the relative performances of the two types of transatlantic trade in terms of the numbers of vessels involved. This in turn provides a context for Graph B which illustrates what percentage of Lancaster's colonial fleet was employed in the African trade at any one time.

That Lancaster slave merchants ever owned anything in the region of a third of the returning transatlantic fleet, as they evidently did in the years 1755 to 1757, might surprise anyone who doubted the slave trade ever played a significant part in the development of Lancaster. The port reputedly entered its golden age of shipping around 1750,[25] and these statistics can only portray the African trade as a sizeable contributor to the pronounced expansion in colonial trade. Admittedly, the size of Lancaster slave ships was generally small at this time. The average vessel during the years 1755 to 1757 weighed sixty-five tons.[26] However, if this was substantially less than the average ship trading with the colonies at this time, which is not known without further research, the slave trade's significance to the port would almost certainly have been compensated for in other ways owing to the complex nature of an undertaking in the Guinea trade.[27] Although the slave trade's share of transatlantic trade never reached such heights again, it did maintain a significant share at least until 1767. This was

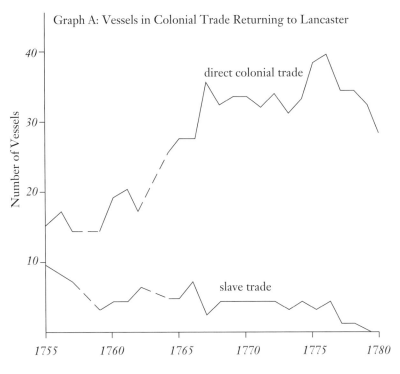

Graph A: Vessels in Colonial Trade Returning to Lancaster

direct colonial trade

slave trade

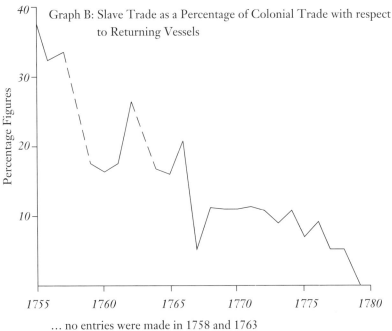

Graph B: Slave Trade as a Percentage of Colonial Trade with respect to Returning Vessels

... no entries were made in 1758 and 1763

178

Lancaster shipping alongside St. George's Quay, about 1790, by G. Yates. The view depicts substantial warehousing around Richard Gillow's noble Custom House, built in 1764 when the slave trade was thriving. *Courtesy of Lancaster City Museums*

most impressive in 1762 and again in 1766. The first date reflects the fact that Lancaster slave merchants had made their highest number of investments ever in the trade during the previous year.[28] Seventeen-sixty-six, meanwhile, witnessed the largest number of slavers returning to Lancaster since 1757. The ten years leading up to 1767 also saw a definite increase in the tonnages of Lancaster Guineamen.[29] This meant that the slave trade was of greater overall dimensions in absolute terms than it had been before, or indeed was ever to be again. Moreover, its percentage of the total incoming tonnage in transatlantic trade at this time may well have been greater than it was between 1755 and 1757, for it seems likely that the size of slaving vessels had increased disproportionately to that of West Indiamen.

In this period, therefore, the slave trade continued or even increased its significance as an area of commercial enterprise for Lancaster merchants. All this was to change in 1767, however, when investments in colonial trade rose sharply to reach unprecedented levels. It was also a year in which the number of homecoming slavers happened to be particularly low.[30] The loss of two, probably three, Lancaster slavers, which had set sail the previous year, was largely responsible for this. The *Nancy II* and probably the *Bridget and Mary* were lost on the African coast, whilst the *Marquis of Granby* was wrecked off Cumberland on its voyage to the Isle de Los. Meanwhile, a fourth vessel

179

clearing that same year had returned to Liverpool.[31] This resulted in the sharp fall in the slave trade's share of transatlantic trade that year, after which a limited recovery took place until the American War of Independence. During these years, however, Lancaster never had as many Guineamen returning up the Lune as it had during previous years of peace.[32] The average size of these later vessels had fallen a little as well. This reduced the slave trade's relative standing in Lancaster's colonial commerce, as did the continuing higher levels of direct trade with the Caribbean islands. The effects of the latter are well illustrated when comparing the slave trade's share of transatlantic trade in 1760 with that of 1770. The number of slavers returning to Lancaster was identical for each of these years (Graph A). Yet, whereas the slave trade had represented almost 17 per cent of colonial trade in 1760, this had fallen to 11 per cent by 1770 (Graph B). After 1776, with the advent of war, the slave trade declined rapidly and despite a brief resurgence in the mid 1780s, so did its significance to the port of Lancaster, as direct trade to the colonies flourished.[33] To summarize, the information shown in Graphs A and B depicts the slave trade as playing a significant and, on occasions, substantial role in the commercial life and development of Lancaster until the mid-1760s. In 1767, however, its representation in the homecoming fleet fell dramatically. Despite a limited recovery, the slave trade's future standing was always offset by the new levels of direct trading with the Caribbean islands.

A brief recourse to the slave trade's performance elsewhere relative to other trades, serves as a useful comment at this point. Richardson has made some similar comparisons for Bristol's trade; though he compares clearances rather than returns and uses figures for overseas trade rather than just colonial trade. His findings show that, for the most part, Bristol slavers constituted 6 to 9 per cent of annual clearances overseas. It rose to 12 per cent of the clearances at the height of Bristol's involvement in the trade around 1730.[34] In table 4.4, Lancaster slavers have been compared to the port's overseas shipping. The figures represent vessels returning to Lancaster.

Table 4.4 *The Slave Trade's Representation in Overseas Trade at Lancaster*[35]

	Overseas Vessels Returning to Lancaster Total Number	Slave Ships Returning to Lancaster Total Number	Slavers as Percentage of Overseas Vessels
1759–1762	108	17	15.7%
1764–1767	166	19	11.4%
1768–1771	178	16	8.9%
1772–1775	193	14	7.2%

These figures suggest the slave trade's representation in overseas trade at Lancaster could have been more prominent than it was at Bristol for a time. However, caution should be exercised in making such comparisons. Bristol slavers were larger than most other ships leaving the port, according to Richardson. Moreover, his figures include the Irish trade. Even so, it seems that, whilst the slave trade's impact on Bristol may have been exaggerated in the past, at Lancaster the very opposite has taken place.

If the slave trade's share of overseas trade was significant for a period, how important was it to Lancaster's merchant society in general, and what role did the African merchants play within this society and in the development of their port? Relevant aspects to consider concern the size of the slave-trading community relative to the merchant community as a whole, and perhaps more importantly, the influence these merchants exerted. Schofield, in his study of the slave trade at Lancaster concludes, "There was never a large community of slave traders among the merchants of the port."[36] Of course one needs to stipulate exactly what type of person one is considering as a merchant. In the eighteenth century a wide variety of people concerned themselves in trade to varying degrees. Any of these might have called themselves merchants and have been listed as such. Even when the term 'merchant' was used more sparingly, the relative involvement and importance of each individual is hard to decipher. Fortunately, there is one useful set of documents which convey information about the more active and influential merchants operating in the Port of Lancaster. These are the Minute Books of the Lancaster Port Commission.[37] Before examining their contents, it would be advantageous to ascertain the African merchants' representation within a somewhat broader merchant group, so as to put their involvement in the Lancaster Port Commission in some sort of perspective. There is a useful list of merchants' and traders' names which appeared as signatures to a letter written in 1766 to one of Lancaster's M.P.s, Sir George Warren, thanking him for his efforts to promote colonial trade at Lancaster.[38] Although its political nature no doubt meant some merchants did not sign it, the letter's seventy-nine signatures suggest it is sufficiently comprehensive to allow for an analysis of the shipowners of the port together with the wholesalers who were involved in export. Thirteen merchants, actively engaged in the slave trade at this time, put their names to the letter, which means they constituted 16.4 per cent of this merchant group: a limited presence perhaps, but one that under-estimates their role in the development of the port according to the Port Commission records.[39]

The Minute Books of the Lancaster Port Commission list the sixteen commissioners or trustees who were elected every three years with the responsibility of performing various functions to improve their port and promote trade. These offices were rotated amongst Lancaster's more active merchants, a group which seemed to number between twenty-two and twenty-eight members. The sixteen commissioners or trustees were elected by fellow members of this group. The lists provide a valuable means of assessing the slave trade's representation amongst this committed and influential organization. Surveying the names of elected port commissioners for the years 1755 to 1782 reveals that Lancaster merchants involved in the slave trade were well represented. The findings are set out in table 4.5. The number of African merchants at Lancaster may not have been large, but they evidently played a very active and prominent role in the management of their port and its trade for some years.

Table 4.5 *Lancaster Slave Traders as Port Commissioners*

Duration of Office	Slave Merchants elected as Port Commissioners	Slave Traders' Percentage of elected Body of Port Commissioners	Additional Commissioners with singular Investments in Slave Trade during their Period in Office
1755–1758	John Heathcote, John Helme, Thomas Hinde, Charles Inman, Robert Thompson, Dodgson Foster.	37.5	
1758–1761	William Butterfield, Thomas Satterthwaite, William Watson, Miles Mason.	25.0	
1761–1764	Thomas Hinde, Miles Barber, Miles Mason, John Watson, Thomas Houseman, Thomas Satterthwaite.	37.5	
1764–1767	Thomas Hinde, William Watson, Robert Dodson, Richard Millerson	25.0	Samuel Simpson, Henry Fell
1767–1770	John Watson, Edward Salisbury.	12.5	
1770–1773	William Watson, Robert Dodson, Richard Millerson.	18.75	Richard Salisbury, John Rawlinson
1773–1776	John Addison, John Watson, Thomas Hinde, Edward Salisbury.	25.0	John Rawlinson, Edward Whiteside, William Lindow
1776–1779	William Watson, Richard Millerson, Thomas Woodburne.	18.75	
1779–1782	John Addison.	6.25	John Satterthwaite

The African merchants' greatest representation as commissioners clearly matches the period when the African trade held its greatest share in the volume of colonial trade, between 1755 and 1767. Their level of involvement and influence is not hard to understand when one considers how few merchants controlled bilateral colonial trade at this time. The Rawlinsons, for example, owned at least eight of the seventeen vessels returning from the West Indian and mainland American colonies in 1756.[40] This would leave the six known slaving partnerships, with vessels involved in the African trade at that time, as constituting a large proportion of the remaining merchants in transatlantic trade.[41] It is also worth remembering, at this point, that investments made in the slave trade generally represented a deeper level of commitment than those made in other trades, since slave-ship proprietors were also, as a matter of course, owners of the cargo as well.[42] This had the effect of concentrating the investments in fewer hands, relative to other trades, and it would have heightened the slave merchants' involvement in, and their awareness of, all aspects of the trade.

From 1767 the representation of slave merchants on the elected committee changed, although, compatible with the volume of trade, their presence was still felt until the American War made its impact. After that time, just the occasional slave merchant appeared on this influential committee, making it clearly indicative of the trade's much reduced role in the port of Lancaster.[43]

No satisfactory attempts can be made to suggest what role the slave trade played, relative to other trades, for casual investors. Eighteenth-century shipping records fail to supply sufficient details for such a survey. What can be said here is that the slave trade clearly did provide investment opportunities for casual investors. They in turn assisted in the effective funding of this trade at Lancaster, and a number undoubtedly made contributions in terms of its provisioning. The fact that the slave trade combined ship and cargo ownership in a single common venture probably meant some wholesalers were involved in ship ownership for the first time.

The aspects of transatlantic trade discussed so far clearly depict the African trade as playing an important role in terms of the amount of commercial activity it generated at the port over a number of years. It provided opportunities for a small but active group of entrepreneurs who undoubtedly played an influential role in the management and development of their port. It would be desirable at this point to give some indication as to the trade's financial value, and better still to be in a position to make comparisons between this and the value of other forms of overseas commerce at Lancaster. Unfortunately, the values of eighteenth-century trade are not at all easy to establish. P. Corfield writes, "Eighteenth-century trade statistics in general provide a better guide to the volume of trade than to its value, as custom valuations were calculated at fixed official rates that did not reflect variations in actual marketability.".[44] Moreover, the lack of slave traders' personal accounts at Lancaster makes detailed quantification in financial terms a very difficult task. What will be attempted, in these circumstances, is to give an indication as to the scale of money passing in and out of the hands of slave merchants in Lancaster, and where possible to relate it to other trades, in particular that to the colonies. Local evidence, though scarce, will be used as and when it is available, together with information about the trade from elsewhere. Features which distinguished the slave trade from other branches of commerce should set it in some kind of context with respect to its relative financial value to the port. Levels of investment will be looked at before the returns from the trade are considered. Evaluation of the latter can only be very limited indeed.

Although only a few examples of initial outlay costs have been found for Lancaster-owned slavers, and these relate to ventures made late in the century when Lancaster slave ships usually cleared from or via Liverpool, it is possible to draw some more general conclusions. A summary of the costs known is set out in Table 4.6. Costs per ton for the various items have been inserted.

Table 4.6   *Outfitting Costs of Lancaster Slave Ships (1788–1791)* [45]

	Ship and Outfit (£ per ton)	Cargo (£ per ton)	Insurance (ship & cargo) (£ per ton)	Total (£ per ton)
Hope II/voyage A (163 tons)	£2850 (£17.5)	£5600 (£34.3)	£507 (£3.1)	£8957 (£54.9)
Hope II/voyage B (163 tons)	£1400 (£8.6)	£4042 (£24.8)	£273 (£1.6)	£5715 (£35.0)
Molly IV (114 tons)	£2420 (£21.2)	£3800 (£33.3)	£373 (£3.3)	£6593 (£57.8)
Golden Age (377 tons)	£4300 (£11.4)	£8677 (£23.0)	£778 (£2.0)	£13755 (£36.4)

How did these figures compare with costs elsewhere? Richardson has indicated average investment costs for Bristol slavers to be about £5,000 per vessel in the mid-century, and after 1783 about £7,300. His average tonnages for Bristol slavers for these two periods were 118 tons and 154 tons respectively which gives costs per ton of around £42 in the mid-century and around £47 after the American War.[46] The figures in Table

184

4.6 show a marked discrepancy between the costs of the *Hope II*'s two voyages and again between those of the *Molly IV* and *Golden Age*, when their respective tonnages are taken into account. The discrepancies are most marked in the 'ship and outfit' column. Here there is a difference of £8.9 per ton between the *Hope II*'s two voyages, whilst the *Molly IV* cost £9.8 per ton more than the *Golden Age*. Such variations must relate to whether a vessel had just been purchased or whether it was being sent on a subsequent venture. In the former instance, costs would reflect the vessel's purchase price whereas in the latter, only the refit costs. If one averages out the 'total' costs of the *Hope II*'s two ventures, the amount per ton would have been £44.95, whilst averaging out all four entries in Table 4.6 gives a figure of £46. More information on these vessels other voyages would no doubt have brought average costs down further.[47] Even so, these figures as they stand are a pound or two less per ton than Richardson's figures for Bristol after the American War, showing that rates continued to be somewhat cheaper in the North-west.

How indicative are these costs per ton of other Lancaster vessels clearing for Africa earlier in the century, when the trade was at its height? Richardson reckons the average cost of a slave ship and its outfit at Bristol in 1749 was £16 per ton.[48] The four later examples in Table 4.6, meanwhile, give variations between £8.6 and £21.2 per ton which average out at £14.7 per ton, slightly less, incidentally, than average costs at Liverpool at this time.[49] As prices would have risen slightly during the eighteenth century, one might suppose that a more realistic figure for the cost of a Lancaster slave ship and its outfit in the mid-century, making allowances for the reduced costs of subsequent voyages, would have been in the region of £12 or £13 per ton. The trade goods of later slavers, meanwhile, probably cost a little more than they would have done in the mid-century. Richardson states that the rising price of slaves on the African coast during the eighteenth century required increasingly large cargoes to be sent out, although the price of trade goods themselves remained remarkably steady.[50] The differences would most likely have been in the region of only a few pounds per ton. Richardson also tells us that the ship and its outfit usually represented a third of the total outlay costs, which is more or less borne out by the figures in Table 4.6.[51] Using this as a yardstick, one might conclude that a typical, initial investment cost in a Lancaster slaving venture during the mid-century years would have ranged somewhere between £36 and £39 per ton. Applying these figures to Lancaster clearances[52] suggests that its townsmen invested between £352,872 and £382,278 between 1750 and 1776, that is during the main years of activity. This averages out at £13,069 to £14,158 per annum and in the peak year of 1761, slave merchants would have invested between £38,880 and £42,120 in equipping their vessels for Africa. Such amounts cannot be regarded as negligible or insignificant.[53]

Insufficient information on the nature of bilateral trade at Lancaster makes a direct comparison between the two branches of transatlantic trade impossible. What can be said, however, is that in terms of financial investment the slave trade would have been proportionally more important than its relative representation in the transatlantic fleet would suggest. Richardson remarks, "Outlays on slaving ventures still represented a larger financial commitment than outport merchants normally undertook when they fitted out ventures to Ireland, Europe or even the Americas".[54] Several differences in the Guinea trade would account for this.

A slaver obviously needed specialist equipment both for trade on the African coast and for transporting its human cargo on the Middle Passage. Trade on the African coast often required longboats as well as firearms and maybe liquor to sweeten the local traders. On the Atlantic crossing a variety of restraints were used, and medical and food provisions were needed.[55] Extra crew members were also required for the management of the live cargo and it was usual for two months wages to be paid out in advance.[56] Another added expense for slave merchants would have been the price of their vessels. Slavers generally required more frequent repairs and replacement, on account of the waters they visited and the long time they spent at sea. Tarleton's evidence on the relative outlay costs of vessels employed in transatlantic trade is illuminating. He reckoned whereas a Guineaman in 1787 cost £15.92 a ton, a West Indiaman only cost £9.34.[57] The figures at Lancaster would have been different, but the ratios may have been similar.

Investments in the slave trade by Lancaster merchants were undoubtedly of significance to the local economy in the third quarter of the eighteenth century. They even reached quite considerable dimensions during peak years of activity. Although a direct comparison with other branches of overseas trade has proved difficult to make, the additional outlay costs required by the slave trade intimate it was proportionally more important as an area of investment than its share of overseas trade would suggest. This is more especially the case, if one is comparing its representation in the returning transatlantic fleet,[58] given the added risks which beset African vessels.

Lack of trading accounts makes it impossible to calculate the levels of returns from the slave trade in any specific way at Lancaster. The diverse nature of the fortunes of African ventures makes generalizations from patchy evidence particularly misleading. It is therefore difficult to assess the trade's impact locally in terms of its financial earnings. Recent research on the slave trade elsewhere, however, particularly at Liverpool, has convincingly shown that overall profits in the trade were much less than had hitherto been claimed. They were most likely in the

King George of Whitehaven fitted out for the slave trade. The wooden barricade on deck, constructed by the ship's carpenter, prevented slaves from rushing to the poop to take over the guns and tiller. *Courtesy of Whitehaven Museum*

region of 8 per cent per annum.[59] This being so, it would seem unlikely that slave-trade earnings at Lancaster had dramatic effects on the local economy that were widely disproportionate to its share of colonial commerce in terms of its volume.[60] Even so, given that on the one hand its share was steady and even quite considerable at times, and on the other that expected profit levels must have been sufficient to entice money away from safer areas of investment, earnings from the slave trade must have played a role in the shaping of the Lancaster economy. A few observations on some of the slave merchants themselves provide a useful comment.

The fact that a solid core of slave traders persisted in the trade so long at Lancaster and became prominent members of their community is strong enough evidence that the trade, despite its misfortunes, to which there is ample testimony in contemporary letters and newspapers,[61] had its sufficient rewards. That the members of one Lancaster partnership were owed as much as £15,000 on an American firm's failure in 1767 is indicative of the scale of the money that was being generated in the trade.[62] The fact that they were able to sustain an eventual repayment of something as low as 9d in the £1 points towards the overall robust financial circumstances of these merchants. Their prominence in the Lancaster slave trade up to this date implies that their financial well-being was largely founded on their previous slave-trading activities, and their willingness to continue in the trade after this incident is evidence of their expectations from the trade. Richard Millerson, for example, the chief representative of this partnership at the time, had shares in at least five slavers after this event and he remained in the trade until his death in 1777.[63]

It should, at the same time, be pointed out that Lancaster slave merchants, as marginal men, would not necessarily have expected immense profits, especially during the earlier years of their trading. They would presumably have been content so long as their returns were sufficiently in excess of the mediocre ones they might hope to make in safer forms of investment. If the returns had been more spectacular, the slave trade might have tempted the more established West India merchants as well.

On an individual basis, the slave trade was clearly more profitable for some than for others. Thomas Hinde certainly prospered more from it than anyone else at Lancaster. Although his business operations were wider than the trade in African slaves, it is clear this trade had not only introduced him to the merchant class but had continued to play a central role in his affairs. The details of his success in the trade, and that of his sons, have already been discussed.[64] The money he and his sons earned at Lancaster then Liverpool, and used to develop the worsted mill at Dolphinholme in 1795, gives some support to the links Eric Williams drew between the slave trade and industrial development. Moreover, the Hodgsons, who had broken their ties with Lancaster much earlier on, so as to pursue their careers in the slave trade at Liverpool, had later returned to invest their "ill-gotten gains" in the Low Mill at Caton in 1784. Thomas Hodgson's commemorative plaque inside the local church at Brookhouse has as part of its inscription:

> After passing the early part of his life in foreign climes he was for many years an eminent merchant in Liverpool and founder of the cotton and silk works in this his native place.[65]

The slave trade, then, clearly had an impact on Lancaster in financial terms, although it would perhaps be misleading to overstress it. What the evidence in this chapter does emphasize, however, is the fact that the slave trade played a much more significant role in the overall structural development of Lancaster and its economy, especially during the 1750s and 1760s, than has generally been realised. This is apparent not only from its share of colonial shipping and the level of investments this represented but also from the prominent part its operators played through the Lancaster Port Commission. Above all, what the slave trade did for Lancaster was to broaden and diversify the opportunities

NEAR THIS PLACE
REST THE MORTAL REMAINS OF
THOMAS HODGSON, OF ESCOW-BECK,
SECOND SON OF ISAAC AND ELIZABETH HODGSON,
FORMERLY OF THE HILL IN THIS TOWNSHIP;
WHO WITH OTHER OF THEIR CHILDREN AND DESCENDANTS
LIE INTERRED ON THE SOUTH SIDE OF THE CHURCH.
AFTER PASSING THE EARLY PART OF HIS LIFE
IN FOREIGN CLIMES,
HE WAS FOR MANY YEARS AN EMINENT MERCHANT
IN LIVERPOOL,
AND FOUNDER OF THE COTTON AND SILK WORKS
IN THIS, HIS NATIVE PLACE.
HE WAS A MAN OF REMARKABLE ENERGY,
AND WARM AFFECTIONS,
GREAT GENEROSITY AND PUBLIC SPIRIT,
AND ARDENTLY DESIROUS TO PROMOTE THE IMPROVEMENT
AND HAPPINESS OF ALL AROUND HIM.
HE DEPARTED THIS LIFE THE 13TH DECEMBER 1817,
IN THE 80TH YEAR OF HIS AGE.
LEAVING TWO SONS, AND FOUR DAUGHTERS.

Commemorative plaque to Thomas Hodgson whose success in the Liverpool slave trade enabled him to return to his native village and invest in a cotton and silk mill there.

on offer to local entrepreneurs. In particular, it gave aspiring merchants the leg-up they needed into the merchant world, a world which otherwise had its limitations at Lancaster. The effect was to aid the town in its development into a moderate but thriving centre of commerce, renowned for its transatlantic trade. This in turn stimulated a number of local industries which soon became well developed. The most lucrative and renowned of these were its ship-building and other related maritime trades, together with its quality cabinet-making. During the last quarter of the century, however, the presence of slave-trade investments by Lancaster merchants, relative to those in bilateral colonial trade, was receding noticeably.

The American War of Independence acted as something of a turning-point in the course of the Lancaster slave trade. However, it would be misleading to attribute the ultimate collapse of the Lancaster trade entirely, or even predominantly, to this one event. The reasons for its decline were much more complex and varied. Moreover, there were signs that certain significant changes were already underway before the war. What the American War did do was to disrupt the trade so as to bring it to a virtual standstill over a period of six years. This in itself inevitably had some repercussions. Most importantly, it opened up new opportunities in other areas of trade which were bound to have ramifications for future investments in the trade. I would argue that the effects of the American War constituted particular elements of two broader developments whose interplay ultimately brought about the demise of the African trade at Lancaster. The first concerned the problems that the slave trade itself was encountering. The other related to the fact that would-be investors were showing much less of a need for the slave trade than they had done in the past. Both these aspects require careful consideration before it can be fully appreciated why and how the slave trade ceased to play a role at Lancaster. The problems encountered by merchants in the African trade will be discussed before the changing areas of investment are considered, along with their implications for slave-trade investments. The immediate effects of the American War on the slave trade make a useful starting point.

This conflict severely impaired the slave trade everywhere, as indeed it did all transatlantic trade. The hostilities first began in April 1775 as the disaffected North American colonies reacted against a recalcitrant mother country. The situation deteriorated in February 1778 when France, resentful of the outcome of the Seven Years War, joined the Americans against the British. The next two years saw Britain's opponents swell to include the Spanish and then the Dutch. In this war Britain's western ports experienced a new threat. A few American privateers succeeded in patrolling the complex waters of the Irish Sea, having tricked local pilots on board.[66] More importantly, a lot of the fighting took place in the Caribbean, because of the participants' sensitivity about their colonial possessions there. Slave ships were particularly vulnerable on their approach to the West Indies whilst carrying their precious human cargoes. Their individual trading schedules meant their protection in convoys was not really practicable.[67] One of the few Lancaster slavers to risk an African voyage in these troubled times exemplifies this particular hazard. John Satterthwaite, one of her owners, on informing his insurers of her fate wrote in March 1782,

> I am sorry to inclose you the Protest for the capture of the *Sally*, Capt.Harrison, which I got last night – She was taken by the French Fleet within as Hour's sail of Basseterre Road, St. Kitts, it's an unlucky circumstance and she wou'd have made a very great voyage. Ship and cargo sold at St.Eustatius (for cash down) for upwards of double the cost near treble – as it is, provided all the Underwriters are staunch I shall lose about £200 by my Share of Her.[68]

Experiences like this one were hardly conducive to making the costly investments a slaving venture entailed. With nearly all the Lancaster slave merchants holding back from making African ventures after 1777, some undoubtedly lost interest in the trade and failed to resume their investments in the trade after the war had ended. Thomas Woodburne, for example, a former captain in the trade, sold his share in the *Sally III* in 1777,[69] before her above-mentioned capture. The evidence shows he had quit the trade for good. Without the problems of the war, it seems more than likely he would have continued in the trade as an experienced and crucial organizer. The reasons why he opted to leave the trade for good whilst Addison and Sawrey picked it up again, after the war was over, are not clear. Meanwhile, conditions during the war certainly did not encourage capital from either casual investors or new ones.

Peace was restored in 1783 with the signing of the Treaty of Paris. The national slave trade resumed, to reach new levels. Curtin estimates that the English slave trade peaked in the 1780s and again in the 1790s, in the years which surrounded the periods of conflict.[70] Lancaster merchants were among those who eagerly seized the opportunity to supply the islands with slaves once more. One or two of their slavers also visited the South Carolina market which had been lost to them during the conflict. Prices would have been more favourable given that the planters were keen to replenish their dwindling stocks. Accordingly, fourteen or fifteen outfits were made by Lancaster slave merchants over the next four years, a level that was not so different from that prior to the war.[71]

However, despite this renewed activity, which was benefitting from the rather unique conditions prevailing in the wake of the war, the fact that the majority of Lancaster slavers cleared via, or directly from, Liverpool[72] signifies that their owners faced particular problems when operating out of their own port. This was clearly not a new phenomenon. It had become a noticeable feature even in the 1770s when twenty Lancaster-owned vessels cleared from or via Liverpool.[73] However, it became more commonplace as the century progressed. There is perhaps no clearer evidence of this than when Thomas Hinde, who had invested in slavers at Lancaster since the mid-century, finally became wholly involved in operations centred on Liverpool. In April 1784 the Lancaster registration of his ship, *Hinde I*, was cancelled and the vessel was re-registered to include his eldest son Thomas, but this time at Liverpool. Thomas junior, having moved to Liverpool, perhaps on his father's wishes or advice, was clearly in a position to manage this slaver's affairs as well as the others he and his father invested in together.[74] Although most Lancaster-owned slavers continued to be registered locally, their dependence on Liverpool as a port of clearance was obvious. Evidently, Lancaster was ceasing to be the viable slave-trading centre it had been in the past.

The reason why Lancaster merchants were making use of the port of Liverpool for their slave-trading operations is of great significance.

This practice was symptomatic of the development of certain fundamental problems within the slave trade at large. Viewing the slave trade nationally, it is clear that Lancaster merchants were not alone in the problems they were encountering. Despite the overall increase in England's participation in the slave trade during the 1780s and 1790s, it soon becomes clear that nowhere outside Liverpool was maintaining or increasing its level of activity during these years. Bristol's share of the trade, which was almost 25 per cent in the early 1750s, fell to just over 10 per cent on the eve of the American War and dropped down to under 2 per cent in the decade before Abolition. London's interest in the trade, meanwhile, became increasingly financial rather than active. On the other hand, Curtin estimates that Liverpool's share of the trade rose from about 69 per cent in 1785–87 to 83 per cent a decade later and to almost 90 per cent by 1802–04.[75] The trade's centralization on Liverpool was undoubtedly the result of the highly competitive nature of the trade by the late eighteenth century.

The cost of slaves on the African coast had soared, as slaves, now scarce near to the coast through years of trading, had to be brought in caravans from further and further inside the interior of West Africa. Even with high prices, the competition for slaves on the coast could be intense at times. As a result, ships generally took longer to fill their holds, and with their heavy overhead costs as well as the problem of tropical diseases, owners saw their profit margins being eroded. What was required under these circumstances was more and more specialization and experience. Liverpool slave merchants, with their long predominance in the trade, clearly became the best equipped and most skilled operators.[76] Thus when the selection of outgoing cargoes and African trading centres became even more crucial, making it imperative to have up-to-date intelligence of trading conditions on the African coast, the frequency of Liverpool clearances meant such information could be circulated here better than anywhere else.

At first it made sense for Lancaster slave merchants to try to capitalize on the relative proximity of Liverpool by using its superior facilities, as and when it was convenient to do so. Ultimately, however, as competition within the trade intensified, they were squeezed out, along with other small-scale operators, and the slave trade at Liverpool became concentrated in fewer and fewer hands until it was dominated by just a few very large Liverpool houses. Lancaster merchants had traditionally thriven on sending small vessels which were able to make short, timely voyages to particular colonial markets. By the later decades of the eighteenth century this type of slave trading had become outmoded, as earlier slaving centres on the Windward Coast of Africa ran short of slaves in favour of regions to the south. That Lancaster slavers were obliged to make for these more

192

southerly destinations is evident in the shipping news provided by the contemporary press. Here, slaving practices were far more suited to the use of large, modern, purpose-built vessels which could transport huge shipments of blacks swiftly across the Atlantic to the big slave markets in the Caribbean. It was a method of slaving hardly known to the Lancaster merchants. Capital outlays on these types of ventures were such a different proposition so as to be entirely beyond the reach of small-scale operators like those at Lancaster.[77] In stark contrast, there was the Lancaster-owned slave ship named *Tom*, which sailed to the Cameroons in 1792. It was a fifteen-year-old, converted West Indiaman which was condemned in Barbados in 1794 after its meagre cargo of just thirty-nine slaves had been sold there. Its cargo had evidently included ivory as well, which was to be shipped back to Lancaster. Its owner, James Sawrey, was clearly trying to compensate for the problems he was encountering in acquiring slaves, by pursuing the produce trade. He made this evident in his letter of instruction to the captain of his previous slaver, the *Hope II*. He wrote,

> We also particularly desire you to purchase all the ivory and dead cargo you possibly can. The article of ivory induced us to send you to the Camaroons in preference to any other part of Africa. Your Com(mission) on ivory or any other Goods the produce of Africa shall be the same as customary out of Liverpool.

As a final brief he added,

> We hope you will be frugal in all your disbursements and in every matter or thing that concern your voyage. Without particular care the ship will loose money.[78]

What the Lancaster slave trade had needed during this period of change was more capital and this meant new operators. Anderson has suggested that Liverpool went ahead in the slave trade because of its enlarged partnership organization, given capital requirements had risen after the war.[79] However, Lancaster partnerships clearly lacked the injection of sufficient new blood at this crucial time. The situation was made worse when two of Lancaster's most active and experienced slave traders, Dodson and Millerson, died during the late 1770s and others, such as William Butterfield and Thomas Woodburne, either retired or simply left the trade. Furthermore, the Guinea captains of Lancaster slavers, who had hitherto progressed to form the back-bone of partnerships in the Lancaster trade, were now either moving to, or even originating from, Liverpool, on account of the trade's operation from there. This meant they were no longer likely to invest in future Lancaster slave ships.[80]

Lancaster's remaining slave traders after the American War, notably Addison, Sawrey and the Watson brothers, had an even greater need for young, ambitious merchants to join them. However, few were forthcoming. Thomas Willock and Robert Worswick were the only new names to join the Lancaster trade in the 1780s. Both were involved in the West India trade and slave trading appears to have been just a subsidiary part of their commercial portfolios.[81] This lack of new blood would be explained both by the deepening problems which faced the slave trade and by the fact that Lancaster had been developing alternative commercial opportunities for young entrepreneurs; opportunities that had not been available in the earlier decades of the century. During the American War, for example, and presumably during the later French Revolutionary Wars as well, privateering proved a very attractive area of investment. Accordingly, in 1781 the Liverpool Advertiser read,

> The Privateering Business goes on very briskly at Lancaster, the merchants entering into the spirit of it are already fitting out several privateers exclusive of the letter of Marque.

It was common practice for the owners of such vessels to be allowed to keep four-fifths of the prize value together with ten pounds for every piece of ordnance.[82] It is perhaps significant that Lancaster slave merchants were tempted into privateering, at least while they were inactivated by the war.[83]

Privateering was not the only opportunity thrown up to Lancaster entrepreneurs by the wars. During the American War there was a greater demand in the West Indies for provisions, as the normal supply from the American colonies was cut off. In 1780 thirty-five vessels sailed from Lancaster having been granted special passes against an embargo.[84] This even continued after 1783 owing to a ban on trading with rebel colonists imposed by the British Government. That Lancaster, as well as other ports, rushed to fill this vacuum is evident from the number of cattle being brought to the town at this time.[85] Meanwhile, through much of the French Revolutionary Wars there are signs that the West India trade flourished.

Aside from these specific opportunities created out of the late eighteenth-century wars, the effects that Lancaster's growing commercial activity had had over a number of decades were evident. It had encouraged the further development of local manufactures, the expansion of wholesaling and the promotion of trading connexions. This inevitably played its part in improving opportunities for young Lancaster merchants wishing to enter colonial trade. A document detailing some outgoing cargoes carried by a number of Lancaster West Indiamen during the early 1780s, together with the suppliers, is evidence that the town and its people were in a better position to provide export goods than they had been earlier in the century. The cargoes were more varied than they had been and the number of local suppliers reflected the expansion of firms which is apparent in the local trade directories of that time. The directory for 1784 listed six woollen drapers, four linen drapers, one silk mercer and four more unspecified mercers and drapers. It also included two cabinet-makers, a firm dealing in earthenware, a hatter, eight ironmongers and eleven tallow-chandlers. By 1799 there were twenty linen drapers, one silk manufacturer, eleven cabinet-makers and ten hatters or milliners.[86] Lancaster's increased prosperity in the West India trade is best exemplified when a tonnage duty, levied on the West Indian trade in 1776, was suspended after seven years because sufficient revenue had already been collected.[87]

Overall, the evidence shows that during the later decades of the eighteenth century, the whole balance of investment opportunities at Lancaster had shifted. Investments in the slave trade were becoming increasingly less viable, as prospects in other areas of colonial trade improved for young, aspiring merchants, who therefore no longer had the same need or incentive to join Lancaster's remaining slave traders. The offspring of Lancaster's most active and committed slave merchants were not tempted to follow in their fathers' footsteps. James Watson, the son of William, who had invested in the slaver *Antelope II* with his father at the age of eighteen in 1770, did not appear in the future registers of Lancaster slavers, except when, on the death of his father in 1794, he inherited his share of the *Molly IV*. The vessel was captured soon after and James Watson's name disappears from the trade for good.[88] Similarly, there are no signs that either Robert Addison or John and Robert Dodson, relatives of the former Guinea captains-turned-owners, went into the African trade at any stage. Their names do, however, appear in connexion with Lancaster's West India trade.[89]

One Lancaster merchant who epitomises how commercial opportunities had changed at Lancaster by the last quarter of the century was John Satterthwaite, son of the disowned Quaker merchant and Guinea factor.[90] Since his father had proved a none too successful merchant, John Satterthwaite seemingly had to make his own way in the world. Like so many young entrepreneurs at Lancaster, he was resident merchant out in the West Indies for a time in the 1770s. In 1777, however, he was back in Lancaster, with his St. Kitts wife and a black woman servant, where, according to his clerk and cousin, John Stout, he made a large part of his fortune between 1779 and 1785.[91] His single investment in a Lancaster slaver in 1781, together with his consideration of investment in another with his brother-in-law, John Backhouse at Liverpool, is evidence that he might well have become a committed

This commemorative ship bowl of 1783, made for the brig *Valentine* which traded between Lancaster, the West Indies and the Baltic, epitomises the increased wealth and confidence of Lancaster's maritime community after the American War. *Courtesy of Lancaster City Museums*

slave merchant, if times had not changed.[92] However, as it was, with England at war during most of this period, John Satterthwaite clearly had little want of the slave trade, more especially given the added risks it carried at this time. Instead, as his surviving letter book illustrates, he used the opportunities the war provided to good effect. In March 1781 he informed his partner, John Robinson, in St. Kitts of their share in three privateers. "The vessels you are concerned with me in here are the *Tom* (Capt. Lee, 80 men), *Admiral Rodney* (Capt. Harrison, 65 men) and *Sally* (Capt. Jackson, 47 men)." He then complained to Robinson, "that none of the privateering accts. are yet entered in the books since Nov.1778." A few months later, he was informing his brokers in Glasgow that "the large ship, the *Stag*, which I wrote you abt. 16 Dec has

Elegant town house on Castle Hill, Lancaster, bought by John Satterthwaite in 1781. He lived here with his family and black servant, Frances Elizabeth Johnson.

contd cruising, in the West Indies and been very successful". John Satterthwaite and his partner had a half-share in this vessel.[93]

His main brush with the slave trade had been through his partner's dealings with Guinea cargoes out in St. Kitts.[94] One might wonder whether Satterthwaite himself had been similarly employed when he was resident there in the 1770s. With friends, as well as a brother-in-law, in the Liverpool slave trade, John Satterthwaite clearly had all the necessary contacts to pursue the African trade further. However, the evidence suggests he flourished rather in Lancaster's thriving West India trade, which reached new levels after the war. His name does not appear in any of the registers of the fourteen or fifteen Lancaster vessels which set sail for Africa at this time.

For John Satterthwaite and other young investors, the African trade had become, at once, unnecessary and unattractive. Under these circumstances the days of the Lancaster slave trade were bound to be numbered. By the late 1780s there remained just a handful of die-hard slave merchants, men who were evidently reluctant to relinquish a trade which had launched and sustained them as colonial merchants over many years. One by one the partners of James Sawrey, the youngest member of this group, died,[95] and, with some disappointing voyages and the renewed war with France in 1793, the forty-nine-year-old captain had little option but to retire too.

The pattern of James Sawrey's career in the Lancaster slave trade summarises the trade's changing role at Lancaster. Slave trafficking had enabled this son of a Hawkshead shopkeeper and brother of a butcher to transcend his marginality to become a member of Lancaster's colonial merchant community. In this capacity he was able to contribute to the development of the town. For example, he bought shares to help fund the construction of the Lancaster canal, an important link for the port.[96] However, his slave-trading career was cut short by the problems that surrounded the Lancaster trade toward the end of the eighteenth century. He was hampered by stiff competition from Liverpool slave traders, as has already been mentioned, and by a dearth of new investors at home. This is obvious in the re-registration of his last slaver, when, after the deaths of his original partners, he was joined by investors from Liverpool, not Lancaster.[97]

The Lancaster slave trade had run its course, its services being no longer regarded as effective or appropriate, except, that is, for one short, sharp and final burst of activity.

Notes to Chapter IV

1. D. Richardson, 'The Slave Trade, Sugar, and British Economic Growth, 1748–1776', *Journal of Interdisciplinary History*, xvii: 4, Spring 1987, pp. 739–69.
2. Edward's figures are taken from Schofield, *Economic History of Lancaster*, p. 27.
3. 5 slavers cleared Lancaster in 1771 according to the Board of Trade's 'An Account of the Tonnage of the several ships cleared from GB to Africa', dated 8 Apr. 1777, P.R.O., B.T. 6/3, Bundle B from 57 to 118, pp. 150–189 (hereafter referred to as B.T., 'Tonnages to Africa'.)
4. P. Gooderson, 'Social and Economic History of Lancaster', unpublished Ph.D. thesis, University of Lancaster, 1975, p. 33.
5. Source, B.T., 'Tonnages to Africa'.
6. These vessels usually returned to Lancaster.
7. Adjustments give Lancaster a total of 103 clearances or 7199 tons and Liverpool 1,579 sailings or 169,578 tons. The total number of sailings for these years is 2,955, the total tonnage is 328,391.
8. B.T., 'Tonnages to Africa', lists the 5 Lancaster clearances as the *Warren*, *Molly*, *Prince George*, *Prince* (should read *Pearl*) and *Sally*. The additional Lancaster-owned vessel recorded in the Liverpool clearances was the *Agnes*. The seventh vessel was the *Nelly*, see *G.L.A.*, 14 Oct. 1771.
9. B.T., 'Tonnages to Africa' gives the *Thetis* and *Lyon* as clearing direct from Liverpool, and the remaining 8 vessels, the *Mary, Cato, Marquis of Granby, Juba I, Molly, Tartar, Britannia* and *Lancaster*, as sailing to Africa from Lancaster. Concerning the *Eagle*, see P/C. Tonnage Book, 7 Oct. 1762, kept at Lancaster Maritime Museum. Lancaster did send ten vessels to

Africa in 1755 and eleven in 1756, but the tonnage for these years was much less, 510 and 548 tons respectively. In 1772 Lancaster had 8 vessels in the trade with a combined tonnage of 620 tons.

10. In 1763, the year peace was restored, London sent 42 and Bristol sent 33 slavers. The following year the figures were 39 and 38 respectively. See B.T., 'Tonnages to Africa'.

11. Liverpool Plantation Registers, 7 May 1761. P.R.O., B.T., pp. 99–129, entitled 'Port of Liverpool: list of vessels sailing to Africa', lists the *Lion* as sailing to Angola for 650 slaves.

12. Schofield, *Economic History of Lancaster*, p. 26. From figures printed by Henry Smithers in 1825.

13. Lancaster's tonnage was 5,665 out of a total figure of 108,952.

14. Schofield, *Economic History of Lancaster*, p. 18. Entitled, 'England Described or the Traveller's Companion', it was based on much earlier sources, written before the slave trade got established.

15. T. West, *A Guide to the Lakes in Cumberland, Westmorland and Lancashire; by the Author of the Antiquities of Furness* (London, 1778), p. 28. Universal British Directory, 1799, vol. 3, 3rd edition, p. 622.

16. Schofield makes direct links between the development of colonial, coastal and European trades. *Economic History of Lancaster*, p. 49.

17. The Lancaster and New Banks were founded in the 1790s. Insurance broking was carried out by a number of firms including Thomas Robinson & Co., Richard Salisbury, Samuel Simpson and Daniel Eccleston. See Schofield, *Economic History of Lancaster*, pp. 52–53; Bodleian Library, MS 477, Sherard and Daniel Eccleston Letter Books 1780–81.

18. Re. *Mary*, see P.R.O., T. 70/29–33, 28 Dec. 1761, Letter from St. James Fort Governor. Re. *Sally*, see Guildhall Library, Lloyds Subscription Book, 8 Apr. 1774.

19. *L.L.*, 23 June 1758.

20. Their combined tonnage was 9,802 tons.

21. Sailors paid 6d per month as an insurance for themselves and their families. A photocopy of these accounts is available at the Lancaster Maritime Museum.

22. P.R.O., Adm. 68/200, London Seamen's Sixpences, 5 Jan. 1762, paid Liverpool.

23. Payments in the Seamen's Sixpence Accounts were generally made soon after a vessel returned to port and the dates and duration of each voyage were always noted. In the Tonnage Registers the dues were often not paid promptly and the dates of the voyage they concerned were not recorded. Sometimes two consecutive entries were made for one vessel with no explanation and although most dues were paid retrospectively some were paid in advance. In the Seamen's Sixpences a ship's place of trade was listed, and in the case of the Guinea trade, few slaving ventures were disguised by reference to their colonial port of call alone. The Tonnage Registers are much less clear. A vessel's place of trade was not given before July 1756 and even after that date a slaver's colonial destination was often the only one mentioned. Finally, the Seamen's Sixpences also record a number of slaving ventures curiously absent from the Tonnage Registers.

These aspects have no doubt contributed to the trade's underestimation in the past.

24. Sources: Information in column 1 is calculated from Schofield's figures on overseas trade which he takes from the P/C Tonnage Registers. See *Economic History of Lancaster*, p. 21. He includes vessels in European trade, but only the very few in trade with Southern Europe were typically smaller. Figures in column 2 are based on my figures taken from the same Tonnage Registers.

25. Schofield, *Economic History of Lancaster*, p. 16.

26. This average is calculated from applying tonnage figures from the P/C Tonnage Registers to the African vessels recorded in the Seamen's Sixpences.

27. See below, pp. 186.

28. See above, pp. 171–172.

29. See above, ch.2, p. 40.

30. Miles Barber, a leading African merchant, had just moved his operations to Liverpool by this time.

31. Re. *Nancy II*, see *L.L.*, 13 Nov. 1767. The loss of the *Bridget and Mary* is suggested by the death of its captain; see Lancs. C.R.O., WRW/A, 1766 (John Matthews). Re. *Marquis of Granby*, see *G.L.A.*, 23 Jan. 1767. Re. *Dove* to Liverpool, see P.R.O., C.O. 5/710, 7 Aug. 1766.

32. Between 1767 and 1774, 43 Lancaster slavers cleared. 31 of their crews paid into the Seamen's Sixpence Accounts, 3 more presumably returned given that they made subsequent voyages. Of the remaining 9 vessels, 5 were shipwrecked or condemned, 1 returned to Whitehaven, having lost part of its cargo, 3 are unaccounted for. The ratio of returns to clearances is similar to that of previous peace-time years.

33. See below, p. 189ff.

34. Richardson, *Bristol Slave Traders*, p. 4.

35. Sources: Column 1, see Schofield, *Economic History of Lancaster*, graph facing p. 21. Column 2, figures are taken from the Lancaster Seamen's Sixpence Accounts.

36. Schofield, 'Slave Trade', pp. 61–62.

37. Kept at L.P.L.

38. L.P.L., Political Scrapbook no. 2 (folio). A Lancaster slaver bearing this M.P.'s name made 6 African ventures from 1770.

39. William Butterfield, Thomas Millerson and Miles Barber did not sign this letter.

40. Re. the 17 returning vessels, see Lancaster Seamen's Sixpence Accounts. For Rawlinsons' vessels, see L.P.L., Journal of Abraham Rawlinson, MS 197 and Free/App. Rolls.

41. The 6 partnerships were, Helme and Fowler, Alman and Co, Dodgson Foster, William Butterfield, Thomas Hinde and Miles Barber, Satterthwaite and Inman.

42. See ch. 2, p. 38.

43. The slave trade was represented intermittently on this committee until its Abolition. Lancaster's last surviving slave merchant, John Cumpsty, served as a commissioner from 1803 to 1806.

44. P. Corfield, *The Impact of English Towns* (Oxford, 1982), p. 90, n.3 (ch. 3).

45. Parliamentary Papers, 1790, XXIX, 698, Accounts and Papers. For *Hope II*'s voyage B see L.P.L., *Hope*'s Package Book.

46. Richardson, *Bristol Slave Traders*, p. 6. Re. average tonnage at Bristol, see Richardson, 'Costs of Survival', p.190.

47. The *Hope II* made 3 slaving ventures before its sale in 1794, whilst the *Molly IV* made 5 before its capture that same year. The *Golden Age* was employed in the slave trade betweeen 1783 and 1792 when it, too, was captured. Although it was registered at Liverpool, its owners were nearly all of the Lancaster area, including Thomas Hinde senior and his son, together with Samuel Simpson of Lancaster and Joseph Fayrer of Milnthorpe.

48. Richardson, 'Costs of Survival', p. 184.

49. *Ibid.*, pp. 184–85. Ship and outfit costs at Liverpool were variously given as £15.92 and £17.50 per ton in 1787.

50. Richardson, *Bristol Slave Traders*, pp. 6–7.

51. Richardson, 'Davenport', p. 70.

52. See above, p. 175.

53. Richardson suggests Bristoleans invested at least £100,000 p.a. in peacetime and probably in excess of £150,000 at the trade's peak around 1730. See *Bristol Slave Traders*, p. 7.

54. *Ibid.*, p. 6.

55. On the nature and implications of these added costs, see Richardson, 'Costs of Survival', p. 184.

56. L.P.L., *Hope*'s Package Book. Sawrey paid £71.5s for the 23 men who were to crew the *Hope* in 1791.

57. Richardson, 'Costs of Survival', p. 184. Tarleton slave traded from Liverpool.

58. See Graph B above.

59. Richardson, 'Davenport', p. 80.

60. The often exaggerated accounts of the impact of the slave trade in the main slaving ports, based on its alleged spectacular profits, has been avoided at Lancaster because of the trade's relative lack of attention.

61. See examples in Hamer and Rogers, eds., *Laurens Papers*, vols. 1–6, and local presses at Liverpool and Whitehaven.

62. This amount represented a third of the total that this firm sunk for. See above, ch. 2, pp. 88–89.

63. Millerson owned *Antelope II* until 1771, *Jenny* until 1776, *Prince George III* until 1770, *Stanley* and *Warren* until 1777. His other partners, Robert Dodson, John Addison, William and John Watson likewise continued in the trade until their deaths. Also see above, ch. 3, p. 151.

64. See above, ch. 3, pp. 141–142.

65. P. Gooderson, 'The Social and Economic History of Caton', unpublished M.A. thesis, University of Lancaster, 1969, p. 28. Re. Low Mill, see Price, *Industrial Archaelogy*, p. 18.

66. P. Crowhurst, *The Defence of British Trade* (Dawson, 1977), p. 67.

67. *Ibid.*

68. John Satterthwaite's Letter Book, 1781–1782, Letter to Bland and

Satterthwaite of London, 5 Mar. 1782. His cousin John was a partner in this firm.

69. See Lloyds Register, 1778.

70. Curtin, *Atlantic Slave Trade*, pp.153–54.

71. Slavers involved in these ventures included *Fenton, Good Intent, Hinde, Molly III, Mungo, Nancy III, Old England, Garnet.*

72. See Schofield, 'Slave Trade', p. 56.

73. See B.T., 'Tonnages to Africa' and B.T. 6/3, 'A List of Vessels that have sailed from this port for Africa 1750–1776'.

74. Re. *Hinde I*'s registrations, see Liverpool Plantation Registers: Lancaster, 4 Oct. 1782, owners, Thomas Hinde Snr., Samuel Simpson and master William Jackson, all of Lancaster; Liverpool, 24 Apr. 1784, owners, Thomas Hinde jr., William Jackson, both of Liverpool with Thomas Hinde the Elder and Samuel Simpson of Lancaster. T. Hinde snr. invested in a number of other Liverpool slavers with his eldest son. In 3 of these, their partners included Samuel Simpson and in 5 of them William Jackson. At least some of the remaining partners had former North Lancashire connexions, for example Moses Benson, Thomas Kirkby and Thomas Parke. The slavers included *Golden Age, King Dahomy, Tarmagon, George, Hinde II* and *Minerva*. For details of their ownership, see P.R.O., T. 64/286, entitled 'List of Slavers from Liverpool, 1789–1795'.

75. Richardson, *Bristol Slave Traders*, p. 5; Lamb, 'Volume and Tonnage', pp. 92–93; and Curtin, *Atlantic Slave Trade*, p. 135.

76. Drake, 'Liverpool–African Voyage', p. 142.

77. The fact that the Hindes continued successfully in the African trade at Liverpool throughout this period is indicative of their financial well-being and status.

78. L.P.L., *Tom's* Papers relating to the sale of its African cargo. Letter to Tobias Collins, captain of the *Hope*, dated 26 Sept. 1791, in *Hope*'s Package Book.

79. Anderson, 'Lancashire Bill System', p. 80.

80. William Jackson and Thomas Kirkby, both natives of Lancaster and captains of Lancaster Guineamen, moved to Liverpool in the 1780s. Their investments in the slave trade there did involve them with other former North Lancashire residents, including the Hindes.

81. Thomas Willock was described as a merchant when made a Lancaster freeman (F.R., 1777/8). He had shares in *Sally III, Hope II* and *Molly IV*. Robert Worswick was resident merchant in St. Kitts in 1788 (Ingram, p. 31) and described as a banker when made a freeman (F.R., 1787/88). He had shares in *Molly IV, Hope II* and *Tom*.

82. E. Wilkinson, *The Port of Lancaster* (Lancaster Museum Monograph, 1982), p. 7.

83. See John Satterthwaite's Letter Book, 1781–82. His letters mention his partnerships with Addison, Sawrey and Willock in privateers.

84. James Monro, ed., *Acts of Privy Council* (Colonial Series), vol. 5, 1766–1783, (H.M.S.O., 1966, reprint), p. 447.

85. Gooderson, 'Lancaster', p. 34 (taken from Ragatz, *Fall of British Planter Class in the Carribean*, pp. 149 and 186).

86. Bodleian Library, Oxford, Sherard MS. and Lancaster Trade Directories, 1784 and 1799.

87. Schofield, *Economic History of Lancaster*, p. 29.

88. Re. *Antelope II*, see Davies-Davenport Papers, Bead Book, 27 May 1770. Re. *Molly IV*, see P.R.O., T. 64/286, 5 July 1794.

89. Robert Addison, son of the slave trader, owned at least 3 vessels, 1789–92. John and Robert Dodson, nephews of the slave trader, owned 8 and 6 vessels, 1795–1806 and 1800–1805, respectively. See Lancaster Shipping Registers.

90. See above, ch. 2, pp. 77–78.

91. Schofield, 'Benjamin Satterthwaite', p. 164 (taken from John Stout, 'A Vindication', privately printed at Lancaster in 1841). Re. his return to Lancaster, see Benjamin Satterthwaite's Letter and Bill Book, Letter to Messrs. Parris Smith and Daniel, 3 Aug. 1777.

92. Re. his share in Lancaster slaver *Sally III*, see his Letter Book, 1781–82, Letter to Bogle and Hamilton, 19 Apr. 1781. His co-owners were Addison, Sawrey, Willock and Captain Jackson. Re. his considered African voyage with John Backhouse, see Letter to Bogle and Hamilton, 10 July 1781.

93. *Ibid.*, Letters to John Robinson and Bogle and Hamilton, 13 Mar. 1781 and 19 Apr. 1781.

94. See above, ch. 2, p. 81.

95. John Addison died in 1788, Thomas Willock in 1790, William Watson in 1793 and John Watson in 1794.

96. L.P.L., Scrap Book, No. 2 (folio).

97. Sawrey's Liverpool partners were Ralph Fisher, John and James Aspinall and John Webster, alongside James Watson of Lancaster. See P.R.O., T. 64/286, 5 July 1794.

Conclusion

The Lancastrians' final encounter with the African trade took place between 1799 and 1808.[1] Its many resonances with Lancaster's earlier experiences in the slave trade offer a good opportunity to review the more important aspects of the town's involvement in slavery.

The conditions under which these last Lancaster slave traders operated were very different from what they had been ten years previously. Opportunities were strongly reminiscent of earlier years. The prospect of the British trade's abolition shifted the balance of investment opportunities in favour of the slave trade once more. Curtin remarks on the surge in annual slave exports in the opening years of the nineteenth century as planters looked to stock up their field gangs.[2] These later slave traders were also able to tap the new colonial markets of Surinam, Berbice and Trinidad, where slaves were eagerly sought and colonial produce was readily available.

What is of most concern here is the fact that these late investors at Lancaster shared many of the characteristics of their predecessors. There were two partnerships at Lancaster at this time. The Freeman Rolls identify the first of these, a partnership involving Nathaniel Calvert, William Ireland, James Overend and Corney Tomlinson. Calvert was the only one to be called a merchant. Of the others, one was a basket-maker and pot merchant, another was the son of a yeoman and the third was a woollen draper.[3] Clearly, these men were marginal newcomers, utilising the trade in African slaves to make their way into colonial commerce. Their initiation to slave trading was not very successful. Their company was declared bankrupt in 1801 and their single slave ship, the *Angola*, was sold.[4] The second partnership was equally representative of the marginal status of most Lancaster slave traders, but much more successful than the Calvert enterprise. This probably owed much to its inclusion of two experienced Lancaster West India captains, one of whom skippered one of their slave ships on a number of ventures. John Lowther and John Nunns were typically joined by a mercer, John Cumpsty. Together they owned four vessels, one of which, the *Johns*, made six consecutive

African voyages, its last clearance being as late as 1808.[5] By then two of the owners had died in the West Indies. Captain John Lowther fell ill on the island of St. Thomas in 1804 and Captain John Nunns died within a few days' sail of Trinidad, while in command of the *Johns*, then carrying its fifth cargo of African slaves.[6] They left John Cumpsty, Lancaster's only surviving African merchant, to enjoy the last benefits that were to be wrung out of an infamous trade that had played a significant role in the development of Lancaster.

A survey of Lancaster in the early 1700s would have given little indication of its future development into an important regional, and indeed national, commercial centre for colonial trade by the third quarter of the eighteenth century. Whilst it may not be possible to predict what would have happened without the slave trade, it is clear that the trade offered two important advantages to Lancaster. It strengthened the local merchant community by recruiting into it men who might have gone elsewhere or remained marginal to this maritime commerce. Perhaps more importantly, it strengthened the whole town's potential to participate fully in the colonial trades.

The slave trade gave new commercial investors a means to benefit from the wealth of the planters and from the produce of their plantations, at a time when local conditions made opportunities in bilateral colonial trade less accessible or attractive for them. Many of these new investors, like Richard Millerson, Robert Dodson, John Addison, James Sawrey, Thomas Hinde and William Watson came from the outlying regions, Furness in particular, and typically featured artisans' and farmers' junior sons, young captains and wholesalers, aspiring to merchant status. As part of a larger merchant community at Lancaster, they fostered and extended trade at home and across the Atlantic, bringing new prosperity and opportunity to the town. Benjamin Satterthwaite expressed this clearly when he spoke of the consequences of William and John Watson's financial difficulties in 1777. He wrote,

> My brother thinks there will be a statute on against them, the *Molly* is discharged again and they're this day unbinding her sails, this affair will be a great hurt to the Town in general, I mean for want of that shipping being employed in it which they did employ, everybody here seem to pity them and to lament the loss of such benefactors to the Town.[7]

Slave traders also played an active role in their Port Commission, which was committed to developing and improving Lancaster's port facilities and to promoting its representation in trading matters of national importance. The dedication of this Commission was to lead to the

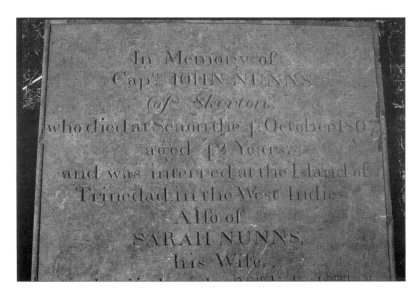

Gravestone in St. John's Churchyard, Lancaster, to commemorate Captain John Nunns who died aboard Lancaster's last slave ship, the *Johns*, in 1807.

building of a fine pier and wet basin at Glasson as well as to the construction of a canal designed to make Lancaster more accessible to suppliers to the north and south. This merchant body was also responsible for making Parliament aware of Lancaster's position on a variety of trading issues, which included their petitioning, alone with Liverpool, against the proposed abolition of the slave trade. Slave traders exerted some influence on the government of their town. A significant number filled some of the top offices in the Lancaster Corporation, several becoming mayors and aldermen on more than one occasion.

In the light of these observations, this study of the Lancaster slave trade has addressed itself to some of the main historiographical issues which surround the slave trade. Although lack of business papers and the varied interests of many Lancaster slave merchants have precluded any detailed or specific comment on the trade's profitability, it has been possible to draw some more general conclusions. Returns from slave-trading ventures were sufficiently attractive to keep existing investors in the trade and to entice new investors to join it. Miles Barber concentrated his capital and energies wholeheartedly on the African trade and Thomas Hinde even continued his investment in slave ships after he could have retired from commerce altogether, or at least found alternatives. Returns from the slave trade also enabled men of marginal status to prosper sufficiently to enter the merchant class and live in some style in fine houses. Many, like Charles Inman and John Addison, set their sons up as colonial merchants and they in turn extended and developed Lancaster's West India trade to reach its climax before the Napoleonic Wars. This study gives more specific details about the trade's structural importance on the shaping of the Lancaster economy. As a small, but significant, branch of Lancaster's transatlantic commerce, the slave trade played its part in shifting the home economy towards industrialisation. In some instances, direct links have been found between slave-trading capital and industrial development.[8] More often, however, the slave trade acted as part of a complex Atlantic economy where colonial trade, the triangular trade included, stimulated home manufactures and was responsible for the establishment of a commercial and financial infrastructure on which future developments could be based.

An important concern of this book has been the organization and management of the slave trade. An analysis of Lancaster ventures has shown that a triangular pattern of trading was both practicable and important for these small-scale operators. When sugar became harder to obtain, Lancaster traders found other useful imports, such as mahogany, rum and dyewoods. This enabled them to maximise their profits on each leg of their enterprise, which was particularly important for marginal operators trading in a competitive field. The experience of the trade's operation at Lancaster stresses the value of managers with first-hand, practical knowledge of the trade, as well as the advantages of certain types of wholesalers in a slave-trading partnership. Thus, whilst wholesalers did indeed form an important group of investors, once the Lancaster trade got underway, it was the former slaver captains who dominated the organization of African ventures. The advantages of good trading links across the Atlantic, both along the African coast and in the colonies, has also been stressed. Although more information on this aspect of the Lancaster trade would be welcome, it has, with the evidence available, been possible to construct a plausible picture of how these important aspects of a slaving enterprise functioned.

The presence of characteristics such as these in the Lancaster slave trade, fortified no doubt by the apparent grit and determination of these opportunists, goes a long way towards explaining how these small-scale operators co-existed with larger competitors, at least until the last quarter of the eighteenth century. When competition did ultimately make the slave trade less viable at Lancaster, the contacts and experiences forged by the African trade meant that other opportunities were on offer to aspiring merchants.

In the context of local history, this research has challenged the low profile previously given to the slave trade in Lancaster's development.

Cable Street, Lancaster in 1807 by J.C. Ibbetson. To the right is Brockbank's shipyard where a number of slave ships were constructed. The large house in the centre belonged to Robert Addison, merchant son of slave trader John Addison who had originated from Ulverston. *Courtesy of Lancaster City Museums*

Its all too ready dismissal in the past can be largely attributed to the confusing picture portrayed by local maritime records, especially those of the Port Commission, and the absence of slave-trading accounts. This book has sought to build on Schofield's earlier work on the Lancaster slave trade, by exploring new avenues in its operation and organization, by analysing its operators far more closely and, most important of all, by assessing its role in the economic development of Lancaster. Lancaster's slave trade has been compared and contrasted to that of other small ports in the region, as a valuable means to explain Lancaster's greater involvement and success in the trade. It was the Lancastrians' awareness of opportunity in colonial trade, tempered by the restrictions that local conditions imposed on this trade, which distinguished them from their neighbours and made the slave trade more attractive to this group of aspiring merchants.

Attaching greater importance to the role of the slave trade in the economic development of Lancaster is compatible with the port's position as Britain's fourth slave-trading port, ahead of other small ports on the west coast. It also makes sense of the following statement, quoted in Hewitson's memoranda,

> Here lived the wealthy merchants who flourished, so it is said, on the slave trade, and who grew rich on their importations of mahogany and rum.[9]

Notes to Conclusion

1. An Act of Parliament, passed in 1799, made it compulsory for slaving vessels to clear from Liverpool.
2. Curtin, *Atlantic Slave Trade*, pp. 154 and 267.
3. F.R., 1793/94; 1783/84; 1787/88 and 1781/82.
4. Re. bankruptcy, see *W.L.A.*, 16 Mar. 1801. For registration and sale of *Angola*, see Lancaster Shipping Registers, 21 June 1799.
5. Their three other slavers were *La Fraternité*, *Britannia II* and *Beaver*. Re. *Johns'* final African voyage, see Lancaster Seamen Sixpences, 13 June 1809.
6. Re. Lowther's death, see *Lancaster Gazette*, 1 Sept. 1804. Re. Nunn's death, see *Liverpool Chronicle*, 30 Dec. 1807.
7. Benjamin Satterthwaite Letter Book, letter to John Satterthwaite, 17 Nov. 1777.
8. See above, ch. 4, p. 188.
9. William Hewitson's *Memoranda*, vol. 1, p. 5 (L.P.L., microfilm).

Appendix A

Cargo Suppliers for *Hope*'s African Voyage in 1792

TRADER	GOODS	AMOUNT	COMMENTS
1. Backhouse and Lowe	rice knives	£29.13s.2d £4.14s.2d	John, Thomas Backhouse and Joseph Lowe, merchants in Liverpool.
2. William Beg	romalls *	£102.10s.0d	Liverpool slave trader.
3. John Blackburn	salt	£80.1s.9d	Of Northwich, with Liverpool Warehouse.
4. Edward Bate	knives & co.	£110.1s.6d	He supplied J. Knight's slaver, *Anson*, in 1771 with knives and flints.
5. John Clowes	battery**	£498.3s.1d	
6. John Copland	beads	£212.10s.11d	A Liverpool slave trader.
7. Ralph Fisher	brass, wire & co.	£84.10s.0d	Of Cheadle.
8. John Fisher	masks	£1.0s.0d	
9. Robert Green	manilloes***	£4.12s.0d	A Liverpool slave trader
10. William Hope	britannias,† shawls and baize	£117.10s.9d	
11. Haworths and Smith	printed cotton	£80.0s.6d	Manchester calico manufacturers. The Haworths may be the same family which had previously had shares in Lancaster slavers and other vessels.
12. James Haswell	rings	£9.7s.1d	
13. Richard Hill	earthenware	£39.3s.4d	There was a Liverpool merchant of this name.
14. John Jackson	flaggons	£66.13s.8d	Lancaster tea-dealer and spirit-merchant.
15. John Kirk	glass	£6.0s.0d	
16. Langton,Birley &Co	canvas	£39.8s.0½d	Sail-manufacturers of Kirkham.
17. Lindsey and Goulden	matts	£9.19s.7d	
18. William Morgan	pipes	£1.1s.3d	
19. John Parr	guns	£337.18s.6d	Liverpool merchant and supplier to J. Knight's *Anson* with pans and cutlasses.
20. Peter Rigby	knives and iron	£137.14s.7d	Probably the son of former Liverpool ironmonger, Edmund Rigby.
21. John Smith	beans and barley	£41.19s.9d	Probably the Lancaster grocer of Penny Street.
22. Sydebotham and Harrocks	earthenware	£10.1s.10d	Of Preston.

23. Taylors and Withington	manor goods (cloths‡)	£413.17s.0d	
24. Robert Tyrer	chests	£25.19s.8d	Lancaster cooper.
25. John Watson	swirles	£7.10s.3d	Probably the Lancaster slave trader.
26. Ann Wood & Sons	caps	£11.14s.6d	
27. Walton, son and Newton	romalls *	£80.10s.10d	Possibly the Manchester fustian manufacturer, named William Walton.

* silk or cotton squares
** metal goods, usually of brass or copper, beaten into shape
*** metal bracelets made of brass, bronze or copper
† fine linen produced in West Scotland and Ireland
‡ included bafts, brawls, chilloes, bejutapants and photacs

Appendix B

Benjamin Satterthwaite

As a Quaker and relative, Benjamin Satterthwaite was resident factor in
Barbados for the Townson-Dillworth-Rawlinson group from 1737 to
1741. Benjamin was a stepson of Miles Townson and a nephew of John
Dillworth, who in turn was related to the Rawlinsons. At this time he
appears to have had no dealings with Guineamen, rather keeping
himself loyal to serving his non-slaving Quaker employers. However,
he was obviously well aware of the slave-factorage business for he
makes several references to Richard Morecroft who "has so many
Guineamen to load".[1] In September 1741 Benjamin took the wayward
step of marrying an Anglican, Jane Casson, daughter of Alderman John
Casson, a mercer of Lancaster. This earned him disownment by the
Society of Friends and lost him his employment with his Quaker
family. In November 1741 Benjamin wrote to Thomas Greenup, an
African captain in Liverpool, "Since I left your town I have been at my
step-father Townson's several times who never offered me a birth
though they're going to fit out a vessel to Barbados and another for
Antigua". Benjamin was employed by his father-in-law for a short time,
but clearly contemplated settling in Liverpool with his wife. In
December 1741 he wrote to Captain Haresnape of Liverpool, "If I can
get imployment in your town I intend to settle there".[2]

His letters show that he sought employment as a factor in the West
Indies, commissioned from Liverpool. He was in Barbados and
Antigua in 1742, then in January 1745 Benjamin was writing for
insurance to cover a vessel, *Ruby*, for Barbados, himself commander. It
carried a cargo for his family's competitor, Myles Birket.[3] Between 1749
and 1751 he was employed as a factor in Barbados for the Lancaster
cabinet-maker, Robert Gillow and his associates. Thereafter, there is a
total break in his letter-writing until 1763, when a Letter Book shows
he was once more in the employment of his Quaker family as factor,
this time in Jamaica.[4] Schofield notes Benjamin's curious absence from
Lancaster records during the 1750s.[5] I would suggest that this was due
to his involvement in the partnership in Barbados which dealt with
slaves, Law, Satterthwaite and Jones.[6] Correspondence from
Benjamin's later Jamaican letters hints at this former partnership and
their dealing in African cargoes in the 1750s. In October 1764
Satterthwaite wrote to Thomas Daniel of Barbados, "I wonder Mr.
Jones should never be so kind to acknowledge the letters I wrote him
from Belfast. Should always be glad to hear of his welfare, pray tender
my compliments to him and Mrs. Jones". Other letters indicate that
Benjamin had strong links with several Liverpool slaver captains, men

with whom one might not otherwise expect him to have had such connexions. For example, in March 1764 he wrote to Captain Samuel Linnecar concerning the state of Linnecar's affairs in Jamaica and concluded that a protested bill might now be paid by a Mr. Ros[s] and that he was enclosing a copy of Mr. Lancelot Graves' last will with the belief that a bail bond would discharge the trust. Then in August Benjamin noted, "I hear my old friend Captain Linnecar is gone to Callabar in a ship from London, pray any kind compliment to Mrs. Linnecar when you see her". It was owing to this friendship that Benjamin agreed to sell a slave, Bryan, for Linnecar's friend, William Dingman of Liverpool, in 1764. Benjamin had trouble selling this slave owing to his poor state, which cost him doctor's fees and his upkeep until he was fit to sell. Benjamin could not think of charging commission, rather thinking "myself well paid if my transactions herein pleases my old acquaintance Captain Linnecar's friend".[7]

The general picture, and this favour in particular, strongly suggest Benjamin Satterthwaite was dealing in slave cargoes in Barbados in the 1750s.

Notes to Appendix B

1. Schofield, 'Benjamin Satterthwaite', p. 142 and see Donnan, ed., *Slave Trade*, vol. 4, pp. 427–31 for Richard Morecroft as slave factor in Barbados.
2. Schofield, 'Benjamin Satterthwaite', pp. 157 and 160. Re. Greenup see Donnan, ed., *Slave Trade*, vol. 2, p. 431.
3. Schofield, 'Benjamin Satterthwaite', p. 163.
4. Gillow Papers, 344/161.
5. Schofield, 'Benjamin Satterthwaite', p. 164.
6. George Law also came from North Lancashire. See Hewitson's *Memoranda*, p.98. Re. their slave dealing: Messrs. Law & Co., of Barbados sent '50 new negroes' to St. Eustatia aboard the *Anna Sibella* in 1752. See P.R.O., C.O. 33/16 (Part 2).
7. Benjamin Satterthwaite's Letter Book, Letters to Daniel, 18 Oct. 1764; Linnecar, 9 Mar. 1764 and to Dingman, 31 Aug. and 1 Oct. 1764.

Appendix C

Samboo's Elegy

The sun descending sheds his parting gleam,
And dew, in tears, weeps for expiring day,
O'er the wave comes the sea-gull's lonely scream
And gentle surges sighing die away.

Solemn the shore, more solemn still this dell,
Scoop'd like a grave its solitary glade,
Where sober contemplation seems to dwell,
For muses' haunts and melancholy made.

Whose sides wild roses, violets, blue bells deck,
And Agrimony, with its golden plumes,
Wild thyme and daisies its green bottom speck,
And dandelion's vulgar stare illumes.

Aw'd by the magic of this sacred ground,
It's venerable far sequester'd gloom,
"The rude forefathers of the hamlet"* found
Its fitness for poor Samboo's lonely tomb.

Wild Afric's torrid realms gave Samboo's birth,
Beneath some cocoa or some palm tree's shade
He nature's child, first crawl'd, then trod the earth,
On Niger's banks, or Gambia's, harmless play'd.

The lion, or the alligator's jaw,
The wolf, or venom'd snake, thy infant years,
Joyful escap'd. But, ah! we little know
Our future destiny of woes and fears.

To manly pith the sinews scarce were grown,
Thy rude shap'd lance had scarcely learn'd to wield,
When by the hellish warhoop thou wert drawn,
Through distant woods to try the doubtful field.

But, ah! by vict'ry or deep ambuscade,
Some of thy tribe bleed in the land where born;
Oh! thus like thee are captive traffic made,
And from their native plains for ever torn.

Heart–broke on Indian Shores thou tread'st at last,
But soon (thy master, lot, and labour known)
Hope chear'd thy soul, thy hopes seem'd all o'erpast,
Thy useful toil, was soon familiar grown.

215

Thy faithful hands the cane or coffee raise,
The burning still**, or cauldren† too, thy care,
But greater bliss, thou here first learnt to praise
This God unknown‡, and supplicate in prayer.

But man's ne'er happy long; –Fidelity,
Like thine, had won thy gentle master's heart,
To his dear native Britain he chose thee
Attendant; never, but with death to part.

From faithful wife and weeping children torn,
Affliction almost rent thy heart in twain;
Yet, by thy master's love, thy woes upborne,
Thou hop'st to clasp him in thy arms again.

Now o'er the Atlantic's troubled deep they haste;
When lo; what crosses human hopes betide;
From fever's rage, or quick consumption's waste,
Samboo saw land, –just entered Lune, –and died.

No knell his fun'ral told –no dirge, no bier,
No white-robed priest trod this unhallowed ground
But his kind master drops the manly tear
And serious rustics sympathize around.

Epitaph

Full sixty years the angry winter wave
Has thundering, dash'd this bleak and barren shore,
Since Samboo's head, laid in this lonely grave,
Lies still and ne'er will hear their turmoil more.

Full many a sand bird chirps upon the sod,
And many a moon-light Elfin round him trips;
Full many a Summer's sunbeam warms the clod,
And many a teeming cloud upon him drips.

But still he sleeps, –till the awak'ning sounds
Of the Archangel's Trump new life impart;
Then the Great Judge his approbation founds.
Not on Man's colour but his worth of heart.

Reverend James Watson, 1796.

* Gray's Elegy   ** distilling rum   † making sugar   ‡ Acts 17,23

Bibliography

I Primary Sources

A. *Manuscript*

Public Record Office
    Admiralty
        Mediterranean Passes.   Adm. 7.
        Protection of Vessels.
        London Seamen Sixpences.
    Board of Trade
        Ships to Africa, 1747–1753.   B.T. 6.
        Tonnages and Clearances to Africa, 1750–1776.
    Colonial Office
        Naval office shipping lists for West Indies
        and Mainland America.   C.O.
    Inland Revenue
        Registers of Apprentices.   I.R.I.
    Treasury
        Letters to the African Company.   T. 70.
        British ships to Africa, 1788–89.   T. 64.
        Liverpool Slavers, 1789–1795.   T. 64.

Lancashire County Record Office
    Statutory Registers of Lancaster's Merchant Shipping.
    Richmond and Chester Wills.
    Lancaster Marriage Bonds.
    Parish Registers and Bishops' Transcripts for Lancaster,
    Caton, Cartmel, Preston, and Liverpool St. Nicholas.
    Debtors Insolvency Papers.
    Documents Deposited, miscellaneous.

Lancaster Public Library
    Sawrey Papers.
    Rawlinson Papers.
    Lancaster Freemen, Apprentices and Waste Rolls.
    Lancaster Port Commission Records.
    Seamen's Relief Book
    Valuation of Yearly Rents.

Bond (Heathcote-Rhodes and Read).
Political Folders and Scrapbooks.

Lancaster Friends' Meeting House
Monthly, Yearly and Preparative Meeting Papers.
Letters and Papers.

Lancaster University Library
Satterthwaite Letter Books.
Gillow Archives (microfilm), ledgers and accounts for
outfitting ships.

Lancaster Maritime Museum
Lancaster Seamen Sixpence Accounts (photocopy).
Lancaster Port Commission Tonnage Book and St. George's
Quay Accounts.

Liverpool Record Office
Liverpool Plantation Registers.
Liverpool Freemen Books.
Committee Book of the African Company.

Guildhall Library, London
Lloyds Coffee House Subscription Books.
Insurance Records (Sun Fire Office and Royal Exchange).

Sheffield City Library
Stanhope-Spencer Collection, Letters to Benjamin Spencer.

Keele University Library
Davis-Davenport Papers, William Davenport's Bead Book,
Trade Accounts, Bill and Waste Books.

Bodleian Library
Sherard Manuscript.

Cumbria Record Office (Kendal)
Parish Registers for Kendal (Holy Trinity) and
Crosby-Ravensworth.
Cumbria Record Office (Carlisle)
Westmorland Probate Records.

B. *Printed*

Parliamentary Papers
Sessional Papers, New Series, items relating to slave trade.

Newspapers
Lloyds Lists, 1741–84.
Lancaster Gazette.
Williamson's Liverpool Advertiser.
Gore's Liverpool Advertiser.

Liverpool Chronicle.
Cumberland Pacquet.

Other Printed Material
    Lloyds' Shipping Registers.
    Lowndes' *London Directory, 1787*.
    Shaw's *Liverpool Directory, 1767*.
    Universal British Directory, 1799.
    William Holden's *Triennial Directory, 1809*.
    Bailey's *British Directory, 1784*.
    Tunnicliffe's *Topographical Survey of the counties of Stafford, Chester and Lancaster, 1787*.
    Lancaster Poll Books, 1768, 1784/86 and 1802.
    Lancaster Parish Registers.
    Ulverston Parish Registers.
    Hawkshead Parish Registers.
    North Lancashire villages (various) Parish Registers.
    Quaker Registers.
    Lancaster Freeman Rolls.
    Lancaster Marriage Bonds.
    Thomas Pennant's *Tour in Scotland, 1774*.
    Thomas West's *Guide to the Lakes in Cumberland, Westmorland and Lancashire, 1778*.
    Lonsdale Magazine.

II   Secondary Sources

A. *Books*

Anstey, R., *The Atlantic Slave Trade and British Abolition, 1760–1810* (London,1975).
Anstey, R., and P. E. H. Hair, eds., *Liverpool, the African Slave Trade and Abolition* (Historical Society of Lancashire and Cheshire, Occasional Series, vol. 2, 1976).
Beckett, J. V., *Coal and Tobacco: The Lowthers and the Economic Development of West Cumberland* (Cambridge, 1981).
Clowse, C. D., *Economic Beginnings in Colonial South Carolina, 1670–1730* (Columbia, S.C., 1971).
Corfield, P., *The Impact of English Towns, 1700–1800* (Oxford, 1982).
Crowhurst, P., *The Defence of British Trade 1689–1815* (Dawson, 1977).
Curtin, P. D., *The Atlantic Slave Trade: A Census* (Madison, 1969).
Davidson, B., *Black Mother* (London, 1980).
Davies, K. G., *The North Atlantic World in the Seventeenth Century* (Minnesota, 1974).
Davies, K. G., *The Royal African Company* (London, 1957).
Davis, D. B., *The Problem of Slavery in Western Culture* (Cornell, 1966).
Davis, R., *The Rise of the English Shipping Industry in the Seventeenth and Eighteenth Centuries* (Newton Abbot, 1962).

Donnan, E., *Documents Illustrative of the History of the Slave Trade to America*, 4 vols. (Washington, 1935 and New York, 1969).

Dunn, R. S., *Sugar and Slaves: the Rise of the Planter Class in the English West Indies 1624–1713* (N. Carolina, 1972)

Fleury, Cross, *Journal* (Preston, 1896–1910).

Fleury, Cross, *Time-honoured Lancaster* (Lancaster, 1891).

Fraser, A., *Will Cause: Tatham v. Wright* (Lancaster, 1834).

Galenson, D. W., *Traders, Planters and Slaves* (Cambridge, 1986).

Gemery, H. A., and J. S. Hogendorn, eds., *The Uncommon Market: Essays in the Economic History of the Atlantic Slave Trade* (New York, 1979).

Hamer, P., and G. C. Rogers, eds., *The Papers of Henry Laurens*, vols. 1–6 (Columbia, S.C., 1968–1978).

Hewitson, William, *Memoranda relating to Lancaster and District* (Lancaster, ca. 1906).

Hughes, E., *North Country Life in the Eighteenth Century*, Volume Two, 'Cumberland and Westmorland 1700–1830' (London, 1965).

Hyde, F. E., *Liverpool and the Mersey* (Newton Abbot, 1971).

Jones, Sir C., *John Bolton of Storrs* (Kendal, 1959).

Kennerley, E., *The Brockbanks of Lancaster* (Lancaster Museum Monograph, 1981).

Mannix, D. P., and M. Cowley, *Black Cargoes: A History of the Atlantic Slave Trade, 1518–1865* (London, 1962).

Marriner, S., *The Economic and Social Development of Merseyside* (London, 1982).

Marshall, J. D., ed., *Autobiography of William Stout* (Manchester, 1967).

Marshall, J. D., *Furness and the Industrial Revolution* (Barrow-in-Furness, 1958).

Martin, B., and M. Spurrell, eds., *The Journal of a Slave Trader – John Newton* (London, 1962).

Monro, J., ed., *Acts of Privy Council*, Colonial Series, vol. 5, 1766–1783 (H.M.S.O., 1966, reprint).

Owen, Nicholas, *Journal of a Slave-Dealer*, ed., E. Martin (London, 1930).

Pares, R., *Merchants and Planters*, Economic History Review Supplement, 4 (Cambridge, 1960).

Pares, R., *Yankees and Creoles: The Trade between North America and the West Indies before the American Revolution* (London, 1956).

Penson, L. M., *The Colonial Agents of the British West Indies* (London, 1971)

Porter, R., *English Society in the Eighteenth Century* (Harmondsworth, 1982).

Price, J. W. A., *The Industrial Archaeology of the Lune Valley* (Centre for North-West Regional Studies, University of Lancaster, Occasional Paper No. 13, 1983).

Ragatz, L. J., *The Rise and Fall of the Planter Class* (New York, 1977).

Richardson, D., *The Bristol Slave Traders: A Collective Portrait* (Bristol Historical Association, 1985).

Schofield, M. M., *Outlines of an Economic History of Lancaster*, Part I, 1680–1800 (Transactions of the Lancaster Branch of the Historical Association, no. 1, 1946).

Shepherd, J. F., and G. M. Walton, *Shipping, Maritime Trade and the Economic Development of Colonial North America* (Cambridge, 1972).

Sirmans, E., *Colonial South Carolina, a political history, 1663–1763*

(Williamsburg, 1966).

Wadsworth, A. P., and J. de L. Mann, *The Cotton Trade and Industrial Lancashire, 1600–1780* (Manchester, 1931).

Wilkinson, E., *The Port of Lancaster* (Lancaster Museum Monograph, 1982).

Willan, T. S., *An eighteenth-century Shopkeeper, Abraham Dent of Kirkby Stephen* (Manchester, 1970).

Williams, E., *Capitalism and Slavery* (London, 1964).

Williams, Gomer, *History of the Liverpool Privateers and Letters of Marque, with an Account of the Liverpool Slave Trade* (London, 1897).

B. *Articles*

Anderson, B. L., 'The Lancashire bill system and its Liverpool practitioners', in W. H. Chaloner and B. M. Ratcliffe, eds., *Trade and Transport: Essays in economic history in honour of T. S. Willan* (Manchester, 1977).

Anstey, R., 'The Volume and Profitability of the British Slave Trade, 1761–1807', in S. L. Engerman and E. D. Genovese, eds., *Race and Slavery in the Western Hemisphere: Quantitative Studies* (Princeton, 1975).

Awtry, B. G., 'Charcoal Ironmasters of Cheshire and Lancashire, 1600–1785', *T.H.S.L.C.*, 109, 1957.

Checkland, S. G., 'Finance for the West Indies, 1780–1815', *Ec.H.R.*, 2nd Series, 10, 1957.

Checkland, S. G., 'Two Scottish West Indian Liquidations after 1793', *Scottish Journal of Political Economy*, 4, 1957.

Craig, R., 'Shipping and Shipbuilding in the Port of Chester in the Eighteenth and Early Nineteenth Centuries', *T.H.S.L.C.*, 116, 1964.

Craig, R., and R. C. Jarvis, 'Liverpool Registry of Merchant Ships', *Chetham Society*, 3rd Series, 15, 1967.

Drake, B. K., 'Continuity and Flexibility in Liverpool's Trade with Africa and the Caribbean', *Business History*, 18, 1976.

Hyde, F. E., B. B. Parkinson and S. Marriner, 'The Nature and Profitability of the Liverpool Slave Trade', *Ec.H.R.*, 2nd Series, 5, 1952.

Ingram, K. E., 'The West Indian Trade of an English Furniture Firm', *Jamaican Historical Review*, 3, 1962.

Inikori, J. E., 'Slave Trade and Capitalism', *Journal of Interdisciplinary History*, 17: 4, 1987.

Inikori, J. E., 'Market Structure and the Profits of the British African Trade in the Late Eighteenth Century', *Journal of Economic History*, 41, 1981.

Jarvis, R. C., 'Customs Letter-Books of the Port of Liverpool', *Chetham Society*, 3rd Series, 6, 1954.

Jarvis, R. C., 'Liverpool Statutory Register of British Merchant Ships', *T.H.S.L.C.*, 105, 1953.

Jones, A., and M. Johnson, 'Slaves from the Windward Coast', *Journal of African History*, 21, 1980.

Klein, H. S., 'New Evidence on the Virginia Slave Trade', *Journal of Interdisciplinary History*, 17: 4, 1987.

Klein, H. S., 'Slaves and Shipping in Eighteenth-Century Virginia', *Journal of Interdisciplinary History*, 5: 3, 1975.

221

MacInnes, C. M., 'Bristol and the Slave Trade', in P. McGrath, ed., *Bristol in the Eighteenth Century* (Newton Abbot, 1972).

Merritt, J. E., 'The Triangular Trade', *Business History*, 3, 1960.

Morgan, N., 'The Social and Political Relations of the Lancaster Quaker Community, 1688–1740', in M. Mullett, ed., *Early Lancaster Friends* (Centre for North-West Regional Studies, University of Lancaster, Occasional Paper No. 5, 1978).

Ostrander, G. M., 'The Making of the Triangular Myth', *William and Mary Quarterly*, 3rd Series, 30, 1973.

Richardson, D., 'The Costs of Survival: the Transport of Slaves in the Middle Passage and Profitability of the Eighteenth-Century British Slave Trade', *Explorations in Economic History*, 24, 1987.

Richardson, D., 'The Slave Trade, Sugar and British Economic Growth', *Journal of Interdisciplinary History*, 17: 4, 1987.

Roper, W. O., 'Materials for the History of Lancaster', *Chetham Society*, New Series, 62, 1907.

Roper, W. O., ed., 'Materials for the History of the Church of Lancaster', *Chetham Society*, New Series, 58, 1906.

Sanderson, F. E., 'Liverpool and the Slave Trade: A Guide to Sources', *T.H.S.L.C.*, 124, 1972.

Schofield, M. M., 'Chester Slave Trading Partnerships 1750–56', short notes, *T.H.S.L.C.*, 130, 1981.

Schofield, M. M., 'The Letter Book of Benjamin Satterthwaite of Lancaster, 1737–1744', *T.H.S.L.C.*, 113, 1961.

Schofield, M. M., 'The Slave Trade from Lancashire and Cheshire Ports outside Liverpool, c.1750–1790', *T.H.S.L.C.*, 126, 1977.

Sheridan, R. B., 'The Commercial and Financial Organization of the British Slave Trade, 1750–1807', *Ec.H.R.*, 2nd Series, vol. 11, 1958.

Sheridan, R. B., 'Rise of the Colonial Gentry: Case Study in Antigua, 1730–75', *Ec.H.R.*, 2nd Series, 13, 1961.

Singleton, F. J., 'The Flax Merchants of Kirkham', *T.H.S.L.C.*, 126, 1977.

Steckel, R. H., and R. A. Jensen, 'New evidence on the Cause of Slave and Crew Mortality in the Atlantic Slave Trade', *Journal of Economic History*, 46, 1986.

Thomas, R. P., and R. N. Bean, 'The Fishers of Men: The Profits of the Slave Trade', *Journal of Economic History*, 34, 1974.

Williams, J. E., 'Whitehaven in the Eighteenth Century', *Ec.H.R.*, 2nd Series, 8, 1955.

C. *Unpublished Theses*

Eaglesham, A., 'The Growth and Influence of the West Cumberland Shipping Industry, 1660–1800', unpublished Ph.D. thesis, University of Lancaster, 1977.

Gooderson, P. J., 'The Social and Economic History of Caton, 1750–1914', unpublished M.A. thesis, University of Lancaster, 1969.

Gooderson, P. J., 'The Social and Economic History of Lancaster, 1780–1914', unpublished Ph.D. thesis, University of Lancaster, 1975.

Index

230